Training for Treason

The Harmful Agenda Behind Education for Sustainability

Holly Swanson

CIN PUBLISHING

Published in the United States by CIN PUBLISHING
Email: cinpublishing@earthlink.net

Training for Treason: The Harmful Agenda Behind Education for Sustainability

Library of Congress Control Number 2012938348

Includes references and index

ISBN: 978-0-9645108-3-8

Contents

1

A Political Movement NOT An Environmental Movement

A tremendous amount of good has come from increased environmental awareness but a tremendous problem has also come to light. Our goal of a healthy environment must now include dealing with a harsh reality, which is; the environmental cause has been hijacked by a radical political movement, with a harmful agenda and the focus has changed.

The environmental cause has been renamed the 'Green movement' for a reason. This name change represents a strategic political alliance to advance an agenda we all need to understand. The Green movement's invasion of the classroom and insistence that America's children, students of all ages, 'go Green' is the strategy to change the role of public education and indoctrinate our innocent children to impose this political agenda. Free thought, individual freedom and a quality education are at risk. Parents, grandparents, family and friends need to be aware of how this harmful agenda affects the hearts, the minds and the future of the children we love.

Today's Green movement opposes just about everything we believe in and this nation stands for. The agenda of the Green movement is a serious problem that affects each and every one of us, especially our children. The Green movement encompasses the undisclosed political agenda behind Education for Sustainability.

We all want clean air and clean water and, are willing to do our share when there is a legitimate need. Distinctions between a legitimate need and a false claim, made by the Green movement to advance their agenda, must be at the forefront of environmental decisions. When we understand the political agenda behind the Education for Sustainability movement, we can help our children and others make critical distinctions between Green politics and legitimate environmental concerns.

In the following pages, fact after fact confirms how the environmental cause and Education for Sustainability programs are being used by the Green movement to deceive students and the American people.

"The great masses of people will more easily fall victims to a great lie than to a small one."

Adolf Hitler

What's wrong with lies? People believe them. Beyond being deceitful, lies cause serious problems. We expect what we are told to be true. We base our decisions on trusting what we are told to be true. Lies have countless ripple effects.

Exaggerated claims and premeditated deception have been used extensively by the Greens to advance their political agenda. A prime example of this is found in the 1989 Green Party Program. The following statements confirm the strategy to use the Greenhouse effect, now called global warming or climate change, to trick the public into supporting the Green Party agenda.

"This urgency along with all the other Green issues and themes it interrelates, makes confronting **the Greenhouse a powerful organizing tool**.

Survival is highly motivating and may help us in building a mass movement that will lead to large scale political and societal change in a very short time.

First of all we would have to inform the public that the crisis is more immediate and severe than we are being told. Its implications are too great to wait for the universal scientific confirmation that only eco-catastrophe would establish."

Green Party Program 1989 (Page 16)

The global warming issue has been used to build a mass movement by scaring people into believing "large scale political and societal change" was necessary. The next statement is from the book, 'The Holes in the Ozone Scare, The Scientific Evidence: The Sky Isn't Falling':

"Witch doctors operate on the basis of asserted supernatural powers that they use to scare and awe their devotees.

Climate catastrophe doomsayers use the same kind of psychological manipulation to achieve their goals. This was revealed by the leading climate modeler in the United States, Stephen Schneider, in an interview with the October 1989 issue of 'Discover' magazine.

Schneider, who works at the National Center of Atmospheric Research at Boulder, Colorado, **said:**

"We need to get some broad-based support to capture the public's imagination. That of course entails getting loads of media coverage. So we have to offer up scary scenarios, make simplified, dramatic statements and make little mention of any doubts we may have... Each of us has to decide; what is the right balance between being effective and being honest."

These statements confirm the premeditated strategy to use the environmental cause to deceive the American people. Over the past 23 years global warming claims have been used to trick people into believing Green demands to avoid climate catastrophe were legitimate. Deception pure and simple and yet, even after 'climate-gate', after the Greens were caught doctoring global warming data, one of the primary excuses to push Education for Sustainability programs into our schools is still global warming.

"I hate deception, even where the imagination only is concerned"

George Washington
Letter to Dr. Cochran, August 16, 1779

Language plays a key role in how the Greens operate to advance their political agenda. Words are powerful tools that can be used to clarify or mask objectives. For instance, the word 'sustainability' has been politicized by the Greens. When a word is politicized it takes on a new meaning, which reflects the goals of the group or cause that is using the term as a 'buzzword' to identify their particular effort. For example, if someone says the word 'pot' what comes to mind, a kitchen utensil or marijuana? If the word 'gay' is mentioned, what comes to mind, a happy heart or a lifestyle choice?

Politicized words mean different things to different people. This is why understanding what the Greens mean by a 'sustainable future' is so important to all of us. The concept of sustainability sounds fine on the surface but the Green definition of sustainability, the one America's children are being trained to embrace, looks like communism with a facelift.

The word 'green' has also been politicized. Green is no longer just a color; it now represents the entire scope of the environmental movement, from Education for Sustainability to the aligned Green Party agenda, which also happens to mirror communism. Many Americans have adopted the Green label without realizing the word 'Green' also stands for those who support the Green Party and are working hard to implement the radical political agenda of the international Green movement in the United States.

More and more people, from environmental activists to world leaders, are recognizing that the environmental cause has been hijacked by extremists and is being used to advance a radical political agenda.

"Founder of Greenpeace Says Movement Has Lost Its Way"

That was the headline on the front page of the April 13, 2002 Medford Mail Tribune based on an interview with Dr. Patrick Moore by reporter Paul Fattig. After 15 years, Patrick Moore, one of the founders of Greenpeace, had left the organization. The article included the following statements by Dr. Moore:

> "I believe we did a lot of great things to raise public awareness." Having said that, **Moore, who spent 15 years with Greenpeace, took issue with what he believes is today's environmental extremism. "**
>
> **"The environmental movement has shifted from being politically centered and science based to having a fairly strong left-wing rhetoric that has more to do with politics than science." ...** "There is no reason why environmentalists should be left-wing."
>
> **"The point is that the world is not coming to an end as some would suggest"**

On October 10, 2004, Senator James Inhofe made the following statement:

> "What we find now is the fleecing of the American public's pocketbooks by the environmental movement for their political use. What we find now is **exhausting litigation, instigation of false claims, misleading science, and scare tactics to fool Americans into believing disastrous environmental scenarios that are untrue**."
>
> US Senator James Inhofe, Chairman
> Environment and Public Works Committee
> Source: http://inhofe.senate.gov/pressreleases/epwgroups.htm

However well intentioned the environmental cause started out to be, it is now being used as a smokescreen to impose the political agenda of the Green movement, Green Party and international Greens. The original goal to take care of the land and the water has been replaced by Green plans to take control of the land and the water. On March 20, 2007, a World Net Daily article titled "Czech prez: Environmentalism is new communism. Biggest threat to freedom, democracy, the market economy and prosperity" included the following statement about environmental extremism:

> "Czech President Vaclav Klaus is warning congressmen that environmental extremism is the modern equivalent of communism."
>
> Source: www.wnd.com

President Vaclav Klaus is a strong voice for reason in the global warming debate and author of the book "Blue Planet in Green Shackles, What is Endangered, Climate or Freedom?" The Green movement has used global warming to create 'climate change hysteria' to justify their demands and scare people and our children into compliance.

Climate Update: Read All About It!

The following April 23, 2012 report, by Marc Morano of the Climate Depot, speaks for itself.

> **"Alert: 'Gaia' scientist James Lovelock reverses himself:** I was 'alarmist' about climate change & so was Gore! 'The problem is we don't know what the climate is doing. We thought we knew 20 years ago' - Climate Shocker: **In 2007, Lovelock Predicted Global Warming Doom: 'Billions of us will die; few breeding pairs of people that survive** will be in Arctic'...
>
> **MSNBC**, perhaps the most unlikely of news sources **reports on what may be seen as the official end of the man-made global warming fear movement.** More MSNBC article excerpts:
>
> **Lovelock pointed to Gore's "An Inconvenient Truth" and Tim Flannery's "The Weather Makers" as other examples of "alarmist" forecasts of the future..."The problem is we don't know what the climate is doing. We thought we knew 20 years ago.** That led to some alarmist books – mine included – because it looked clear-cut, but it hasn't happened," Lovelock said.
>
> **"The climate is doing its usual tricks. There's nothing much really happening yet. We were supposed to be halfway toward a frying world now," he said. "The world has not warmed up very much since the millennium. Twelve years is a reasonable time... it (the temperature) has stayed almost constant,** whereas it should have been rising ...."
>
> "... **'I made a mistake'** - As "an independent and a loner," he said, he did not mind saying "All right, I made a mistake." He claimed a university or government scientist might fear an admission of a mistake would lead to the loss of funding."
>
> Source: http://www.climatedepot.com/a/15621/Alert-Gaia-scientist-James-Lovelock-reverses-himself-I-was-alarmist-about-climate-change--so-was-Gore-The-problem-is-we-dont-know-what-the-climate-is-doing-We-thought-we-knew-20-years-ago (or) http://www.climatedepot.com

How many times, despite objections, has Al Gore's movie 'An Inconvenient Truth' been shown in classrooms since its release in 2006? How many children, over the past 6 years, have been 'scared Green' by this movie? How many children still believe the world is coming to an end because of this movie?

How has this reckless use of fear in the classroom affected our children's hope for the future? The "Inconvenient Truth" does not belong in K-12 classrooms. Many warned that climate change should not be taught as factual reality in the classroom because the jury was still out, but this issue was pushed into our schools anyway.

This admission by one of the leading climate alarmists, James Lovelock, can help students, teachers, parents and others recover from 'climate deception' and to understand why climate change needs to be removed from the K-12 educational realm. Every school and every teacher that has shown the "Inconvenient Truth" and pushed students to reduce their carbon footprint ought to announce James Lovelock's admission of error and then eliminate climate terror curriculum in K-12 classrooms.

The Education for Sustainability movement has also used climate terror as the excuse to push their program into our schools and the plan is to make Education for Sustainability the new mission of public education.

> "All who have meditated on the art of governing mankind are convinced that the fate of empires depends on the education of youth."
>
> Aristotle
> The Rebirth of America

Education for Sustainability Basics

Education for Sustainability is the name of a political movement and the name of the curriculum this movement is pushing into schools across America. Education for Sustainability is a plan to hijack public education, drastically alter the curriculum and use every subject to train America's children, students of all ages, to align with the political agenda of this movement. To understand the harmful political agenda behind the Education for Sustainability movement, we need to take a close look at:

- the political objectives of this program
- the political ideology behind this program
- the difference between a quality education and this program
- the intended outcome and its effect on our children, families and nation

Although the Education for Sustainability movement shares a similar name with the United Nation's program 'Education for Sustainable Development', the evidence in the following pages will confirm, the agenda behind the US based

Education for Sustainability movement did not, as we have been led to believe, come from the 1972 United Nation's Environmental Summit, but from a document that was prepared in advance of that event, to influence that event.

That document outlined many of the goals and strategies to create a sustainable society that are now being implemented; including the plan to use education to indoctrinate students to impose this agenda. This document first appeared in 'The Ecologist' magazine in 1972. The 'Ecologist' magazine and its founder, are credited with igniting the environmental, now Green movement. This document is the 'Blueprint for Survival' and it is also recognized for inspiring the founding of the international Green Party. The devil is in the details.

The objectives of the Education for Sustainability movement in the United States have Green Party fingerprints all over them. Although not every single detail of the Green Party program is visible in every single aspect of the Education for Sustainability movement; the core themes, values and aims are clearly the same.

Education for Sustainability groups pretend the 1972 United Nations summit is where the ideas about sustainable development began and point to other events following that summit to justify pushing an international curriculum into our schools. The Greens forgot to mention their connection to the 'Blueprint for Survival' and the link between this document and the political agenda of the Green movement, the Green Party and the Education for Sustainability movement.

Blueprint Basics

The following statement, from 'The Ecologist' magazine, introduces the 'Blueprint for Survival'.

> "A Blueprint for Survival occupied the entire issue of 'The Ecologist' Vol. 2 No. 1, January 1972, **in advance of the world's first Environment Summit: the 1972 UN Conference on the Human Environment**, in Stockholm.
>
> **The principal authors were Edward Goldsmith and Robert Allen**, with additional help from Michael Allaby, John Davoll, and Sam Lawrence.
>
> So great was demand for A Blueprint for Survival that it was republished in book form later that year by Penguin Books, on 14 September 1972."
>
> Source: http://www.theecologist.info/key27.html

A few of the political objectives, the authors of the 'Blueprint for Survival' outlined in the Preface, included the following:

- give rise to a national and international movement
- form a movement that would be the dawn of a new age
- assume political status
- movement's success depends on formulating a new philosophy of life
- formulate a precise and comprehensive plan, to bring about the kind of society, in which a new philosophy of life can be implemented

Source: http://www.theecologist.info/page34.html

What Happened Next?

The 'Blueprint for Survival' included recommendations for the decision makers attending the world's first Environmental Summit. Then, the 'Blueprint for Survival', co-authored by Edward Goldsmith, became a "key text" for the environmental, now Green movement and also led to the formation of a political party, which was later renamed the Green Party. Edward Goldsmith played an instrumental role in founding the Green Party. Following are a few facts about the 'Blueprint for Survival', the environmental movement and the Green Party.

- **In 1969, Goldsmith established 'The Ecologist' magazine** "which would for decades provide a platform for his views. Funded by his brother, the late billionaire financier Sir James Goldsmith".

  Source: http://www.independent.co.uk/

- Goldsmith "...**ignited the modern environmental movement in 1970** by founding 'The Ecologist' magazine..."
- "Soon after founding 'The Ecologist', **Goldsmith co-wrote 'A Blueprint for Survival'** ..."
- The "**Blueprint led to the foundation of the People Party** (later the Ecology Party **and finally the Green Party**) for which Goldsmith stood unsuccessfully in the 1974 general election at Eye, Suffolk."
  - "...He stood as **a Green Party candidate..."**

  Source:http://www.edwardgoldsmith.org/938/eco-hero-edward-goldsmith/

- Goldsmith "... was a "**founding member of the political party "People"** (**later renamed the** Green Party), itself largely **inspired by the Blueprint."**
- Goldsmith was a "**deep ecologist and systems theorist**..."

- **"The Blueprint"** ... **"became a key text for the early Green movement..."**

Source: http://en.wikipedia.org/wiki/Edward_Goldsmith

- **Goldsmith regarded "himself as one of the founding fathers of what in time became the Green Party."**

Source: http://www.independent.co.uk/

The 1972 'Blueprint for Survival' helps explain why the objectives of the environmental movement mirror the agenda of the radical Green Party and, why forty years later, the Green Party and Green movement now share the same name. Goldsmith's magazine, 'The Ecologist' is recognized for:

- igniting the 1970's environmental movement, now Green movement

The 'Blueprint for Survival', co-authored by Goldsmith, is also recognized for:

- becoming a key text for the environmental movement
- inspiring the founding and philosophy of the Green Party

These credits, from different sources, suggest that the 'Blueprint for Survival' was the basis for the political agenda of the Green movement and the Green Party. The political impact of the 'Blueprint for Survival' was and is far reaching. The September, 2002 edition of 'The Ecologist' magazine reported:

> "Originally published in January 1972, A Blueprint for Survival went on to become, **one of the decade's most important environmental books** selling 120,000 copies in 17 languages, **and influencing the formation of Green Parties around the world."**

The Ecologist (VOL 32 NO 7) September 2002 (page 27)
Source: http://www.theecologist.org

The 'Blueprint' is considered "one of the decade's most important environmental books" and has influenced the "formation of Green Parties around the world."

The political agenda of the Green Party and logically the Green movement is based on the 'Blueprint'. The Earth Charter and the Education for Sustainability movement are also aligned with Green Party goals. We are dealing with a political movement not an environmental movement. We are dealing with the implementation of a political agenda.

The first section of the 'Blueprint for Survival' (#110) outlined the goal to create a sustainable society.

"We believe that a growing number of people are aware of this choice, and are more interested in our proposals for **creating a sustainable society**..."

Source: http://www.theecologist.info/page33.html

The 'Blueprint' strategy was to formulate a 'precise and comprehensive plan' to mentally prepare people to accept a new philosophy of life and the implementation of a radical political agenda. The environmental cause has been the excuse to demand change and get people to embrace being Green. This opened the door to adopting the Green definition of a sustainable lifestyle and Green philosophy of life. Sustainability is the buzzword to mask imposing radical change. Education for Sustainability is part of the conditioning process and implementation plan. The political agenda and new philosophy of life are based on the Green Party and Earth Charter.

Although tweaked and re-tweaked over the years, the aims of the Greens still reflect goals outlined in the 'Blueprint'. The links between the goals of the Education for Sustainability movement and the Green Party are unmistakable.

Understanding that we are dealing with the implementation of a political agenda is a vital part of removing Education for Sustainability programs from our schools and preventing the Greens from continuing to use the environmental cause as a smokescreen to take control of our lives, our children's lives, our lands, our communities and our nation.

In addition, since the 'Blueprint for Survival' was prepared for the 1972 United Nations Environmental Summit; it is likely this document influenced the United Nation's ideas about sustainability. This helps to explain why the United Nation's sustainability agenda mirrors the goals of the international Green Parties, Earth Charter and communism. The Green Party of the United States is also part of the international Green Parties Network.

Earth Charter: Quick Study

The Earth Charter is the pet project of Mikhail Gorbachev and Maurice Strong and a few other leaders of the international Green movement. Since his supposed disposition from power in the Soviet Union, the former communist dictator has positioned himself as a leader of the US Green movement. Gorbachev's projects and organizations include, the Earth Charter, Green Cross International and Global Green.

Gorbachev's 2006 book the 'Manifesto For the Earth' is about the Earth Charter. The back cover of the 'Manifesto' features the following statement:

"To complete the Declaration on Human Rights and the Charter of the UN **he has co-authored the remarkable Earth Charter**..."

Gorbachev co-authored the Earth Charter. This is important because Earth Charter goals mirror Green Party goals and communism. The Earth Charter is based on 16 main principles and over 50 sub-principles or goals. A quick study of the general aim of the Earth Charter follows:

Most of the leading groups in the Green movement and the Education for Sustainability movement have endorsed the Earth Charter, which indicates they support an agenda which mirrors Green Party goals and communism. What does the endorsement of the Earth entail? The following excerpts are from the Earth Charter's official statement of endorsement and specify the commitment endorsers have made.

> **"Endorsement of the Earth Charter by individuals or organizations signifies a commitment to the spirit and aims of the document**. It is an indication that they intend to utilize the Earth Charter in ways that are appropriate given their situation."
>
> **"Endorsement also means a commitment to work for the implementation of the values and principles of the Earth Charter and a readiness to cooperate with others in this endeavor."**
>
> "You can use the following sample:
>
> > "We, the undersigned, endorse the Earth Charter. **We embrace the spirit and aims of the document. We pledge to join the global partnership** for a just, sustainable, and peaceful world and **to work for the realization of the values and principles of the Earth Charter."**
> >
> > Additionally, **it is expected that an Endorser will:**
> >
> > - **Actively promote the Earth Charter** and follow the Action Guidelines.
> > - Contribute to the Earth Charter Initiative and to Earth Charter-inspired action projects in whatever way is most appropriate.
> > - **Implement the Earth Charter in your professional work** and personal life."
>
> Source:http://www.earthcharterinaction.org/content/pages/Endorse.html

Guide and Assess the Conduct of ALL Individuals

Earth Charter endorsers support the following political objectives:

> **"We urgently need a shared vision of basic values to provide an ethical foundation** for the emerging world community."

"Therefore, together in hope we affirm the following interdependent principles for a sustainable way of life as **a common standard by which the conduct of all individuals, organizations, businesses, governments, and transnational institutions is to be guided and assessed."**

The purpose of the Earth Charter is to become international law which is confirmed on page 4 of the Earth Charter, which states:

"In order to build a sustainable global community, **the nations of the world must** renew their commitment to the United Nations, fulfill their obligations under existing international agreements, and **support the implementation of Earth Charter principles with an international legally binding instrument** on environment and development."

A "legally binding instrument" is a law. Endorsers of the Earth Charter support the implementation of the Earth Charter as international law, which means if ratified, the Earth Charter could replace the United States Constitution as the law of our land.

The Education for Sustainability movement is using public education to align students with the Earth Charter. We need to take a closer look at the following Earth Charter objective and understand the message to our children is submit.

"...the conduct of all individuals, organizations, businesses, governments, and transnational institutions **is to be guided and assessed."**

It is critical that we realize our individual conduct cannot be 'guided and assessed' unless it is 'monitored' on a regular basis by someone. In addition, why bother to monitor or access conduct, unless there is a reason, such as a plan to enforce required conduct? This Earth Charter mandate would apply to our personal lives, organizations, businesses and to our government. This is not freedom.

The Earth Charter is already being used as an Education for Sustainability teaching guide in many of America's schools. What better way to foster world communism than to present a political indoctrination scheme as education?

Education for Sustainability is the Green movement's vehicle to get Green Party politics taught as curriculum in America's public schools.

Hidden In Plain Sight

The big push for Education for Sustainability in the United States began in the early 1990's. Since then, the Green movement has transformed 'environmental education' into what is now, the Education for Sustainability movement. The Greens have put Education for Sustainability on a fast track to become the new mission of public education. This is a major concern because Education for Sustainability is rooted in the ideology of the Green Party, which makes it a political indoctrination program.

A concise look at the difference between an 'education' and Education for Sustainability comes from the Sustainable Oregon Schools Initiative, a program started by Governor Ted Kulongoski in 2003. This program was originally called the Sustainable Schools Project.

The following statement, which includes the original bold emphasis placed on the words FOR and ABOUT by the Sustainable Oregon Schools Initiative, clarifies the difference between a lesson ABOUT sustainability and a political advocacy lesson FOR sustainability.

> "Education **ABOUT** sustainable development **is an awareness lesson** or theoretical discussion."
>
> "Education **FOR** sustainable development **is the use of education as a tool to transform our societies** to achieve sustainability."
>
> Sustainable Oregon Schools Initiative - October, 2009
> Source: http://www.sustainableschools.org

The difference is clear. Education FOR Sustainability is "a tool" to train students to align with an agenda that will result in the transformation of our society. Is transforming our society, to achieve the Green definition of sustainability, the purpose of public education? No. The Education for Sustainability agenda mirrors Green Party goals, which is perhaps why the strategy of this political movement aligns with the 1989 Green Party plan:

> "**Greens see education as a transformative agent** in which primary, secondary and higher education as institutions represent only one important arena. Authentic education directly arises from and informs human experience at the grassroots level".
>
> Green Party Program 1989 (page 25)

The Education for Sustainability plan to use education to transform America matches the Green Party plan to use education to transform America. Both of these plans align with how Communist leaders used education 'as a tool' to transform society by indoctrinating students to adopt the goals of one political party, the Communist Party. The following statement confirms this point.

"From the moment they seized power **Communist leaders stressed the importance of education**, and **regarded it as a tool for the transformation of society."**

Education for Communism
Communism: What it is and How it Works
Schlesinger/Blustain (page 133)

The plan this decade is to train students to align with the Green Party. The agenda of the Education for Sustainability movement is political, not environmental and not educational. The leading national and international organization in the Education for Sustainability movement is Second Nature which was founded in 1993. The President of Second Nature, Anthony Cortese, clarified their mission and the purpose of Education for Sustainability during a 1996 interview when he said:

"And humans are guided by a whole set of beliefs and values, and those come from culture, from religion, from social, economic, and political structure. We need to change all of those."

Anthony Cortese, CEO Second Nature
Conservation Matters Magazine - Spring 1996
Conservation Law Foundation Publication
Source: http://www.clf.org/../CM/archive.htm (or) http://web.archive.org/web/19991023112303/http://www.clf.org/pubs/cortes.htm

The political objective of the Education for Sustainability movement is to change the "cultural, religious, social economic and political structure" of our nation by using this curriculum to indoctrinate or train ALL of America's children to align with this agenda as the following statement shows.

"Why Is a Sustainable School System Important? **K-12 school/districts and schools** serve their communities and play a critical role in the sustainability effort.

They should be striving for sustainability because: They **are in the best position to reach ALL children with an education for sustainability, setting them up to create a sustainable future."**

Sustainable Oregon Schools Initiative
Source:http://www.sustainableschools.org/discover-sustainability/sustainability-in-schools

This plan to set-ALL-children up to conform to the demand that they must help create a sustainable future is a political not an educational objective. Education for Sustainability is a political movement masquerading as an educational movement. This is a plan to use our schools like they do in communist countries, to transform America by training our children to support one political party.

A plan of this magnitude did not fall out of the sky. A plan to change every major area of life in America, including the personal beliefs of the American people, would require specific objectives; predetermined outcomes, an implementation program and plenty of funding to get the job done. This would also require a 'Blueprint' and leadership.

Second Nature is recognized as the leading organizer of the Education for Sustainability movement and it is important to understand the background of this organization. The following statement is from Second Nature's brochure 'ABOUT OUR FOUNDER' which states:

> **"Since its inception in 1993, Second Nature has been a major driving force transforming the education**, research, operation, and community outreach of the higher education sector in order **to create a healthy, just and sustainable society for everyone.**
>
> **At a time when few saw the urgent need to find more sustainable ways to meet human needs and creating a thriving society, Anthony Cortese envisioned** how higher education, as the educator of all societies professionals and leaders and the generator of the knowledge on which we thrive, could lead this effort and **become a model for all of society.**
>
> **With the encouragement and support of Senator John Kerry and Theresa Heinz Kerry, Second Nature was created to make this vision a reality."**
>
> Source: http://www.secondnature.org/documents/brochure_final_pdf

This statement suggests Anthony Cortese started Second Nature and was the driving force behind establishing the Education for Sustainability movement.

The following statement is from the 1996 Conservation Matters interview with the then CEO of Second Nature, Anthony Cortese who said:

> "After I left Tufts, **Senator John Kerry**, who has been a longtime environmental supporter and advocate, **called me and said he wanted to start a nonprofit organization** to really push sustainable development. **He asked me if I would help organize it, and he decided to call it Second Nature."**
>
> Anthony Cortese, CEO Second Nature
> Conservation Matters Magazine - Spring 1996
> Conservation Law Foundation Publication
> Source: http://www.clf.org/../CM/archive.htm

Why doesn't Second Nature acknowledge that Senator John Kerry started Second Nature because he wanted to push sustainable development and, that even the name of this organization is Senator Kerry's idea? Why doesn't

Senator Kerry want credit for his brainchild? In addition, why doesn't Second Nature credit Senator Kerry and Theresa Heinz Kerry for their leadership role since 1993, to establish Second Nature as THE leading organization in the Education for Sustainability movement, rather than barely mentioning them for "providing encouragement and support?"

Encouragement and support sounds like an understatement. Another important fact regarding the history of Second Nature is that unlike many start-ups, Second Nature began with a 'no worries' multimillion dollar funding guarantee so they could concentrate on executing the plan to change our culture, religion, society, economy and government. The following statement confirms ample funding was in place to advance transformative change.

> "**We began with a multimillion dollar, ten-year outreach and advocacy effort to catalyze such transformative change,** change that would have universities produce students prepared for character and citizenship as well as commerce and career in the 21st century."
>
> **Second Nature - History**
> Source: http://www.secondnature.org

Where is Second Nature today? The following excerpts, also from the Second Nature brochure, confirms the groups leadership position in the Education for Sustainability movement and the objective to make their agenda the "fundamental purpose of all learning" so the "sustainability perspective will be 'second nature' for all graduates, in all they do."

> "**Second Nature is the international leader** in building momentum, leveraging collaborations and catalyzing change to move higher education toward sustainability.
>
> **We believe that creating a thriving, enduring society is the fundamental purpose of all learning; sustainability should be the foundational principle** of higher education. We call this **Education for Sustainability (EfS) - a movement that has grown synonymous with Second Nature.** We mobilize higher education leaders and policy makers to advance sustainability imperatives and inspire higher education to embrace sustainability as a core concept."
>
> "**We are the primary force in the nation and worldwide** engaging higher education senior leadership (presidents, trustees, business officers, and provosts) to make sustainability a strategic imperative for their institutions."
>
> "**In addition to building the EfS movement**, as a convener and collaborator, Second Nature continues to work with individual schools to advance their efforts on campus and in the classroom."
>
> "We worked with the Campaign for Environmental Literacy on recent amendments to the Higher Education Act that **authorized $50 million**

annually for college and university sustainability programs, the first federal funds directed in support of EfS."

"With your help, **Second Nature will continue to play its leading role** in developing strategies to make this a reality—**so that a sustainability perspective will be 'second nature' for all graduates, in all they do."**

Second Nature
Source: http://www.secondnature.org/documents/brochure_final_pdf

Free Thinking Americans or GREEN-BOTS?

In the above statement, Second Nature clarified that the intended outcome of Education for Sustainability is to indoctrinate students to the degree "that a sustainability perspective will be 'second nature' for all graduates, in all they do".

This confirms Education for Sustainability is a plan to train students, all of America's children, to have only ONE perspective when it comes to sustainability and to automatically apply that ONE way of thinking to "all they do" in life.

Robots are programmed to respond to commands. Education for Sustainability is a tool to program students to obey Green commands for "all" they do in life, all their life choices. The objective is to mass produce manageable, limited thinking, conforming students or 'GREEN-BOTS' that will automatically eat Green, live Green, worship Green and vote Green.

Since Education for Sustainability is rooted in Green Party ideology, this is also a program to train children to be loyal to everything Green, including the Green Party. This is a cunning strategy to gain a free political advantage and foster single party rule at the expense of free thought and individual freedom.

The Greens have targeted and relentlessly pressured students to 'go Green' and conform to the Green's definition of a sustainable lifestyle for many years. We need to understand the Greens have manipulated student's beliefs. Students need to understand the Greens have manipulated their beliefs for political gain.

There are multiple groups involved in the Education for Sustainability movement which are aligned with the political objectives of Second Nature. Position statements by Second Nature along with statements by Anthony Cortese, the President of Second Nature, are cited throughout this document because, in Second Nature's own words:

"**Second Nature is the international leader** in building momentum, leveraging collaborations and catalyzing change to move higher education toward sustainability."

> We believe that creating a thriving, enduring society is the fundamental purpose of all learning; sustainability should be the foundational principle of higher education. We call this **Education for Sustainability (EfS) - a movement that has grown synonymous with Second Nature."**
>
> "**We are the primary force in the nation and worldwide** engaging higher education senior leadership (presidents, trustees, business officers, and provosts) to make sustainability a strategic imperative for their institutions."

Second Nature continues to play the leading role in developing, organizing and implementing the objectives of the Education for Sustainability movement. In addition, statements by Anthony Cortese and Second Nature provide past and present insights, which clarify the ideology, the alliances and the political agenda of this movement.

Inculcate: Instill, Beat, Hammer, Pound, Repeat

The following statement is from 'Earth Rising' by Philip Shabecoff, published in 2000. The aim of this book was to define the future agenda of the Green movement based on multiple interviews with leaders of major environmental groups, the Green Party and others in leadership roles. Shabecoff wrote:

> **"Anthony Cortese, president of Second Nature, a Boston based organization dedicated to inculcating the importance of "education for sustainability**" in professionals in higher education ...contended:
>
> **"The current educational system, Cortese said, reinforces "the deep cultural belief that humans are separate from nature."** Secondly, instead of being taught in **holistic and interdisciplinary ways,** we are taught in separate little compartments, math is separate from physics is separate from reading, is separate from chemistry. ... we don't make connections between economics, biology, politics, engineering."
>
> "... **Cortese is trying to persuade school administrators ... to ... integrate ecological and environmental material into every element of their curricula**".
>
> Earth Rising (page 70-71)

Anthony Cortese is obviously recognized as a leader in the Green movement. One of the future agenda items identified in the book was, the Greens were going to concentrate on education.

The strategy, according to Cortese, was to inculcate "the importance of 'education for sustainability' in professionals in higher education", so they would "integrate ecological and environmental material into every element of their curricula".

Cortese said "The current educational system reinforces "the deep cultural belief that humans are separate from nature" which indicates his opposition to that belief. To change this core belief, Second Nature and the Education for Sustainability movement are using 'systems thinking' and our public education system to instill the Green belief that man is part of nature. The Education for Sustainability movement intends to make this belief part of the new philosophy of public education.

> "We advocate giving high priority in both funding and public attention to the sciences that involve **interconnectedness of systems and interdisciplinary studies**
>
> Green Party Program 1991 (page 33)

The "interconnectedness of systems" is systems thinking. The systems thinking mindset is man is part of nature, which is the core philosophy of the Green Party. The Greens oppose the belief that man is separate from nature or above nature.

> **"The content of learning must embrace interdisciplinary systems thinking** to address environmentally sustainable action on local, regional and global scales
>
> Anthony Cortese
> Leveraging Change: The Role of the University in a Sustainable Future
> MIT panel on Alliance for Global Sustainability January 2000
> Source:http://www.secondnature.org/history/writings/speeches/leveraging_change.html

Education for Sustainability and systems thinking are training tools to impose "deep cultural change" in America. Second Nature's strategy to build support for the Education for Sustainability movement was to target professionals in higher education and convince them to use their influence to advance the agenda of the Education for Sustainability movement. Additional steps to advance this agenda include:

- training leaders in higher education in systems thinking so they would in-turn impose that mindset on students in the classroom and on campus practices

- presenting the Education for Sustainability agenda as a necessary mindset to save the earth

Do those who joined forces with Second Nature understand the political agenda behind this program is to change our culture, religion, society, economy and form of government? Do they realize the plan to impose this agenda is to indoctrinate or 'inculcate' our children to adopt the mindset of the Green Party?

Inculcate is the perfect word to describe the mission of Second Nature and the Education for Sustainability movement. The term 'inculcate' means instill, beat, hammer, pound, repeat and indoctrinate. The aim of Education for Sustainability is to become the new foundation of all learning in our schools, which means Green goals for sustainability would be taught in every subject from preschool through university. This is a plan to hijack public education and use the classroom to beat, pound and hammer students every single day until they tap-out, say uncle, give up and conform to the Green worldview that they are part of nature.

Students have been betrayed by the Greening of public education. If we were in these student's shoes, and had been unfairly targeted and programmed to be a GREEN-BOT, we would appreciate a loving hand off the Green bandwagon. We would also hope that once our parents, grandparents, teachers, citizens, community and political leaders understood the indoctrination problem, they would come to our rescue and expel this program. After this program was expelled, we would need time to 'UN-BOT' and pick-up our hopes and dreams.

Public education was intended to provide students with basic skills and knowledge which included a healthy appreciation for America's founding principles. We can and must return our schools to safe havens of learning.

A New Story

Two of the stated goals of Education for Sustainability are to change our system of government and religious beliefs. Obviously, these are political not educational objectives. Training student's to embrace the Green Party worldview that man is part of nature; the earth is a living organism (life form or living being) and humans are just another species is the strategy to replace the belief in God's word, that man was given dominion over nature and charged with being a good steward.

> **"We have to make the human relationship to the environment, values and ethics a central part of teaching in all the disciplines** ...We have to understand that **we are an integral part of nature** and that we are co-evolving **with other species** in the biosphere."
>
> Anthony Cortese
> Leveraging Change: The Role of the University in a Sustainable Future
> Source:http://www.secondnature.org/history/writings/speeches/leveraging_change.html

There is a big difference between a worldview which promotes appreciation, respect, responsibility, love and care for the natural world based on the belief man is separate from nature and, the Green's worldview that man is part of nature. The following excerpt, from an interview with deep ecologist and leading environmentalist, John Seed, helps clarify the difference.

> "John Seed gave up his practice of insight meditation **after the rainforest suddenly took over as his teacher of truth.** In the last decade, since hearing the call of the wild, **Seed has become a leading environmental activist as well as a theoretician and teacher of deep ecology.**
>
> He travels around the world organizing and leading groups called **Council of All Beings, a workshop he developed with Joanna Macy** based on her Despair and Empowerment work. The Council of All Beings uses ritual, visualization, movement and breath work **to help people overcome their narrow anthropocentric views, and to actually experience interconnectedness with the earth** and other life forms. According to Seed, **this radical change in human consciousness is required if nature is to survive.**
>
> John Seed's own story reveals that **the natural world will teach us all the dharma we need to know,** if only we listen deeply enough."
>
> "...I find myself surrendering completely to the rain forest. The closest thing to meditation practice for me now is, **to lie down in the forest when it's dry, cover myself in leaves and imagine an umbilical cord reaching down into the earth.** Then I visualize myself as being one leaf on the tree of life, both as myself personally and as a human being, and I realize that the sap of that tree runs through every leaf, including me, whether I'm aware of it or not."
>
> 'The Rainforest As Teacher'
> John Seed interview by Wes Nisker
> Spring 1992 'Inquiring Mind' (Volume 8, #2)

As unusual as this description of the practice of deep ecology might sound we need to realize this is the mindset behind the systems thinking, man is part of nature, Humanist worldview of the Education for Sustainability movement. This is the mindset behind being Green. This is the mindset behind the Green movement Green Party and the Earth Charter. This is the mindset behind ecological wisdom and the environmental literacy programs taught in our schools.

> "The **Green principle of ecological wisdom** always occupies the primary position because it means far more than mere environmentalism or saving what's left. The **Greens have in mind deep ecology**. Deep ecology encompasses the study of Nature's subtle web of interrelated processes"
>
> Charlene Spretnak
> The Spiritual Dimension of Green Politics (page 23)

The Education for Sustainability movement's use of the Earth Charter as a training guide is a direct promotion of the deep ecology, Humanist mindset of the Greens. The Earth Charter US campaign uses guided meditations in deep ecology, based on the book by John Seed and Joanna Macy, "Thinking Like a Mountain: Towards a Council of All Beings", to train students and others to understand and adopt the principles of the Earth Charter.

Political Reality

The purpose of the Education for Sustainability movement is to change America's culture, religious base, society, economy and form of government. Anthony Cortese revealed another piece of the strategy to achieve these goals when he said, during a 2001 presentation on Sustainability & Ethics, that:

> **"We need a new story**. The new story is the kind of story that Eric Chivian and David Orr were telling this morning. It is a story about how **we are part of nature**." - "... and the **planet as a living organism**. And, **that's a big worldview change.** And that change will not come easily.
>
> **I encourage all of you that have any influence, in or over the education system to help work on it, because there is no higher leverage point than changing the mindset of people.** And if we don't change the mindset of the people who are coming out of the colleges ... out of these K-12 schools and colleges today ... then what happens is, we just keep fighting the same battles over and over again."
>
> Anthony Cortese
> Speech: Sustainability & Ethics
> Oregon Sustainability Forum, 2001

Education for Sustainability is a program to completely change America by politically indoctrinating, socially engineering, brainwashing or otherwise training America's youth to adopt a new worldview, the Green Party worldview. Making Education for Sustainability programs the focus of public education is the same as making the Green Party worldview the focus of public education. 'Systems thinking' is THE TOOL to change the beliefs of America's children.

Removing the belief in God from the hearts and minds of America's children is a TOP priority for this political movement. The key to America's strength is America's moral foundation. The key to destroying America is to destroy the moral foundation of America's youth. Our TOP priority must be to protect our children from this movement and rekindle our moral base.

A quick note: This is also one of the reasons for Green festivals. These events are designed to promote the idea of celebrating the earth and being Green. The purpose is not just to introduce innovative products but that is part of the draw. Green festivals are recruiting events. The objective is to get the public to link innovative ideas to being Green and the political views of the speakers to saving the earth. Green festivals are a lot like poison oak; it is an event where Green ideas can rub off and spread. The aim is to get adults to try on the Green mindset and children to adopt the Green mindset.

If Education for Sustainability was about saving the environment, and not a tool to impose the political agenda of the Greens, then why is changing our culture, religion, society, economy and form of government the objective? Can't we take care of the environment and believe in God at the same time? Yes. Do we need to throw out the US Constitution to address an environmental concern? No. The Greens have kept this overall plan quiet so they could instigate multiple changes in each of these areas to advance their goals hidden behind multiple assertions that change was needed to save the earth.

The international platform of the Global Greens or the "Charter of the Global Greens" was adopted in 2001. The Green Party of the United States is an arm of this international political party. The following statement, from the Preamble of the 2001 Global Greens Charter states:

> "Assert the need for fundamental changes in people's attitudes, values, and ways of producing and living."
>
> Source: http://www.globalgreens.org/blobalcharter-english

The Green Party is asserting that we need to change our values in hopes we will blindly accept that claim and take up their values and support their objectives. Convincing people to voluntarily change their values and their lives is a clever and easy way to impose a dictatorial political agenda. This Green strategy sounds like what Krushchev planned when he said, 'we will take you over from within without firing a single shot'.

2

Assertions Are Not Facts

The Green's political strategy matches the assertions and objectives of the Education for Sustainability movement. The following statement was made by Anthony Cortese during a 2001 presentation on 'Education for a Sustainable Future'.

> "Um, in effect **we have to reinvent the world socially, economically and technologically.** William McDonough, a green architect and the Chairman of our Board of Directors, says you have to take the filters out of the pipes to put the filters in our minds. **And that's the change that we really need to make, the shift in worldview.** Now, **this shift in worldview** is not going to come easy, you know, because **it means a change in thinking, values and action**."
>
> "... **Change in mind set requires a sustained, long-term effort to transform education at all levels**."
>
> Anthony Cortese, President Second Nature
> Speech: Education for a Sustainable Future
> Oregon Sustainability Forum - September 6, 2001
> Transcript (page 4)

The Greens would like us all, especially students, to blindly accept these assertions. This plan, to use public education to change student's worldview, thinking, values and actions through a sustained long term effort is a brainwashing scheme carefully hidden behind multiple assertions. An assertion is not a fact. The strategy of the Green Party and the Education for Sustainability movement are the same, assert the need for change.

The Green Party has been intentionally presented as the tiny, weak environmental party so people do not notice that the environmental movement is pushing Green Party ideas into our classrooms and into our lives. The US Green Party signed a "Common Ground" statement with the European Greens in 1999, an official statement that they are working together.

The implementation of the Green agenda, or Green Communism, in the United States is a calculated plan and a joint political effort. The Greens have pulled together behind the Education for Sustainability movement.

This political movement has several key components which include, but are not limited to the following:

- Blueprint for Survival
- Green Party
- Green environmental movement
- Earth Charter
- Humanism
- Communism
- United Nations (UNESCO – Agenda 21)

Over the past several years the Greens have escalated fears of environmental ruin, with a concentration on global warming, to create the false perception that the scope of environmental education had to be expanded dramatically. This is what opened the door to introduce the Education for Sustainability movement and to start pushing this invasive program into our schools.

The stage has been set for the current push to make Education for Sustainability the new mission of public education and sneak this Green Party training program into our schools.

If Education for Sustainability became the new mission of education, it would mean that every subject, at every grade level, as well as all daily school practices, would be used to align students with Education for Sustainability agenda. Students would not be able to escape the indoctrination process and that is the political objective. The tentacles of this indoctrination program would have a substantial ripple effect.

Green Party Advantage at Taxpayer Expense

Another statement made by Cortese during that 2001 event, adds more clarity, he said.

> "US Senator John Kerry and I started Second Nature eight years ago because **we felt that we needed a massive change in mindset**. And **we needed to work on higher education because higher education trains all the professionals in society** and the people who are leading all of our institutions, **all the future K-12 teachers.** They train all, and also **set-the-kids-up for our framework for learning**
>
> Anthony Cortese, Second Nature
> Oregon Sustainability Forum
> Sustainability & Ethics - September 2001

This statement exposes the plan to impose massive political change in the United States by targeting and training teachers to set-kids-up to adopt the mindset of the Education for Sustainability movement. The ripple effect of this program is aimed at changing the mindset of parents, faculty, administrators and ultimately the American people. Because the Education for Sustainability agenda mirrors the goals of the Green Party, the result of this training program would be to produce a Green voting block; which would give the Green Party a national political advantage at the taxpayer's expense.

Greening America's schools is part of the strategy to saturate public education with Green demands for students to go Green and for schools to adopt sustainable practices. The saturation strategy keeps faculty and students so busy conforming, that they do not realize they are being trained, or training themselves, to be GREEN-BOTS. The never ending assertion that students must help create a sustainable future, or risk environmental disaster, keeps survival at the forefront of their minds which is the primary motivation to conform to the Green way of thinking.

Education for Sustainability is not a lesson, at an age appropriate level, about an environmental topic; it is a plan to politically indoctrinate America's children. Following, is a partial list of goals from the 1990-1991 Green Party program. These goals confirm the Green Party plan, to use education and the idea of creating a sustainable society to advance their agenda, directly aligns with the mission and ideology of the Education for Sustainability movement.

> **"A Green educational policy will be based on** modeling and **teaching the following values**:
>
> - reverence for life in all its forms and its **interconnectedness**
> - ecological wisdom and a **sustainable life-style**
> - bioregional awareness and perspectives should be incorporated into many aspects of the school curriculum and should include **direct experience of nature as an interactive whole**
> - the **local environment should be the core of the curriculum**
> - we support expansion of the traditional concept of the classroom: bringing in plants and animals, growing food and an increased use of the schoolyard, nearby woodlands and neighborhoods
>
> Green Party program 1990-1991 (pages 12 & 13)

This list shows what teaching Green Party ideology in the classroom would look like and it looks just like Education for Sustainability. It is clear that many of these ideas have been pushed into our schools over the past 20 years.

Following is another Green Party policy statement that also aligns with the Education for Sustainability agenda.

> "We advocate a diverse system of education that would introduce children early to the wonders of the Great School (Nature), and would cultivate the wisdom of **eco-education, eco-economics, eco-politics, and eco-culture."**
>
> Green Party Platform 2004 (page 17)

The political objectives of Education for Sustainability are to use public education to train students 'they are part of nature' as the method to change our culture, economy and government. This sounds a lot like the Green Party plan for an eco-education, designed to create eco-economics, an eco-culture and eco-politics or an eco-government.

The following list represents a few basic comparisons between the educational goals of the Green Party 20 years ago and the Education for Sustainability agenda today.

Green Party Education Goals	**Education for Sustainability**
• interconnectedness, whole systems	• systems thinking, interconnectedness
• ecological wisdom	• sustainability, environmental literacy
• adopt a sustainable lifestyle	• adopt a sustainable lifestyle

Education for Sustainability is a plan to take advantage of the captive audience that enters the classroom and use the power of education to change student's beliefs, values and behavior.

The Education for Sustainability movement has selected the Earth Charter as a training tool. The following statement is from Second Nature's 2000 website. Second Nature used EFS to abbreviate Education for Sustainability.

> "EFS Writings: **EFS Charters and Declarations**
>
> **The following documents serve as Education for Sustainability (EFS) guidelines or commitments** for higher education institutions and their stakeholders."

This statement was followed by a short list of the 'guidelines or commitments' Second Nature recommends, which included the Earth Charter and Agenda 21.

Source:http://web.archive.org/web/200011210857/http://www.secondnature.org/programs/starfish/biblio.nsf/www/vbefscharters

Second Nature was advocating the use of the Earth Charter as an approved 'guideline or commitment' for the Education for Sustainability movement in 2000. Like Education for Sustainability, the goals of the Earth Charter are rooted in Green Party ideology. The purpose of the Earth Charter is to become international law so the goals of this document could be enforced worldwide. Who authorized the use of the Earth Charter as curriculum in America's schools? Gorbachev's Earth Charter has been used in multiple schools to align students with this document since at least 2000.

Who is responsible for pushing the Earth Charter into our schools? Part of the answer to that question is found in an article by the University Leaders for a Sustainable Future or ULSF. One of the primary goals of the University Leaders for a Sustainable Future is to train our children to support the aims of the Earth Charter. The following statements, from an October 2000 ULSF article, "Higher Education and the Earth Charter", confirm the plan.

> "Completed this year, the Earth Charter has emerged as a potent force for change in the way we think about ourselves and the Earth. **It is useful not only as a guide to our governments, institutions and communities, but as a learning tool in our schools and universities."**
>
> "**The Earth Charter Education Project - Conducted by ULSF**, the Earth Council and other organizations, **will develop and disseminate a range of educational materials for all ages to promote the** understanding of the global challenges we face, the **values and principles contained in the Earth Charter, and how the Earth Charter can be used to help bring about the transformations necessary** to attain a more sustainable way of living."
>
> "The Earth Charter Initiative can assist in awakening these values and providing a blueprint to a compassionate and sustainable future for all life on earth."
>
> Declaration Article Index (Volume 4, Number 1)
> Source: http://www.ulsf.org/pub_declaration_othvol41.htm

It is important to note that ULSF works closely with Second Nature and is a leading organizer of the Education for Sustainability movement.

> "ULSF is a member of the Alliance for Sustainability through Higher Education, a collaborative group of organizations with a common goal to catalyze an international movement for sustainable development and environmental literacy. Other member organizations include:
>
> - Center of Respect for Life and Environment (CRLE)
> - Consortium for Environmental Education in Medicine (CEEM)

- Management for Environment and Business Institute (MEB)
- National Wildlife Federation Campus Ecology Program
- Second Nature

Source: http://www.center1/ulsf/index.html
(or) http://www.ulsf.org (1996-1999)

Most of the major Education for Sustainability groups such as Second Nature and the University Leaders for a Sustainable Future have endorsed the Earth Charter. Green groups and Green strategies overlap in many areas because Education for Sustainability is the vehicle to advance multiple pieces of the Green agenda, in multiple areas, all at the same time. Each piece of the Education for Sustainability agenda is aimed at culminating in rapidly changing our culture, religion, society, economy and form of government.

The Education for Sustainability movement, the Earth Charter, the Green Party and the Green movement all work together and are a political movement, pretending to be an environmental movement. Most of the leading groups in the Green movement have also endorsed the Earth Charter. The following statement confirms the Earth Charter is part of the Green Party program.

> **"We must build on the "Earth Charter"** that came out of the 1992 U.N. environmental Earth Summit. New definitions of what constitutes real security between nations must be debated and adopted by the foreign policy community."
>
> Green Party Program 2000
> Section D: Foreign Policy

The goals of the Green Party and Earth Charter align. The 2010 Green Party program also includes the above statement. The Education for Sustainability plan to train America's children to align with the Earth Charter is the same as training America's children to align with the Green Party.

Although the Earth Charter is presented and promoted as non-biased, regarding politics and religion, that is not the case. The Earth Charter US is an implementation arm of the international Earth Charter.

The Earth Charter US confirmed the religious bias of the Earth Charter, from what the values are based on, to revealing that 'Systems Thinking' is THE TOOL to implement the earth-based Humanist worldview, in the following statement:

"The progressive sciences have joined with the ancient Eastern teachings and the wisdom traditions of earth-based cultures (a true merging of science and spirituality) to form a systemic/holistic approach to understanding life." ... **"Systems theory** enables us to see that everything in the universe is both a part in a whole and a whole unto itself."

Earth Charter US
The Art of Earth Chartering (page 6)
Source: http://earthcharterus.org

The Earth Charter is a spiritually and politically biased document. Earth Charter principles align with systems thinking and earth-based beliefs, which are the common denominators for the Education for Sustainability movement, the Green Party and the Green movement. These groups are politically and philosophically aligned. The Earth Charter is not a God friendly document, it stands for:

- progressive sciences and ancient Eastern teachings
- wisdom traditions of earth-based cultures
- merges science and spirituality for a new understanding of life
- systems theory or systems thinking

This sounds like the 'new philosophy of life' called for in the 'Blueprint for Survival'. It also sounds like the Communist Party goal, entered into the Congressional Record in 1963, to "...replace revealed religion with 'social' religion".

Using our schools to train America's children to adopt systems thinking and an earth-based Humanist worldview is the strategy to train our children to be against the founding principles of our nation which include the religious base. Using our schools to train America's children to adopt the goals of the Earth Charter is the strategy to train our children to oppose the United States Constitution and support international law.

This combination also trains America's children to adopt Green Party ideology which parallels the communist model of education designed to produce support for one single party and a dictatorial system of government.

We all enjoy the right, as do our compatriots, to express ideas and to discuss or advocate different points of view. That's free speech, free thought and individual freedom. The Education for Sustainability movement is putting these treasured freedoms at risk because this program is designed to indoctrinate our children to adopt Green Party ideology instead of thinking independently.

The United Nations is advocating Education for Sustainability programs worldwide but is not the source of this agenda or the culprit pushing this program into America's schools. The driving force behind pushing Education for Sustainability programs into our schools is the Green movement, Education for Sustainability groups, the Green Party and Earth Charter endorsers.

Education for Sustainability: Green Party Not Agenda 21

The plan to use education to train students to adopt sustainability goals did not originate as alleged, from Chapter 36 of the United Nation's Agenda 21 document or a UN Environmental Education Conference in 1977. The plan to use education to indoctrinate students to obey sustainability rules was outlined in the 1972 'Blueprint for Survival', which was prepared 5 years earlier for the first UN Environmental Summit.

> **"A 'Blueprint for Survival' was published in January 1972 occupying all of 'The Ecologist'**, Vol. 2 No. 1, **in advance of the world's first ever Environment Summit**: **the 1972 UN Conference** on the Human Environment, in Stockholm.
>
> **So great was the demand for the Blueprint that it was subsequently republished in paperback** by Penguin books on 14 September 1972."
> ..."The principle authors were Edward Goldsmith and Robert Allen ..."
>
> Source: http://www.theecologist.info/key27.html

The concept behind Education for Sustainability, to impose a sustainable or stable society by indoctrinating students, was outlined in agenda item #276 in the 'Blueprint for Survival', which states:

> "It is self-evident that **no amount of legislative, administrative or industrial change** will create **stable communities if the individuals who are meant to comprise them are not fitted for them.**
>
> **As soon as the best means of inculcating the values of the stable society have been agreed upon, they should be incorporated into our educational systems.**
>
> Indeed, **it may not be until the generation of 40-50 year olds have been educated in these values** (so that as far as possible everybody up to the age of 50 understands them) **that stable communities will achieve sufficient acceptance for them** to be permanently useful."
>
> "Towards the stable society: strategy for change"
> Source: http://www.theecologist.info/page32.html

The 1972 'Blueprint for Survival' inspired the environmental movement and led to the founding of the Green Party. This link explains why the goals of the Green movement and the Green Party align. The concept of sustainability or Education for Sustainability also stems from the 'Blueprint for Survival'. This explains why the objectives and ideology of the Education for Sustainability movement also align with the political agenda of the Green movement and the Green Party.

Agenda 21 is a purposeful document that promotes the adoption of the United Nation's goals for sustainability, or Green Communism, worldwide. Agenda 21 is a roadmap, not the driver. Education for Sustainability groups gladly point to Chapter 36 of Agenda 21 as a reference, because it provides them with an excuse for their actions. Pointing to Agenda 21 is also a Green strategy to keep the focus on how to deal with that overwhelming UN plan and off the root of the problem, which is communism, and the out of control Green movement that is imposing Green Communism in our backyard. It was the Green movement that pushed environmental education into America's schools. It was the Green movement that used the environmental cause as an excuse to push Green political activism into the classroom. The Green movement was changing the role of public education years before Agenda 21 emerged in 1992.

Our number one priority must be to save our children from being further indoctrinated by the Green movement, which is now using Education for Sustainability as the tool to train our children to be GREEN-BOTS. To stop the indoctrination of our children we must stop the problem at the source.

During the week of January 23, 2012 an Op-Ed piece by Congressman Wally Herger titled "What's all the buzz about Agenda 21?" appeared in Yreka's Siskiyou Daily News. A few excerpts from Congressman Herger's article follow:

> "While this document was agreed to by the United Nations, the United States is a party to the agreement only by our membership in the UN. For the agreement to become legally binding it would require submission to the U.S. Senate for ratification by the President. This has not occurred. Again, "Agenda 21" is not legally binding on the United States."
> "Let's not be distracted by Agenda 21, because it is not a threat in and of itself, but let's rather continue to battle the mindset that underlies it and all of the other policies and laws that have done so much harm over the years to rural America -- radical environmentalism.
>
> The Heritage Foundation supports this approach, stating in a recent report that opponents of Agenda 21 should "not allow it to divert them from opposing the more ubiquitous, overarching agenda of homegrown environmental extremists". The true fix to extreme environmentalism is continued education of ordinary Americans, updating the laws and the

> judicial system that have crippled our resource base, and perhaps most importantly, a new Administration that shares our philosophy."
>
> "If we truly want to make a difference in our local economy, we need to focus our time and attention on reforming our own laws and regulations. The current dispute over the Klamath dams has everything to do with United States law, and nothing to do with the United Nations."

In this statement, Congressman Herger, a veteran representative, issued a very important warning, an accurate assessment and a strategic recommendation. The American people need to realize that environmental extremism is Green communism and is propelled by the Green movement not a radical fringe. The Education for Sustainability agenda; to change America's values, culture, religion, society, economy and our form of government is the epitome of political extremism.

A little more history, the 1972 'Blueprint for Survival' laid out an agenda for the environmental movement to follow. That same year the Communist Party USA was preparing to hijack the environmental cause and use that issue to impose communism. Gus Hall, National Chairman of the Communist Party USA from 1959 to 2000, made the following statements in his 1972 book 'Ecology'.

> "This is true in the struggle to save the environment ... we must be the organizers, the leaders of these movements ... Human society cannot basically stop the destruction of the environment under capitalism. Socialism is the only structure that makes it possible"

The Communist Party planned to take control of the environmental cause in the very beginning and in 1972, the same year the 'Blueprint for Survival' was released; the Communist Party instructed their allies to:

- infiltrate the environmental cause
- become the leaders and the organizers of the environmental movement
- use the environmental cause to advance socialist policies
- assert the environment cannot be saved under capitalism
- use the environmental movement to impose socialism then communism

The 'Blueprint for Survival' called for creating sustainable societies and led to the founding of the Green Party. It is no accident that the agenda of the Green Party mirrors communism.

Speaking of communism; on March 20, 2012, a Glenn Beck TV post, by Tiffany Gabbay included the following statements.

> "Glenn contends that those seeking to dismantle the American way are "no longer progressives." Instead, the left has successfully morphed into what it has always intended to be: Full-fledged Communists."
>
> "Glenn informed viewers that progressives' "road" has come to an end, and thus, it is now time to "start studying Communism."
>
> Source: http://www.gbtv.com

'Training for Treason' is a resource, which confirms how Education for Sustainability is being used to indoctrinate America's children to adopt the philosophy of Green Communism and how that political agenda is being implemented, in multiple areas, across America.

It is critical to understand where the United States government stands on the issue of Education for Sustainability. The Obama Administration and the US Department of Education are in complete support of advancing the goals of the sustainability movement through our public education system.

A leading group in the US based Education for Sustainability movement is the 'US Partnership for the Decade of Education for Sustainable Development' - US Partnership - for short. The aim of the US Partnership is to impose the objectives of the United Nation's Decade on Education for Sustainability in the United States. The US Partnership featured a link to a letter from the US Secretary of Education Arne Duncan to the "Attendees at the UNESCO World Conference on Education for Sustainable Development" which was held on March 31, 2009. Long story short, in that letter Secretary Duncan stated:

> "President Obama also intends to make our country one of the leaders in responding to global climate change. Our goal is to ensure that we use some alternative sources of electricity, and we aim to reduce our greenhouse gas emissions.
>
> **These major changes require educating our people - both students and adults - about the importance of environmental sustainability** and training our people in this developing field.
>
> **We intend to do everything in our power to encourage education for sustainability.**"
>
> Source: http://www2.ed.gov/about/inits/ed/internationaled/unesco-letter.pdf
> (Bold emphasis added)

This statement by Secretary Duncan that, "we intend to do everything in our power to encourage education for sustainability" is a serious commitment. The plan to train students and the American people to conform to the Education for Sustainability agenda makes it absolutely imperative that we all understand exactly what this agenda means to our children, to our families and to the future of freedom.

After posting Secretary Duncan's letter, the US Partnership featured the following news release on their website:

> **"September 21, 2010 - Secretary of Education, Arne Duncan gives keynote address at Sustainability Education Summit –**
>
> **"Today, I promise you that [the Department of Education] will be a committed partner in the national effort** to build a more environmentally literate and responsible society...
>
> **We must advance the sustainability movement through education**... **Education and sustainability are the keys to our economic future-and our ecological future...**
>
> We are proud to be... joining you in this work, and **hopeful about the impact we will make together**."

Source:http://www.ed.gov/news/speeches/greening-department-education-secretary-duncans-remarks-sustainability-summit
US Partnership Source:http://www.uspartnership.org/main/view_archive/1
Letter Source: http://www2.ed.gov/about/inits/ed/internationaled/unesco-letter.pdf

This statement indicates the Administration considers "education and sustainability" the key to our economic future". Does the Obama Administration realize the aim of Education for Sustainability and Earth Charter partners is to impose a zero growth economy?

The following excerpt is from a 1997 document from Gorbachev's organization Green Cross International titled "The Earth Charter: The Green Cross Philosophy", which states:

> "Principle 7: **Zero-Growth** of Material Economy
>
> (a) Even allowing for rapid technological improvements, resources are finite. A basic sustainable level of per capita material consumption will have to be reached in accordance with the Earth's natural resource constraints. This requires both increasing the material consumption of the people now living in poverty and the reducing material over-consumption by the rich minority. Full life-cycle accounting practices and resource and energy efficiency need to become integrated at all levels, and in all activities, of the economy."

Source: http://www.earthcharter.org/resources/essays.htm

Another confirmation a zero growth economy and a political transformation are part of the Education for Sustainability agenda comes from the 'Youth Sourcebook on Sustainable Development. (Winnipeg: IISD, 1995), which states"

> "NATURAL RESOURCES
> **Political Transformation**
>
> The technology used should be appropriate and simple. **Production should be mainly from local materials and for local use**, not for exports to rich consumers; it should provide a community which is in harmony with nature and which is **self-sufficient**.
>
> **Such no-growth economics cannot be achieved without revolutionary political transformation** involving the demise of power groups with vested interest in maintaining the status quo. ..."
>
> "...The alternative can only be made possible if there is grassroots democracy, economic decentralization and regional **and local self-sufficiency."**
>
> Source: http://iisd.ca/youth/ysbk037.htm.

The plan to impose a zero growth economy also aligns with agenda item #166 from the 1972 'Blueprint for Survival' which states:

> **"Our task is to create a society which is sustainable** ..."
>
> "... Such a society by definition **would depend not on expansion** but on stability."
>
> Blueprint for Survival

The concept of zero growth aligns with the concept of a non-expanding or non-growing society. These ideas to create a sustainable society are not spontaneous but concepts from the 'Blueprint for Survival' which inspired the Green Party. The sustainability agenda now being imposed throughout America is the execution of the Green Party agenda.

The Greens have done a good job over the past few decades of gradually introducing Green ideas, from sustainability to self-sufficient communities, so these ideas appear to be spontaneous responses to environmental concerns. This approach keeps people from considering these ideas represent the execution of a long-term political agenda that was laid out 40 years ago.

The Greens are training students to believe that a 'revolutionary political transformation' is necessary to save the planet. This is the why the radical political goals of the Education for Sustainability movement are to change our culture, religion, society, economy and form of government.

Another revealing look at the politics behind the Education for Sustainability movement comes from the notes, documenting the proceedings of a US Partnership meeting, held in February 2005, regarding their progress to advance the Education for Sustainability agenda. An excerpt from those notes, a progress report from the US Partnership's Higher Education Action Team, follows:

> "US Partnership for the Decade of Education for Sustainable DevelopmentNotes from February 2005 Partner Forum - Posted by Heather, 02/28/05 (10:20 AM)
>
> **Higher Education Action Team**
>
> "Higher Education Action Team (David Blockstein): Debbie Rowe, Wynn Calder and myself, have visited more than 50% of the leaders of higher educational associations who are here in the DC area. These people are heads of associations that represent university and college presidents. There has been great receptivity to the USPDESD.
>
> There is a group of six of these organizations headed by the American Council on Education that is especially interested. They are trying to figure out how they can best be involved. Certainly they can work as communication channels to the colleges and universities, and they can officially recognize the Decade and its goals. **Every one of the folks they've met has asked how to assure that education for sustainable development is not just seen as something on the left side of the political spectrum.** It is important that this be, and be perceived as, a bi-partisan, broadly supported effort."

If a 'leftist' political agenda was not obvious, why would "**every one of the folks"** they met with, immediately see the Education for Sustainability movement was **"on the left side of the political spectrum"** and ask "how to assure" that Education for Sustainability would not be seen as leftist?

> **"It turns out that virtually the whole political agenda of the progressive left can be fit inside the word 'sustainability'."**
>
> Peter Wood, President,
> National Association of Scholars
> 'How Many Delawares?' March 6, 2008
> Source: http://www.nas.org/

The political agenda attached to the Education for Sustainability movement is not just a wee bit left, it is far left. Education for Sustainability is not an educational breakthrough; it is a program designed to train students of all ages to align with one political ideology, which mirrors Green Party goals and communism.

If this indoctrination scheme is not addressed and these programs are allowed to remain in our schools, the political agenda of the far left will define our children's future, our future and the future of our nation. Expelling Education for Sustainability programs is one of the most important duties of our time. Training America's children to align with one political party puts free thought, individual freedom, the voting process and our Republic at risk. We must uphold the principles upon which this nation was founded.

> "We hold these truths to be self-evident, that all men are created equal, that they are endowed by their Creator with certain unalienable Rights that among these are Life, Liberty and the pursuit of Happiness."
>
> United States Declaration of Independence, 1776

Boldly speaking, our forefathers made it abundantly clear that this nation was founded on moral principles that were based on a belief in almighty God. The success of this nation stems from that belief and worldview. Life is not perfect and mistakes have been made, but by and large, the success of this great nation is due to the initial grounding in moral principles based on God's word.

We are a melting pot and in a free nation, people can believe differently, however, preserving the moral base upon which this nation stands is essential. Every other country protects and preserves their base, because that base is what makes them, them. We need to remember who we are and make protecting and preserving our base a national priority. The Greens plan to use Education for Sustainability and systems thinking to change and destroy America's base. Constitutional principles, founding beliefs and national pride must once again be part of our children's education or our base will disappear.

> **"We must rededicate ourselves to the great principles of our Constitution... our nation needs the services of organizations who will remain vigilant in the defense of our principles."**
>
> President John F. Kennedy

The Education for Sustainability movement has generated support for this program by selling the idea of 'sustainability' without publicizing the plan is to use this program as a tool to change our culture, religion, society, economy and our form of government. Changing the United States government would require eliminating the US Constitution and the freedoms that go with it. What form of government do the Greens have in mind? The following definitions offer a quick look at distinctions between communism, socialism and capitalism.

Communism:	Government control of production and distribution
Socialism:	Public control of production and distribution
Capitalism:	Individual control of production and distribution

It is important to consider, as we review this list, that the Communist Party pushes socialism not communism as the following statement confirms.

> "A better and peaceful world is possible – a world where people and nature come before profits. That's' socialism. That's our vision. We are the Communist Party of the USA"
>
> Communist Party USA
> Source: http://www.cpusa.org

The Communist Party uses socialism as their vision because it sounds less threatening than communism. First we do not need to change our government system. Our government system is the greatest, but we need to clean out the corruptive forces that have gained a strong foothold. The value of understanding the Communist Party uses socialism to soften their agenda is to realize the Green Party also calls for socialism or public control of production and distribution. Actions speak louder than words and the Green's have used the environmental cause to increase, not decrease, government control of production and distribution.

Along those same lines, we the people, did not build the Education for Sustainability movement nor ask that this agenda be pushed into our schools and forced on our children. Special interest groups, like Second Nature, get the credit.

We need to understand the details of the Education for Sustainability program so we can recognize this agenda when we see it. A good place to start is to understand why systems thinking and the man is part of nature idea is such an important part of this program.

> **"All students would understand that we are an integral part of nature.**"
>
> Anthony Cortese, Second Nature

Dr. Corliss Lamont is a leading authority on the subject of Humanism. The back cover of Lamont's 1990 book "The Philosophy of Humanism" (Seventh Edition) features the following review by the New York Times and comments about the author:

> "In a work that has become standard text and reference in the ongoing national debate that swirls around secular humanism, Lamont offers a vigorous argument for **a philosophy that advocates happiness in this life rather than hope for a heaven in an afterlife."**
>
> New York Times

> "Dr. Lamont has long been associated with Humanism, and authored the standard text on the subject, 'The Philosophy of Humanism' in 1949." ... "Dr. Lamont was a director of the American Civil Liberties Union from 1932 to 1954."

Dr. Lamont was the director of the ACLU for 22 years and the author of multiple books including, "You might Like Socialism". The top 2 principles of the 1933 'Humanist Manifesto' listed on page 286 of Lamont's book, 'The Philosophy of Humanism' follow:

> • **First:** Religious humanists regard **the universe as self-existing and not created**.
>
> • **Second: Humanism believes that man is part of nature** and that he has emerged as the result of a continuous process.

The number one Humanist belief is that God did not create the universe and the number two belief is that man is part of nature. Cortese said, "All students would understand that we are an integral part of nature".

Systems thinking is the method to embed Humanist's beliefs in Education for Sustainability curriculum and train our children, starting in kindergarten, to believe that saving the earth requires they accept they are part of nature so they will deny God and reject America's founding principles. This method also sets students up to accept or support a different form of government.

This political agenda may not belong in the classroom but it is already in many of our schools and universities. One of the Ten Key Values of the Green Party is the 'man is part of nature' Humanist worldview. Training "all students" to align with this worldview is the same as training all students to be against God and country.

In the introduction to the 'Philosophy of Humanism', Lamont stated "the supernatural aspects of Christianity" were regarded as a "poetic myth". Lamont also outlined specific methods to advance Humanism through education and stated on page 274, that:

> **"Humanist education naturally accents social rather than individualistic aims.** This implies both more attention to social studies, such as economics, politics **(including civil liberties),** and sociology, and **inclusion in the curriculum** of **courses on ethics in order to train the youth of a nation in the broad Humanist attitudes of loyalty to the social group and to humanity.**
>
> Humanism would also greatly extend **the teaching of science and scientific method putting emphasis on the student's learning to think**

> **straight**, but not neglecting the inculcation of basic facts." – "... **stress complete cultural democracy** ..."

Lamont pointed out that an educational program designed to train students to think like a Humanist would include:

- using ethics courses to train students in Humanist attitudes
- training students to be loyal to a social group rather than pursue individual aims
- using a scientific method as a basis for decision making

Lamont's ideas parallel the Education for Sustainability ideas outlined below:

- Green America's schools and create a new social group
- Train children to be activists loyal to the Green social group
- Train children they must save the earth and skip their dreams
- Use systems thinking as a scientific method for decision making
- Train students they are part of nature, promote Humanism

Another example of how Education for Sustainability aligns with the goals of a Humanist education:

> "... an emphasis on **the separation of humans from the rest of nature**, compartmentalized learning - where we learn everything in silos; individual specialization and success; and **the absence of explicit ethics and values** in learning, **the dominant educational model is reinforcing the current inequitable and unsustainable worldview."**
>
> Anthony Cortese, Second Nature
> Speech: Education for a Sustainable Future
> Oregon Sustainability Forum
> September 6, 2001 - Transcript (page 5)

This statement by Cortese suggests an education that 'separates man from nature' is an unsustainable worldview and, that an education with explicit ethics that promotes 'man is part of nature' is a sustainable worldview.

A Wolf in Sheep's Clothing

The following statement, featured in the November 2002 issue of 'Sustainability News' from (OSU) Oregon State University, quotes Anthony Cortese on a few key goals, regarding the Education for Sustainability agenda. These goals also parallel Lamont's Humanist education plan to discourage individual aims and train students to focus on group goals. The OSU newsletter states:

> "What would transformational change look like? According to Cortese, it would reflect a **complete shift in thinking, values and action.** ... Communities would change from being auto-centered to people centered, the market would serve the people rather than the other way around.
>
> Emphasis on **individual success would diminish;** we would **focus on community success**. We would work to **promote democracy and human rights**."

This statement verifies the plan to use the power and influence of public education to impose a predetermined political agenda on students, citizens and communities. The strategy to redesign student's thinking, values and actions so they will conform and support the implementation of this sustainability agenda in their communities is evident.

This statement also outlines the sustainability objective to force communities to become people centered not auto centered. This would require policies to force the reduction of, or elimination of, the current use of personal automobiles. The plan to use Education for Sustainability to push this agenda on citizens and to foster a complete shift in students' thinking, values and action shows no respect for free thought and individual freedom.

The following chart compares the basic ideas Lamont specified for a Humanist education with the Education for Sustainability goals outlined by Cortese.

Lamont's Humanist Education	**Education for Sustainability**
• Social aims not individualistic aims	• Diminish value of individual success
• Humanist ethics, loyal to social group	• Humanist ethics, loyal to Greens
• Accent social aims	• Focus on community success
• Stress complete cultural democracy	• Promote democracy
• Civil liberties (human rights)	• Promote human rights
• Use a scientific method	• Scientific method, systems thinking
• Train students to think straight	• Change thinking, values and actions

The use of a 'scientific method' is a high priority in a Humanist education because science is used to train students to make decisions based on attaining goals void of God's moral compass.

Second Nature and the Education for Sustainability movement use the Natural Step, a systems thinking program, to train students to make decisions based on 4 principles or goals. This Natural Step process appears to be based on a similar 4 step process, which was agenda item #210 in the 1972 'Blueprint for Survival'. The 'Blueprint's' 4 step process follows.

> "The principal conditions of a stable society-one that to all intents and purposes can be sustained indefinitely while giving optimum satisfaction to its members - are:
>
> 1. **minimum disruption of ecological processes**;
>
> 2. **maximum conservation of materials and energy**-or an economy of stock rather than flow;
>
> 3. a **population in which recruitment equals loss** and,
>
> 4. a social system in which **the individual can enjoy**, rather than feel restricted **by, the first three conditions."**

Next is the summary of the current Natural Step's 4 step process.

> "The Natural Step is a framework that can help guide our actions toward sustainability. It calls out four system conditions that define sustainability in scientific terms. In a sustainable global society, the ecosphere is not subject to systematically increasing:
>
> 1. Concentrations of substances extracted from the earth's crust. Examples: Fossil fuels, metals, and minerals
>
> 2. Concentrations of substances produced by society (synthetics) Examples: Persistent substances (DDT, PCB's...), plastics, Freon
>
> 3. Degradation by physical means. Examples: Over-harvesting (forests, oceans...), eliminating biodiversity and in that society
>
> 4. People are not subject to conditions that systematically undermine their capacity to meet their basic needs. Examples: Overpopulation, unlivable wages, environmental and social inequity"
>
> *Developed in 1989 by Swedish oncologist Karl-Henrik Robert and a peer group.
>
> Source: http://www.sustainableschools.org/

It is important to recognize the similarity of these 2 programs; not only because the Natural Step reflects the Blueprint's concept but also, because they are both designed to control people and restrict activities. In addition, the Natural Step process is a key part of the Education for Sustainability training program. A good example of how students are trained to conform, is a Natural Step process called 'backcasting'. According to the Natural Step, the definition of 'backcasting' is:

> "**Backcasting**: A fancy word for a strategic planning method where a successful future is envisioned first. The current reality of today is then assessed against the vision.
>
> Source: http://www.naturalstepusa.org/

By definition, this practice trains students to equate a 'successful future' with a sustainable future. Second, it trains students that a successful future depends on applying this 'planning method' to their lives. Third, it trains students to conform and not to do anything outside the guidelines. 'Backcasting' allows any idea, subject or situation to be used to manipulate and intimidate students to change their thoughts, values and behavior.

What happens if student's dreams and ideas do not fit within the box outlined in the Natural Step principles? You guessed it, if it does not fit, forget it. Restricting free thought and individual freedom to impose this political agenda is not education, nor the role of public education. This is political indoctrination. Of interest, Anthony Cortese is a founding member of the Natural Step US, according to his bio, as an Advisor for Living Routes, an Ecovillage program.

Population Control

A major goal of the Greens and the Education for Sustainability movement is population control or population stabilization. Considering the "Blueprint for Survival" prompted the founding and agenda of the Green Party, it is only wise to understand Green goals for population control. One of the 'Blueprint's' top 4 system goals includes a population where "recruitment equals loss", which indicates the birth of a baby requires the death of another. Please think about what that would mean in practice.

Following are two other population control goals, listed in agenda item #257 in the 'Blueprint' regarding "ending population growth". One of these goals, the call for our government to provide free contraceptives, just made national news.

Both of the following political goals reflect the implementation of the Green's population control agenda.

- **provide, at local and national levels, free contraception**
- **provide contraceptives free of charge, free sterilization, and abortion on demand**

Overpopulation is also one of the issues identified in the Natural Step process. What are students being trained to support regarding the environment and population control? Jonathon Porritt is a former Chairman of the Green Party in Europe. The 'Times Online' featured an article about Jonathon Porritt on February 1, 2009 titled "Two children should be limit, says green guru" which included the following statement:

> "Jonathon Porritt, who chairs the government's Sustainable Development Commission, says 'curbing population growth through contraception and abortion' must be at the heart of policies to fight global warming."
>
> Source: http://www.timesonline.co.uk/

Global warming is the reason to limit families to 2 children and Green Party leader Jonathon Porritt is now the chair of the government's Sustainable development Commission. Sustainability is the vehicle to impose the Green's political agenda. No surprise that stabilizing the population is also part of Education for Sustainability agenda. The following statement sheds light on where the Greens plan to be in the future and Cortese credits the "world's most progressive" thinkers for their assistance with the report.

> "... **The world population is stabilized at a level that is within the short and long term carrying capacity of the earth's finite resources.** The market is the servant in aligning social, economic and natural systems for mutual benefit and sustainability."
>
> Anthony Cortese, Second Nature
> Visions of Sustainability in 2050
> Source: http://www.secondnature.org

Is the goal of a stable population in a self sufficient and sustainable community one where recruitment equals loss? Now is the time to find out.

3

Premeditated Deception

"Leveraging Change: The Role of the University in a Sustainable Future" was the title of a January 2000 speech Anthony Cortese presented for an MIT panel on the Alliance for Global Sustainability. Meanings of the word 'leverage' include influence or force. The title of the presentation reflects the message.

In this presentation Cortese called on higher education to get involved and to use their influence to advance the goals of "sustainability education" or Education for Sustainability. Cortese also revealed a key strategy the Education for Sustainability movement was using to get students and others on board. Cortcsc said:

> "We do not change by negative information. **If we have learned anything in the environmental field, we have learned that more negative doom-and-gloom is not going to make change**. We must tell the truth, and the truth is that we are in trouble. But **we must also paint a picture of a future that is so desirable that people will want to move from where they are now to that new future - a sustainable future."**
>
> **"Let us imagine a society that has all present and future humans healthy and where they have their basic needs met, have fair and equitable access to Earth's resources, have a decent quality of life** while we preserve the biologically diverse ecosystems on which we all depend."
>
> Anthony D. Cortese, President, Second Nature
> Leveraging Change: The Role of the University in a Sustainable Future
> Source:http://www.secondnature.org/history/writings/speeches/leveraging_change.htm

In this statement Cortese pointed out, that the leaders in the Green movement figured out their negative 'doom and gloom' strategy was not working, so they added a new slant which Cortese described when he said:

> "... **we must also paint a picture of a future that is so desirable that people will want to move from where they are now to that new future** - a sustainable future."

This is another form of manipulation. Forecast doom to scare students into compliance or forecast bliss, with a false promise, hooked to compliance. The political goal is the same, impose change and control people's lives. The Education for Sustainability strategy is to paint an imaginary picture of a sustainable future that sounds 'so desirable' that students will want to live there. Fabricating a whopping tale about a fantasy future and then presenting it to students as a factual alternative to planetary ruin, is not education but rather, an abuse of power and a violation of trust.

If I told a class of children, I envisioned a place where toys grew on trees and all they had to do to get there, was to make a few sacrifices ... would that be education? No. Imagination is a powerful tool of persuasion. We know toys do not grow on trees. Persuading children to make sacrifices to attain an unrealistic goal is indoctrination not education.

If I told a class of college students, I envisioned a future where everyone was healthy and life was bliss, and all they had to do to get there was make some sacrifices ... would that be education? No. Persuading students to make sacrifices to attain an unrealistic goal, such as a future where everyone is healthy and life is bliss, is just as unrealistic as promising children that toys grow on trees. This is indoctrination not education.

The strategy to paint a fantasy future, which Cortese outlined in 2000, is one of the main ways the Education for Sustainability movement manipulates students to change their behavior. The following excerpt, from Second Nature's current 'Vision & Philosophy' statement, confirms this is still the Education for Sustainability movement's political strategy.

> "We imagine a just and sustainable future. We envision a world where **all members of humankind are healthy**, **live in socially vibrant** and culturally diverse **communities** have personal and economic security ...
>
> Source: http://www.secondnature.org

The fairy tale image of a sustainable future is a tool of deception to trick students and others into making sacrifices, changing their lives to align with Green Party goals in the present, so the Greens can control the lives of the American people now and in the future.

Following is an example of how the fantasy future tactic can be introduced and used in a classroom situation to shape political beliefs and change student's behavior.

- First, guide students to talk about what is bad in the world and ask a question like, what do you think the world will be like in 50 years? This sets the tone for a doom scenario based on the assumption, if we have this problem now just imagine how bad it will get in 50 years. Then encourage a doom and gloom forecast to create sadness, frustration and anger towards our nation.

- Next, guide students with another question like, what do you want the future to look like in 50 years? Then talk about a positive vision of a future that sounds just like paradise, where the earth is saved, everyone is happy and label that a 'sustainable future'. Then ask who wants to live in that future?

- Then, empower students with the idea that they can create that future by eating less cheese burgers or walking to school. Whatever the assigned task, the goal is to get students to agree to change their behavior in the present.

- Finally, direct students to a sustainability guide, such as the Earth Charter, and encourage students to adopt the Green's definition of sustainability. In the case of the Earth Charter, that would also include supporting international law over the US Constitution.

The Education for Sustainability plan is to use public education to train students to dedicate their lives to creating a sustainable society. This plan matches the Green Party goal to use education to emphasize the challenge of creating a sustainable society.

> **"Greens advocate holistic education emphasizing the challenge of creating a sustainable, just, and peaceful society** in harmony with the Earth and its life."
>
> Green Party Program 1990-1991 (page 13)

The concept of creating a sustainable society has been part of the agenda of the international Green Party since about 1974. One of the most important things to understand about the word sustainability is that is directly connected to the radical agenda of the international Green Parties. This word represents the goals of a political movement not an environmental cause. The Education for Sustainability movement is advancing the Green Party plan by using education to 'emphasize' the need for students to dedicate their lives to creating a sustainable society.

The sustainability movement includes a condescending and condemning attitude towards students who do not wish to participate. Students have been subjected to ridicule, peer pressure and grade discrimination for not conforming to the views of Green teachers. The political objective is to change student's behavior and the end justifies the means.

> **"Our most stalwart concept,** the one that we hold forth for future leaders in the Education for Sustainability movement, **is that the entire education experience must change behavior."**

"...the educational experience **of all students must be aligned with the principles of sustainability ..."**

Second Nature Vision & Philosophy 2011
Source: http://www.secondnature.org

Trash the present, paint a picture of an imaginary but desirable sustainable future and manipulate students to conform to every Green demand is the game plan. We all need to realize we are dealing with a political movement not an environmental movement.

"Manipulation is persuading people to make up their minds while withholding some of the facts from them."

Harold Evans
British Journalist, 1971

It all comes down to moral character and truth or deception? The fantasy future is a harmful political strategy to take advantage of students for political gain. The following 2001 statement, made by Anthony Cortese, reveals another very important part of the Education for Sustainability movement's political strategy.

"**Most people are focusing on policy issues, how to change the politics in Washington**, and ...**when, in fact,** in the long term, **if we're talking about sustainability in the long term, we've got to change the way we think because it's the only way we'll change our behavior.**

Now, higher education is important for all levels of education because it prepares most of the professionals who develop, lead, manage, teach, work in, and influence society's institutions in K through 12 education. **We're going to replace twenty two million K through 12 teachers** in the next [ten years?] and **if we begin at the beginning of the pipeline training them properly,** there we have a chance of making a difference. Besides **training the future teachers**, higher education strongly influences the learning framework of K through 12 education."

Anthony Cortese, President of Second Nature
Speech: Education for a Sustainable Future
Oregon Sustainability Forum
September 6, 2001 - Transcript (page 5)

The first statement by Cortese, leaves little doubt the goals of Education for Sustainability are political. While most people are focused on changing policy in Washington, Second Nature's strategy is to indoctrinate students as the way to impose their political agenda below the public radar.

In addition, the statement "if we begin at the beginning of the pipeline training them properly" confirms Education for Sustainability is indeed, a "training" program". A key part of the strategy to impose the Green agenda nationwide is to train students headed for a career in education to think properly. This movement is targeting future teachers, so those teachers will go out and train students in their classrooms, to think properly, which in this case, means to eat Green, live Green, worship Green and vote Green.

> "The philosophy of the classroom in one generation will be the philosophy of government in the next."
>
> Abraham Lincoln

Lincoln's words ring true today. The harmful political agenda behind the Education for Sustainability movement does not belong in America's schools as this political indoctrination program puts free thought, individual freedom, the voting process and our form of government at risk.

Many parents plan and save for years so they can send their children to college; believing that a college education will give their children an opportunity to fulfill their dreams. Students go to college with the expectation of learning, pursuing their dreams and achieving success.

The Education for Sustainability agenda, from painting fantasy futures to backcasting, is an underhanded scheme to change student's thinking, demand conforming behavior, trash their dreams and use them to produce predictable political support for the anti-American agenda of the Greens.

Our children are being led to believe that the environment is in ruin and their only hope is to go Green. The weight of the world is a heavy burden to put on great big shoulders, but putting that burden on little tiny shoulders, is eco-child abuse. The Greens have maintained a high level of stress in the classroom for many years, which is a brainwashing technique. After a certain level of stress, students may adopt the Green demand or belief, just to relieve stress. Stress, fear and celebrating nature all play a key role in changing student's beliefs.

Humanism Goes Green

The Green movement has stretched and twisted the environmental cause in many different ways to promote Green Party ideology. Using famous people's birthdays to mark an occasion to celebrate the earth is one of the tactics. After explaining the goals of a Humanist education, Corliss Lamont, author of the 'Philosophy of Humanism' discussed the Christian myth of celebrating Easter and Christmas, followed by a few suggestions on ways to celebrate Humanism, stating:

> "The essential function of artists and writers in a Humanist society will be to **work out rituals and ceremonies that are consistent with the central**

tenets of Humanism. Such ceremonies should appeal to the emotions as well as the minds of the people, capturing their imagination and giving an outlet to their delight in pomp and pageantry."

"Easter can be humanistically utilized to **celebrate the rebirth of the vital forces of Nature** and the renewal of man's own energies. In fact, according to the anthropologists, Easter probably originated in just such a way. **Humanism will likewise naturally make much of the birthdays of outstanding leaders** of the human race, and of other important anniversaries."

Corliss Lamont
The Philosophy of Humanism (pages 276- 277)

Earth Day celebrations match Lamont's description of celebrating nature. The first Earth Day was held specifically on April 22, 1970. April 22nd is the Father of Communism, Vladimir Lenin's birthday. Earth Day fits the plan to celebrate Humanism and the accomplishments of leaders you admire, like Lenin. It also sheds more light on why the Earth Day Network is an Earth Charter partner organization. The Earth Charter reflects Humanism, communism and Green Party ideology.

Of interest, many people involved in the first Earth Day event in 1970 have commented, they never understood why Earth Day "had" to be held on that particular day. After learning it was Lenin's birthday it made sense. Earth Day events have captured people's imaginations, partly because it was heavily promoted in the 90's as the way for people to show support for the environmental cause. The following Green Party statement reflects a deep ecology or Humanist worldview.

"Spirituality for Greens is thus a way of being in the world that acknowledges and celebrates our connectedness to the Earth ..."

Green Party Program 1990-1991 (page 32)

Humanism adds a new dimension of understanding the purpose behind the "All Species Parades" held on Earth Day. Children are dressed up like different animals for this parade and run around pretending to be that animal species. This is a subtle way to implant the Green belief in children's minds, they are part of nature like other animals.

We do not have to embrace the idea that we 'are' animals, to love animals or to take care of the animals and the environment. The purpose behind this objective is political, it is to destroy America's base.

Earth Day is a political event for the Greens and needs to be removed from our schools. Earth Day events can easily be held off school grounds so student participation is an option not a mandate. Currently, Earth Day events are one of the biggest events on school grounds along with Halloween.

Earth Day, The New Children's Crusade!

"If the millions of school kids who now raise Earth flags, plant trees and march in 'All Species parades' get their way, Earth Day will soon be bigger than Christmas."

Mike Weilbacher
E magazine - April 1993

The Greens, not children, have raised the Earth flag in the classroom and transformed Earth Day into Earth Week, then Earth Week into Earth Month and, now are advancing the 'Every Day is Earth Day' mindset. The Greens, not children, have made Earth Day bigger than Christmas in our schools. Christmas is barely allowed, let alone, celebrated in our public schools.

Dr. Lamont's book, 'The Philosophy of Humanism' includes a list of 15 beliefs from the 1933 version of the Humanist Manifesto (first published in the 'New Humanist' (Vol. VI, No.3, I) in 1933). A few of the ideas which parallel the Education for Sustainability mindset follow:

"First: Religious humanists regard **the universe as self-existing and not created**. (Page 286)

"Second: **Humanism believes that man is part of nature** and that he has emerged as the result of a continuous process." (page 286)

"Eighth: Religious humanism considers the complete realization of human personality to be the end of a man's life and seeks its development and **fulfillment in the here and now**. This is the explanation of the humanist's social passion." (page 287)

"Ninth: **In place of the old attitudes involved in worship and prayer** the humanist finds his religious emotions expressed in a **heightened sense of personal life** and in a **co-operative effort to promote social well-being."** (page 287)

"Fourteenth: The humanists are firmly convinced that existing acquisitive and profit-motivated society has shown itself to be inadequate and that **a radical change in methods, controls and motives must be instituted. A socialized and co-operative economic order must be established to the end that the equitable distribution** of the means of life be possible. **The goal of humanism is a free and universal society in which people voluntarily and intelligently co-operate for the common good.** Humanists demand a shared life in a shared world." (page 288)

Education for Sustainability is a program to change our culture, religion, society, economy and government, by training our children to adopt the Green alternative in each of these areas. In his 1995 book, 'The Search for a New Civilization', the former communist dictator of the Soviet Union, Mikhail Gorbachev states:

> "**The greening of politics** is a new view of the problem of consumption and its rationalization..."
>
> "**The greening of politics** affects approaches to tackling many social problems connected...with damage to people's health as a result of the harm already done to the environment."
>
> **"The greening of politics means maximum support for scientific research** and **fundamental disciplines that study the biosphere and its ecosystems."**
>
> **"The greening of politics is an affirmation of the priority of values common to humanity, enriching education and upbringing with ecological content from childhood onward** and **developing a new modern attitude toward nature**. At the same time **the greening of politics is the** return of humankind to the **awareness humanity is a part of nature.** The moral improvement of society ... is inconceivable without this."

The new civilization Gorbachev envisions is Green and the ideas are based on the same man is part of nature, Humanist worldview of the Green Party. Most communists share the Humanist belief that God does not exist. In this statement, Gorbachev combined Green politics with the idea man is part of nature and a plan to use education to promote that mindset.

His general plan included:

- Green political values are the priority
- use ecological values in education and upbringing, from childhood onward to develop a new modern attitude toward nature
- use green politics to build awareness humanity is part of nature

Gorbachev's plan to use education to influence or Green children's upbringing sounds just like the purpose of Education for Sustainability. The plan is to make Education for Sustainability the new mission of public education and Green our children's upbringing from preschool through University.

Since his supposed disposition of power, Gorbachev has become an international leader in the global Green movement. His promotion of "green politics" speaks clearly to his alignment with the aims of the Green Parties. Gorbachev is recognized as the co-author of the Earth Charter, which mirrors Green Party goals and communism. What are Gorbachev's plans for the Earth Charter?

> "My hope is that this charter **will be a kind of 'Ten Commandments', a 'Sermon on the Mount' that provides a guide for human behavior** toward the environment in the next century and beyond".
>
> Mikhail Gorbachev
> Los Angeles Times, May 1997
> Source:http://web.archive.org/web/20000531004758/http://www.gci.ch/GreenCrossFamily/gorby/newspeeches/interviews/laTimes.html

Beyond the arrogance of this remark is the underlying political objective. Gorbachev inferred in this statement, that the Earth Charter could replace the Ten Commandments, as a "guide for human behavior". How could that happen?

The Earth Charter was selected by UNESCO as an Education for Sustainability guide in 2003. UNESCO, the lead organization for the United Nations Decade on Education for Sustainability, officially recognized the Earth Charter as an 'ethical framework' to teach sustainability. The resolution stated:

> **"The Earth Charter Initiative seeks to collaborate with the efforts of the** United Nations Decade of Education for Sustainable Development. In October 2003, UNESCO adopted a resolution **"recognizing the Earth Charter as an important ethical framework** for sustainable development."
>
> **The resolution affirms member states' intention to "utilize the Earth Charter as an educational instrument,** particularly in the framework of the United Nations Decade for Education for Sustainable Development" (Resolution Reference 32C/ Resolution 17*)."*
>
> Source: http://portal.unesco.org/education/en/ev.php (or)
> http://www.earthcharterinaction.org/content/categories/Education/

The Education for Sustainability movement points to the UN Decade for Education for Sustainable Development to justify using the Earth Charter in our schools. Second Nature was already recommending the Earth Charter as an Education for Sustainability teaching guide in 2000.

If the Education for Sustainability movement is allowed to use the classroom, from preschool through college, to train our children to adopt Earth Charter principles for a sustainable future, then the Earth Charter would guide their beliefs. Teaching the Earth Charter in our schools is the way to replace the Ten Commandments and the US Constitution in the hearts and minds of America's children.

A quick summary, the Education for Sustainability movement is using our schools to foster a nationwide shift in values by:

- advocating the philosophy of the Green Party
- aligning students with the Greens with every 'go Green' message
- pushing students to eat, live, worship and vote Green
- advocating a Humanist worldview is necessary to save the earth
- pushing students to adopt Earth Charter principles

The Earth Charter is recognized as the ethical base of the Green Party and plays a key role in advancing the political agenda of the national and international Greens.

Orion Magazine has used their influence to promote the endorsement of the Earth Charter. The Orion Grassroots Network, over 870 organizations, has endorsed the Earth Charter. In 2001, Orion Magazine featured the cover story "Green Across the Globe ... Activists from over seventy nations met in Australia last year to forge a global Green network".

This article, by Polly Stupples, provided an insider's look at the Global Greens Conference, from the Global Greens Charter, the "political manifesto" of the global Greens, to her personal decision to join the Greens. Regarding the Earth Charter and the Green Party alliance, Stupples wrote:

> **"The Earth Charter outlines a new ethic; the Greens Charter outlines pragmatic political steps that embody that ethic."**
>
> 'Green Across the Globe' by Polly Stupples
> Orion Magazine: Winter, 2002
> Source: http://www.orionmagazine.org/index.php/articles/article/108/

If the principles (ethics) of the Earth Charter represent (embody) the political agenda of the Global Green parties, then there is no real difference between Earth Charter and the political agenda of the Green Party US which is part of the international Green network.

"Founded in 2001, the Global Greens is the international network of Green parties and political movements and represents more than 70 Green parties and political movements, in Asia-Pacific, Africa, Europe and the Americas, **including the Green Party of the United States.** The parties and movements have united behind the Global Green Charter."

Green Party of the United States
Press release: December 7, 2007
Source: http://www.gp.org/press/pr_2007_12_07.shtml

The Green Party US is working with the Global Green parties to advance an international agenda in the United States. The Global Greens Charter is based on several documents including the Earth Charter Benchmark Draft II, April 1999.

As the Orion magazine article 'Green Across the Globe' points out, the Earth Charter represents the political agenda of the Global Greens. The use of the Earth Charter as an Education for Sustainability guide is the same as training our children to be for the Green Party and, for the Earth Charter instead of the US Constitution. The following statement is from an Education for Sustainability leader on changing or 'Greening' the US Constitution, which it states, "is an evolving document".

"The U.S. Constitution is not just words on paper. It is an evolving document. In Bruce Ledewitz's words, it "need not be interpreted to stand mute while the environment and the interests of the future are sacrificed." ... **"It is time for our understanding and refining of that document to be reconciled with our knowledge of natural systems** and our growing awareness of obligations and rights that extend broadly throughout the community of life and outward in time as far as the mind dares to imagine."

David W. Orr
'Law of the Land' article Orion Magazine - January/February 2004
Source: http://www.orionmagazine.org/index.php/articles/article/133/

David Orr, a Professor of Environmental Studies and Politics at Oberlin College, is a nationally known leader in the environmental and Education for Sustainability movements. Orr serves on Board of Advisors for the Center for Environmental and Sustainability Education at Florida's Gulf Coast University, right along with the Executive Director of the Earth Charter US campaign, Richard Clugston, Coordinator of the Earth Charter Scholarship Project at the Center.

Source: http://www.fgcu.edu/CESE/Advisors.html

The Center for Environmental and Sustainability Education confirmed their commitment to advancing the goals of the Earth Charter through education in the following statements.

> **"In 2009, Florida Gulf Coast University signed on as an affiliate of the Earth Charter,** in recognition of the fact that this global charter encompasses FGCU's mission. **Here at the Center for Environmental and Sustainability Education we are committed to upholding the values and pursuing the mission of the Earth Charter Initiative.**
>
> Source: http://www.fgcu.edu/CESE/earthcharter.html

David Orr's leadership role at the Center for Environmental and Sustainability Education indicates he supports the aims of the Earth Charter and supports the use of public education to impose that agenda. Following is a statement about an Earth Charter celebration hosted by the Center for Environmental and Sustainability Education, in February 2009. This report indicates the Earth Charter has been advocated on that campus for 10 years.

> **"To help celebrate ten years of the Earth Charter, the Center for Environmental and Sustainability Education at Florida Gulf Coast University held its own Earth Charter +10 week on campus to commemorate the momentous occasion"** ... "The week was meant to raise awareness about the Earth Charter and to display FGCU's commitment to the principles of the Earth Charter."
>
> Source:http://www.earthcharterinaction.org/content/articles/610/1/Center-for-Environmental-and-Sustainability-Education-at-FGCU-holds-EC10-Week/Page1.html

Using the Earth Charter as a sustainability guide in our schools is wrong because the aim of the Earth Charter is to become international law over the US Constitution, and because this is the same as teaching Green Party goals, including the man is part of nature or Humanist worldview as curriculum.

> **"Human societies must operate with the understanding** that **we are part of nature**, not separate from nature."
>
> Green Party Platform 2010
> Ten Key Values: Ecological Wisdom

In his 1995 book 'The Search for A New Civilization' Gorbachev states:

> "At the same time, **the greening of politics is the return of humankind to the awareness humanity is a part of nature.** The moral improvement of society ... is inconceivable without this."

In this statement Gorbachev combined Green politics with the idea that the only way to morally improve society was the "return of humankind to the awareness humanity is a part of nature". If humanity has to return to a Humanist worldview, where is humanity now? Perhaps humanity believes in God's word, that man has dominion over nature, and is charged with being a good steward. It is important to understand where the Green Party stands on the religious beliefs of the American people and how that aligns with Gorbachev's worldview.

> "Consumerism and other addictions, **religious escapism, rigid adherence to dogmatic beliefs**, militarism, social oppression, pursuit of power for its own sake, cynicism, and violence **are all indicative of a social failure to meet our spiritual needs** for a fundamental sense of connection and meaning."
>
> Green Party program 1990-1991
> Spirituality (page 32)

> "Elimination of displays of; religious symbols, monuments or statements on government buildings, property, websites, money, or documents."
>
> Green Party program 2004
> Social Justice (page 22)
> Source: www.GP.org

> "Restoration of the Pledge of Allegiance to its pre-1954 version eliminating the politically motivated addition of 'under God'."
>
> Green Party Platform 2004
> Social Justice (page 23)
> Source: www.GP.org

The objectives the Green Party and aligned Green movement help us understand where the push, to change America's founding principles, comes from. Paving the road to communism requires eliminating America's religious base.

The Green Party directly aligned with Gorbachev and the international Earth Charter in 2000. The following position statement is from the Foreign Policy section of the 2000 Green Party Platform.

> **"We must build on the "Earth Charter"** that came out of the 1992 U.N. environmental Earth Summit. New definitions of what constitutes real security between nations must be debated and adopted by the foreign policy community."

The Global Green Charter, the platform of the international network of Green Parties, also aligns with the Earth Charter. The goal of the Earth Charter is to become international law and the basis of global government. The Earth Charter is based on 16 principles with multiple and far reaching sub-principles for each one of the 16 principles.

Following are a few Earth Charter quotations which outline key objectives:

- **Humanity is part of** a vast evolving universe
- Recognize that peace is the wholeness created by right relationships with oneself, other persons, other cultures, other life, **Earth, and the larger whole of which all are a part.**
- **Fundamental changes are needed in our values, institutions, and ways of living.**
- Promote the **equitable distribution of wealth within nations and among nations**.
- **We urgently need a shared vision of basic values to provide an ethical foundation** for the emerging world community. Therefore, together in hope we affirm the following interdependent principles for a sustainable way of life as **a common standard by which the conduct of all individuals, organizations, businesses, governments, and transnational institutions is to be guided and assessed.**
- In order to build a sustainable global community**, the nations of the world must renew their commitment to the United Nations**, fulfill their obligations under existing international agreements, **and support the implementation of Earth Charter principles with an international legally binding instrument** on environment and development.

This list of Earth Charter requirements are supported by those who have endorsed the Earth Charter. Multiple schools are already using the Earth Charter to train our children to adopt these requirements. A concise recap of what these Earth Charter goals would mean if applied or enforced in our lives follows. We would need to:

- abandon America's founding principles
- change our values, institutions and ways of living
- redistribute America's wealth within and among nations
- adopt Earth Charter principles as our new ethical foundation
- accept or adopt Humanism
- conform to the Earth Charter guidelines for a sustainable lifestyle

- accept our personal conduct, and the conduct of others, including organizations, businesses and our government, is to be monitored guided and accessed to ensure compliance

- accept the Earth Charter as law over the US Constitution and make it legal to enforce Earth Charter principles as law

Doesn't sound like freedom to me. These Earth Charter objectives look like a plan to take over our nation and control our lives, because it is a plan to take over our nation and control our lives. The objectives of the Earth Charter reflect the communist mindset of conquest and enslavement. We must remove this document from our schools.

The plan to change our government is not only an Education for Sustainability objective; it is a stated goal of the Earth Charter USA campaign. The following statement, from the 1999 Earth Charter USA campaign, which was later renamed the Earth Charter US campaign, confirms this political objective.

> "**Welcome to the Earth Charter** USA website. I invite you to become involved in the Earth Charter USA Campaign." ... "**Change your lifestyle, your profession** and **our government** to support a sustainable future."... "We want individual citizens to weigh in on behalf of those values, policies and practices necessary to **redirect our politics** and economy toward sustainability."
>
> Richard Clugston, Director
> Earth Charter USA campaign - 1999
> Source: http://www.earthcharterusa.org/campaign_content.html

The Earth Charter US campaign is working with an international political movement, as is the Education for Sustainability movement, and actively working to change and replace our government, with the Earth Charter. There is no allegiance to the United States of America here. These groups are aiding and comforting an enemy actively seeking to supplant the US Constitution and gain control over the lives of the American people. What shall we call that?

America's Founding Fathers based our government on love of God, love of freedom, respect for the individual and created a legacy of freedom of the people, by the people and for the people. They based America's foundation on a moral foundation based on the belief in God, the Bible and the Ten Commandments. We do not need a new ethical foundation or vision of shared values to guide us. We have the Bible. We do not need a new common standard to 'guide and access' our individual conduct. We accept personal responsibility and honor free thought and individual freedom. We do not need the Earth Charter. We have the United States Constitution, the Declaration of Independence and the Bill of Rights.

There is no question there are problems to solve and issues to deal with but the Earth Charter is not the way to fly. The Earth Charter requires the "equitable distribution of the wealth within nations and among nations". What part of this demand is not a dictatorial, communist-like plan to take money away from the American people?

When disaster strikes, where do the eyes of the world turn? The people of this nation give and give to help those in need. We are kind, generous and loving people. The long standing reputation of giving people the shirt off our backs stems from America's initial and enduring moral base. Preserving our moral base is essential and rejecting the Earth Charter, Education for Sustainability and going Green is a good place to start.

Many parts of the Earth Charter agenda are directly aligned with the political and philosophical agenda of the Green Party, including the following Green Party statements supporting the redistribution of the wealth.

> "...equitable distribution of the resources and productive power"
>
> Green Party Program 1989 (page 27)

> "Foreign policies should further encourage an equitable global distribution of wealth"
>
> Green Party Program 1990-1991 (page 19)

The plan to redistribute the wealth has been used before to fan the flames of discontent and impose a radical political agenda. We need to remember history and learn from the mistakes of others. The idea of redistributing the wealth to save the earth was used decades ago.

> "We see that the primary cause for the existing tensions lies in the unfair distribution of the riches of the earth."
>
> Adolf Hitler
> My New Order

Adolf Hitler used the "unfair distribution' of the riches of the earth" to manufacture jealously and hostility to justify the claim that it was necessary to take radical action in the name of saving the sacred soil.

The Earth Charter and the Greens are using a copycat strategy, based on the same concept of the unfair distribution of wealth and the same claim that it is necessary to take action to redistribute the wealth in the name of saving the earth.

This decade Education for Sustainability is the tool to fan the flames of discontent and convince America's youth the redistribution of the wealth, or equitable access to the Earth's riches is necessary.

> **"Let us imagine a society that has all present and future humans ... have fair and equitable access to Earth's resources ..."**
>
> Anthony Cortese, Second Nature
> Leveraging Change: The Role of the University in a Sustainable Future
> MIT panel: Alliance for Global Sustainability. January 2000
> Source:http://www.secondnature.org/history/writings/speeches/leveraging_change.htm

We need to recognize the Green's copycat political strategy and reject it. This is not to, in any way, infer that the Greens are planning to repeat the Holocaust; it is to point out the use of a similar political strategy and a psychological trap to avoid.

4

Implementation Gang

Earth Charter endorsers support the political agenda of the international Greens. Leading groups in the Education for Sustainability movement and the Green movement that have endorsed the Earth Charter, include:

- North American Association of Environmental Education
- Second Nature
- Center for Ecoliteracy
- Earth Day Network
- Sierra Club
- National Wildlife Federation
- Orion Magazine and the Orion Grassroots Network (over 800 groups)
- Natural Resource Defense Council
- Wilderness Society
- Wildlands Project
- World Resources Institute
- Center for the Respect of Life and the Environment
- Rainforest Action Network
- Northwest Earth Institute
- International Baccalaureate Organization
- Global Exchange
- Friends of the Earth
- Institute of Humanistic Science
- Living Routes - Ecovillage Education
- Center for a New American Dream
- University Leaders for a Sustainable Future

Sources: http://www.earthcharterus.org/the-charter/featured-endorsers (or) http://www.earthcharterinaction.org/database/list.php?country=United States# (or) http://web.archive.org/web/20100302065521/http://www.earthcharterus.org/the-charter/featured-endorsers

As endorsers, each of these organizations has pledged to advance the objectives of the Earth Charter in their work. This means all endorsers involved in education have pledged to use their influence to promote and/or implement the Earth Charter agenda in America's schools and elsewhere.

The following statements are from the 'Earth Charter Adaptation for Younger Children'. This lesson confirms how children are being manipulated to see the Earth Charter as their only hope for survival. In addition, and very importantly, the following statements confirm the intended political outcome.

- We are living at a very important time and **we must save the Earth**
- **The Earth Charter says what we must do to save the world**:
    - respect nature
    - respect human rights
    - organize that everyone has what they need and always lives in peace.
- **The Earth Charter will** help to conserve and **improve the world in** which we live
- **The Earth Charter must be law for all countries and all peoples.**
- The Earth Charter was first written in 1992. **We ask for it to be approved, accepted and put into practice by every country of the world."**

  Source:http://www.earthcharterinaction.org/invent/images/uploads/Adaptation%20for%20younger%20children%20_English.pdf

This Earth Charter message for little children convinces them to pledge allegiance to the Earth Charter by emphasizing the following points:

- "The Earth Charter says what we must do to save the world."
- "The Earth Charter must be law for all countries and all peoples."

The assertion that the Earth Charter "says what we must do to save the world" is a sneaky way to use fear of environmental ruin to scare children into believing that the Earth Charter must become "law for all countries and all peoples". These assertions train children to see the Earth Charter as the source for guidance on how to save the world.

Because the Earth Charter represents the values of the international Green Party, it also trains students to align with the Green Party agenda.

"The Earth Charter outlines a new ethic; the Greens Charter outlines pragmatic political steps that embody that ethic."

Source: http://www.orionmagazine.org/index.php/articles/article/108/

Earth Charter Partners

The Earth Day Network is an Earth Charter Partner which means:

- **Earth Charter USA Partners are organizations that are committed to promoting Earth Charter values and using the Earth Charter in their education and advocacy work.**
- **Through the Earth Charter USA Partners, the ideas of the Earth Charter are spread more quickly** and national support for the Earth Charter becomes stronger.

Source: http://www.earthcharterusa.org/aboutus.html

The Earth Day Network has been an Earth Charter Partner since about 2001 and is still an Earth Charter Partner. It is important to note that the door swings both ways. The Earth Charter is also listed as a Partner organization of the Earth Day Network, which means these two groups are on the same team.

Since the Earth Charter represents the goals of the Green Party; then it follows that the Earth Day Network is using Earth Day events, in schools across America, to advocate that political agenda to students.

Sources: http://www.earthday.org/partners?page=1 (or)
http://www.earthday.org/partner/earth-charter-initiative

The Earth Day Network is a powerful tool and voice for the Earth Charter. Greening America's schools is a major focus of the Earth Day Network. According to a February 2, 2012 news brief from the Earth Charter, "ECI Secretariat wishes you all a Happy New Year. See our priorities for 2012", the number one priority of the Earth Charter is Education for Sustainability.

With the alliance and priorities of these groups in mind, please note what Greening America's economy really means. Following is the number one goal from the Earth Charter booklet, "earthsummit2012 Principles for the Green Economy":

"Principles for a Green Economy

1. Equitable distribution of wealth. Promote the equitable distribution of wealth within nations and among nations, to reduce disparities between rich and poor, and **achieve social and economic**

justice, within a sustainable and fair share of the world's resources and leaving sufficient space for wildlife and wilderness."

Source: http://www.unep.org/civil-society/Portals/59/Documents/13_GMGSF/additional_Resources/Principles_for_a_green_economy.pdf (or) http://www.stakeholderforum.org/fileadmin/files/Principles%20FINAL%20LAYOUT.pdf

These Earth Charter aims match Lenin's call for 'Peace, Bread and Land for All' as well as echo the aims of the Education for Sustainability movement outlined by Anthony Cortese in 2000, when he stated:

"Let us imagine a society that has all present and future humans healthy and where they have their basic needs met, have fair and equitable access to Earth's resources, have a decent quality of life while we preserve the biologically diverse ecosystems on which we all depend."

Anthony Cortese, President, Second Nature
Leveraging Change: The Role of the University in a Sustainable Future - January 2000, Cambridge, MA
Source:http://www.secondnature.org/history/writings/speeches/leveraging_change.htm

The purpose of Education for Sustainability is to change our culture, religion, economy and system of government. The current focus of the Earth Day Network is, among other things, to Green our schools. The purpose of the Earth Charter is to guide and access the conduct of individuals, businesses and governments, in other words, control our behavior. The groups that are in the process of taking over public education have endorsed this international document. It is important to realize that before individual conduct can be guided, individual conduct would have to be monitored and accessed.

America's children are already being trained to accept their behavior and choices should be monitored, accessed and guided. Elementary age children are even being asked to present their lunches for inspection so a Green teacher can review the contents and decide if the food choices are deemed sustainable. This harmful practice uses ridicule and peer pressure to embarrass children to never take anything deemed unsustainable, like a pre-packaged goodie, in their lunch again. This is another example of eco-child abuse and the end justifies the means strategy. The plan is to condition children to accept dictatorial control over every aspect of their lives.

The Earth Charter is a plan to control all our lives. The more we compare the objectives of the Education for Sustainability movement to the agenda of the Earth Charter and Green Party, the more we can see they are the same. The following quotation is from a March 30, 2002, World Net Daily, article by Joan Veon, titled "Sustainable Development".

> **"In the interests of the present and future generations**, the necessary steps are taken ... to protect and make scientific, **rational use of the land and its mineral and water resources**, **and the plant and animal kingdoms to preserve the purity of air and water, ensure reproduction of natural wealth, and improve the human development**."

Which Green group wrote this? The language to "protect and make scientific rational use of the land and its mineral and water resources" sounds like the mission statement of the Education for Sustainability movement, the Green movement, Green Party or the Earth Charter. Protecting the environment for future generations sounds Green but the above statement is a description of land use under communism from the 1977 Constitution of the Union of Soviet Socialist Republics, the USSR.

Are any of the ideas from the 1977 communist Constitution reflected in the Earth Charter, co-authored by the former Soviet dictator Mikhail Gorbachev?

<u>Communist Constitution USSR 1977</u>	**<u>The Earth Charter</u>**
In the interests of present and future generations, the necessary steps are **taken ...**	Secure Earth's bounty and **beauty for present and future generations** ... (page 2)
to protect and make scientific, rational use of the land and its mineral and water resources and the plant and animal kingdoms to preserve the purity of the air and water...	**Preserving a healthy biosphere with all its ecological systems, a rich variety of plants and animals, fertile soils, pure waters, and clean air...** (Preamble)
ensure reproduction of natural wealth...	Protect Earth's life support systems,maintain biodiversity, **preserve our natural heritage**... (page 2)
improve the **human development**	**Ensure** that economic activities and institutions at all levels **promote human development in an equitable** and sustainable **manner**... (page 3)

Source: http://www.earthcharterinaction.org

No wonder Gorbachev is happy with the Earth Charter, it includes the ideas from the 1977 Communist Constitution. Incorporating the language of communism into the goals of the Earth Charter leaves the door wide open to interpret those goals just like Communist leaders interpreted those goals. The inclusion and similarities are not an accident. These goals are being advanced under the banner of a sustainable future. Please read the following Earth Charter objective out loud with the above information in mind.

> "... we affirm the following interdependent principles **for a sustainable way of life** as **a common standard by which the conduct of all individuals, organizations, businesses, governments,** and transnational institutions **is to be guided and assessed."**

If America's children are trained, from preschool through college to adopt Earth Charter principles, they will accept this level of control over their lives and they will support this level of control over our lives in the not too distant future.

The political agenda of the Earth Charter and the international Greens stands against what America stands for. The Greens have gained a powerful foothold in many of our schools. It is time to set our children and their non-Green teachers free from the clutches of what has become a Green monster in charge of education. We need to work with administrators, teachers and school boards to remove Education for Sustainability programs and return our schools to safe havens of learning for our children.

We, as our compatriots, enjoy the right to advocate our opinions, which is freedom of speech. The Greens cannot be allowed to invade our schools and train our children to align with Green Party goals because that is political indoctrination.

Target and Train

The following excerpts, from a 2001 speech by Anthony Cortese, reveal key goals and strategies of the Education for Sustainability movement; including the plan to use education to change the mindset of students is preferred to trying to change policies in Washington DC.

> "... an emphasis on **the separation of humans from the rest of nature**, compartmentalized learning - where we learn everything in silos; individual specialization and success; and **the absence of explicit ethics and values** in learning, **the dominant educational model is reinforcing the current inequitable and unsustainable worldview.** As David Orr has said; the crises we face, one of mind, perception..."

> "...As they said in Apollo 13, "Houston, **we have a problem." And it's not an environmental problem;** it's a design problem. **It's a worldview problem.** Now, interestingly enough, **if you're going to change the mind**

set, higher education plays a profound and pivotal, but largely overlooked, role in the transition to a sustainable society.

Most people are focusing on policy issues, how to change the politics in Washington, and ...**when, in fact**, in the long term, **if we're talking about sustainability in the long term, we've got to change the way we think because it's the only way we'll change our behavior**.

Now, higher education is important for all levels of education because it prepares most of the professionals who develop, lead, manage, teach, work in, and influence society's institutions in K through 12 education.

We're going to replace twenty two million K through 12 teachers in the next [ten years] and **if we begin at the beginning of the pipeline training them properly, there we have a chance of making a difference. Besides training the future teachers, higher education strongly influences the learning framework of K through 12 education."** (Transcript page 5)

"All students would understand that we are an integral part of nature" (Transcript page 10)

"We're called Second Nature. We're Senator John Kerry's idea." (Transcript page 18)

Anthony Cortese. Second Nature
Speech: Education for a Sustainable Future
Oregon Sustainability Forum: September 6, 2001

Cortese confirms, once again, Second Nature is Senator John Kerry's idea and, that Education for Sustainability is a well organized political movement that is using public education as a tool to dictate the thinking, values and behavior of future teachers so they will pass those values on to America's children.

60's Revolutionaries, Alive, Well and Green

"We, in the green movement, aspire to a cultural model in which killing a forest will be considered more contemptible and more criminal than the sale of 6-year-old children to Asian brothels."

Carl Amery
Founding member of the German Green Party,
Quoted in Mensch & Energie, April 1983
Source: TargetOfOpportunity.com

This statement is truly shocking. We all, especially those wearing the Green label like a badge of honor, cannot afford to pretend this is just a crazy, off the cuff remark by a wild man. This statement was made by a founding member of the German Green Party. As a representative of the Party, Amery probably would not risk making such a vile remark to emphasize the cultural model the Party was aiming at, unless there was some grain of truth to it.

Our special love of the great outdoors, the creatures and family pets has been skillfully manipulated to keep the focus off the political realities and pit falls associated with the Green movement. We need to look at where the Greens are headed based on what they have said. Is this what 'part of nature' ideology is about? There is no sign of God in Amery's remark. In Germany, people made the fatal mistake of ignoring what Adolf Hitler said he was going to do until he did it. We cannot afford to bury our heads in sand. What cultural model are the Greens heading for?

The leaders of the Green movement pushed environmental education programs into our schools, which led to Education for Sustainability and the plan to make the Green agenda the central focus of all education. The Department of Education is now on board to Green our children. How Green leaders define a sustainable lifestyle is vitally important as it sheds light on where the movement is headed.

Fritjof Capra is a leader in the Green movement, a Green Party organizer and the co-author of the 1986 book 'Green Politics'. The following excerpts are from Capra's December 1, 2002 article "Where Have All the Flowers Gone? Reflections on the Spirit and Legacy of the Sixties", Capra said:

> "What happened to the cultural movements of the sixties? - Our subculture was immediately identifiable"... "It had its own rituals" ..."**fascination with spirituality and the occult**..." ... "Rock music and **psychedelic drugs** were powerful bonds" ... **"casual communal nudity and freely shared sexuality."**
>
> "... **Green Politics** - In the sixties we questioned the dominant society"... "we lived" ... "our protest rather than" ... **"systematizing it".... "During the 1980's and 1990's,** the **Green movement** became a permanent fixture of the European political landscape..." **... "They are the political embodiment of the core values of the sixties.**
>
> "At the turn of this century, an impressive **global coalition** of nongovernmental organizations (NGOs), many led by men and women **with deep personal roots in the sixties**, **formed around the core values of** human dignity and **ecological sustainability.** In 1999, hundreds of these grassroots organizations ... prepared for the joint protest actions at the ... World Trade Organization (WTO) in Seattle."
>
> ... **"This** new form of **alternative global community**, sharing core values **... is one of the most important legacies of the sixties.**

"If it succeeds in reshaping economic globalization ... to make it compatible with the values of human dignity **and ecological sustainability, the dreams of the "sixties revolution" will have been realized: Imagine no possessions, I wonder if you can ..."**

Fritjof Capra is the co-founder of the Center for Ecoliteracy, one of the leading organizations in the Education for Sustainability movement. Capra works with David Orr, Anthony Cortese, the Bioneers and others to advance the political agenda of the Green movement.

Capra, a self-proclaimed 60's revolutionary, said in the 60's they "lived" their protest rather than "systematizing" it. Systematizing means organizing. Systemizing a protest, as used in this context, would suggest reorganizing to achieve the same goals using a different approach. Education for Sustainability is a systematized and organized way for the Greens to use education to brainwash their way to power, instead of protesting the streets.

A quick recap of Capra's message:

- 60's subculture included the occult, communal nudity, freely shared sex and drugs
- Green politics and Green movement ARE the 'political embodiment' of the core values of the 60's
- 60's radicals lived their protest rather than systematizing it
- 60's leaders now in global coalition, focus is ecological sustainability
- If Greens and global coalition succeed, goals of the 60's achieved
- imagine no possessions ...

Capra said, "Our subculture". Capra's leadership role in the Green Party and the Education for Sustainability movement, plus these statements about the 60's revolutionaries, suggest that Education for Sustainability is their vehicle to systematically indoctrinate America's children to impose the revolutionary goals of the 60's presented as steps toward ecological sustainability.

Along the same lines, the Education for Sustainability movement is pushing 'Ecovillage' study programs. Ecovillages are basically glorified communes where students can go to supposedly learn about sustainable living. Eco-villages could also be described as a place to learn about group think, living with less and how to get along on a work farm. Ecovillages and Capra's description of his 60's subculture lifestyle bring forth images of the hippie communes of the 60's and 70's. Communism was the goal then and appears to be the goal now.

Lenin based many of his ideas on the Paris Commune. The ninth plank of Lenin's 1917 April Theses states the:

> "...party program to be changed to include the demand for a 'Commune' state modeled after the Paris Commune."
>
> The Life and Death of Lenin
> Robert Payne (Page 334)

All Aboard: Destination Green Communism

The Greens use trendy sounding ideas like an 'eco-village or Ecovillage' to entice students to jump on board the sustainability train without realizing they are being used and that train is headed for a communist destination. The purpose of Education for Sustainability is to dictate student's beliefs and control their choices so they will submit to Green demands. Ecovillages devalue independence, systems thinking advances Humanism and group think prepares students to accept drone status. Education for Sustainability is a plan to take control of America's future by taking control of America's children.

Small children, young adults and even college students do not enter the classroom prepared to resist this Green Party indoctrination program. The American standard of a Party neutral or politically neutral public education was established to shield children from a harmful political indoctrination program like Education for Sustainability. That American standard is an essential safeguard to free thought, individual freedom and the democratic process. We must insist upon a return to this standard immediately. Students of all ages are being trained to eat Green, live Green, worship Green, and vote Green.

The Green propaganda machine has created a never ending string of environmental fears to justify a never ending string of political demands to implement their agenda. Painting a 'simply marvelous' picture of a sustainable future is just another way to use 'hope plus fear' to bully students and adults into supporting the Green agenda or face extinction. The Education for Sustainability movement is using our schools to pressure our children to adopt the international agenda of the Greens. If we take a step back, we can see it.

The Ecovillage concept is also part of promoting self-reliant sustainable communities, cooperative communities or transition towns. The Greens use the term 'self reliant' because it speaks to our sense of independence but behind this ploy is a communist strategy. The Greens are painting happy pictures of close knit communities to create warm feelings. This approach keeps people from thinking about where the ideas come from and where this is headed. Setting a target date to impose this piece of the Green agenda was planned back in 1972.

> "...target date for basic establishment of network of self-sufficient, self-regulating communities."
>
> Blueprint for Survival - 1972
> Towards the stable society: strategy for change
> Source: http://www.theecologist.info/page32.html

The idea of establishing self reliant communities has been popularized by the Greens over the last several years. This is a step to mentally prepare the American people for the Greens to take control of their communities and in turn begin to take control of production, distribution and transportation. The Communist Party is known for planning 50 years in advance of taking control. The following statement shows the plan to impose, what became the Green Party agenda, was also planned years ago.

> "...formulate a precise and comprehensive plan, to bring about the kind of society, in which a new philosophy of life can be implemented."
>
> Blueprint for Survival 1972 - Preface
> Source: http://www.theecologist.info/page34.html

The 'precise and comprehensive plan' to impose a new philosophy of life in America is the push to impose the sustainability agenda, which looks just like Green Communism, in schools and communities nationwide. Realizing the Green movement is a political not an environmental movement is necessary to understand the Green agenda and to recognize how it is being implemented.

For instance, the Green's call for a switch to local food production and to become self reliant communities is not about health or well being. This is a political goal to gain control of what is produced and transported across the nation. When we understand the hidden objective is to replace local supermarkets with local farmers markets, the steps to impose that agenda are easier to see. Farmers markets are great but so is the ability to go to the market and buy coffee or bananas. Locally grown is part of the strategy to dismantle American agriculture, which currently provides our nation with a stable supply and a fine selection of foods no matter the season or where we live. Our current system of food production also provides enough food to share with those in need should a disaster strike.

Steps to control production, distribution and transportation are not limited to agriculture and other industries. Green plans include ending private property ownership and reducing fossil fuel use; to limit personal mobility and the use of private automobiles.

Another reason for the Green promotion of locally grown foods is to use this romantic concept to socialize the land base and justify 'taking' or controlling private property. How could that happen? The push for locally grown foods includes getting local farmers to agree to produce a certain amount of certain foods. If a local farmer were to produce, say 15% of a given food item, the community would learn to rely on that 15% as part of the local food supply.

What happens if a farmer decides to grow roses on their land instead of providing that 15% of food for the community? If that 15% of food cannot be replaced locally, the farmer's land would be subject to eminent domain, to ensure that 15% of food for the community was guaranteed.

The Greens are enlisting the support of farmers and gardeners to support self sufficient communities and locally grown foods. This is a copycat strategy to get people to, in the name of saving the earth, support a political agenda they may not understand. Hitler also took advantage of farmers.

> "Hitler found the farmers some of his strongest supporters. He singled them out as guardians of the holy soil."
>
> Alfons Heck
> A Child of Hitler

In addition, the Education for Sustainability movement has made school gardens in style. What is wrong with training students to work in school gardens? Why would the Center for Ecoliteracy, which was founded by 60's radical and Green Party organizer Fritjof Capra, emphasize school gardens as part of Green schooling and Education for Sustainability?

Gardening is one of my favorite things but that said, we need to understand the political purpose behind this part of the Green agenda. The following excerpt, from a March 5, 2011, New York Times article "In New Food Culture, A Young Generation of Farmers Emerges" by Isolde Raftery, sheds light on this issue.

> "...**Mr. Jones, 30, and his wife, Alicia, 27,** are among an emerging group of people in their 20s and 30s who have chosen farming as a career. Many shun industrial, mechanized farming and **list** punk rock, **Karl Marx** and the food journalist Michael Pollan **as their influences**."

Why is Karl Marx a role model for young farmers in America? Greening our schools and advocating an agenda that mirrors communism is the answer. The political purpose behind the push for school gardens is to train students to produce food as a group and to prepare them to produce food for the community on a work farm. This is a practice in communist countries. Farmers beware. Hate to say it, but the Green push for local food production is not to help farmers. It is to use farmers for publicity and limited production, then take control of the farmers land and the rest of the land base.

We are not to the work farm stage yet, but if we allow the Greens to continue to use our schools to indoctrinate our children to support Green communism, work farms are on the horizon. We must understand America's young people, in their 20's, 30's and 40's, have been targeted and unfairly influenced to support communist ideas. We need to spend our time and energy on removing Education for Sustainability programs from our schools and avoid condemnation or arguments with those who have been influenced to idolize Karl Marx. We need to give our young people some space and time to heal.

The GREEN-BOT re-education scheme began in the 1970's and has been on the rise in America's classrooms ever since. In the 1990's the environmental movement shifted into high gear with massive public relations campaigns featuring celebrities to help make being an environmentalist fashionable. Soon the environmental movement was strategically renamed the Green movement, but the Green Party link to that name change was not mentioned. Celebrities who promote 'being Green' now (or then) may not realize they are also being used to indirectly promote the Green Party agenda.

Over the years Green marketing campaigns have, as intended, taken the focus off the facts and fair mindedness to reduce environmental issues to fear mongering, sympathy ploys or popularity contests. The Greens have used owls, fish and flies to mask taking control of people's lives and livelihoods, when it never should have been an either/or situation. The Green label has been used repeatedly to justify shameful treatment of the American people. The plan to Green our schools is a plan to train our children to wear the Green label with pride so they will support Green control of their lives, our lives and single party or Green Party dictatorial rule over the future of our nation.

The Green label reminds me of the 'Sound of Music' and how quickly life changed when the call to save the soil outweighed common sense and human decency. The Green label also symbolizes merging the call to save the earth with the Green Party. The Greens are also using the classroom and a similar form of psychological programming, to pressure students to wear the Green label only. We must help our children understand how to reject the Green label because it is part of a harmful, dictatorial, freedom killing, anti-God, anti-American agenda.

How serious is the psychological programming? A quick check; ask your child, grandchild and yourself this question: are you Green or, are you an American? If there is any hesitation to answer, the psychology of the Greens is working. Here's another one. Are you Green or, are you for God? There is a big difference and a child might hesitate because they think they can be both, but that is not the case.

We must help our children understand, and the 'Sound of Music' might help, that the Green label is not the same as being an American. Being an American stands for God, County, Freedom and so much more. Being Green stands for the Green Party and for a political movement that opposes everything this nation stands for and we believe in. This reality is exemplified by the Education for Sustainability movement's goal to change America's culture, religion, society, economy and form of government.

To get back to an America that is united, we must lose the Green label and start dealing with the Green movement as a political movement not an environmental cause. Losing the Green label, and encouraging everyone we know to do the same, is a simple but effective way to help our children, ourselves and our compatriots break free from the Green propaganda machine.

The Green propaganda machine sells romantic sounding ideas, like self-sufficient communities, to get people to hop on board the sustainability train without revealing where that train is headed. This approach lulls people into a trust mode and blurs all the warning signs that show this train is headed for Green Communism not an environmental utopia.

> "It is possible to lead astray an entire generation, to strike it blind, to drive it insane, to direct it towards a false goal. Napoleon proved that."
>
> Alexander Herzen
> Russian Journalist - Political Thinker

This statement by Alexander Herzen is a great summary of how the environmental cause has been deliberately used to mislead, deceive, confuse, manipulate and blind people to the implementation of the Green Party agenda.

An American or A Green Citizen?

A national plan to promote Green ideology to America's children is in the works. The Secretary of the US Department of Education, Arne Duncan, has announced the department will be a committed partner in producing "the next generation of green citizens".

The following excerpts are from the September 21, 2010 speech: The Greening of the Department of Education: Secretary Duncan's Remarks at the Sustainability Summit. Secretary Duncan said:

> "This week's sustainability summit **represents the first time that the Department is taking a leadership role** in the work of educating the next generation of **green citizens** and preparing them to contribute to the workforce through green jobs. President Obama has made clean, renewable energy a priority because, as he says, it's the best way to "truly transform our economy, to protect our security, and save our planet."

Educators have a central role in this. A well educated citizen knows that we must not act in this generation in ways that endanger the next. **They teach students about how the climate is changing**. They explain the science behind climate change and **how we can change our daily practices to help save the planet**. They have a role in preparing students for jobs in the green economy.

Historically, the Department of Education hasn't been doing enough in the **sustainability movement**. Today, I promise you that **we will be a committed partner in the national effort to build a more environmentally literate and responsible society**."

Source:http://www.ed.gov/news/speeches/greening-department-education-secretary-duncans-remarks -sustainability-summit

This is a plan to manufacture a nation of 'green citizens' loyal to all things Green. The U.S. Department of Education has committed to using their influence and financial power to train America's children to be Green and to stand as 'green citizens' under a national Green banner.

The Education for Sustainability movement is not like the space race or the civil rights movement. Education for Sustainability is a biased political movement that is using public education to build support for an agenda that mirrors Green Party goals and communism; with the stated goal to change our government, culture, religion, society and economic system. This political agenda does not belong in our classrooms.

The Department of Education's promise to produce the next generation of "green citizens" is chilling and cannot be ignored. This directly aligns the Department of Education with the Green movement and the Green Party. The term 'Green' is not just a word anymore; it is THE term that represents the Green Party and international Green Parties. This action by the Department of Education cannot be dismissed as an environmental decision because the word Green stands for the Green Party. Would it be acceptable for the Department of Education to launch a:

- Democrat Ribbon Schools program?
- Republican Ribbon Schools program?
- Libertarian Ribbon Schools program?
- Socialist Ribbon Schools program?
- Communist Ribbon Schools program?

No, all hell would break loose. If the Department of Education used the name of another political party to identify a public education awards program, it would align that awards program with that one party. What would the response be if the Department of Education announced a new 'Communist Ribbon Schools' program and a special award for the most communistic school and student body in America?

Would that fly? No. It would not be acceptable for the Department of Education to align with one party or use a national school awards program to unfairly influence America's children to align with that one party. This type of alignment could not be tolerated because the Department of Education would be directly and indirectly, fostering single party rule, which would put our form of government at risk. If this common sense standard applies to all other political parties, it also should apply to the Green Party.

The "Green Ribbon Schools" program aligns the Department of Education with the Green Party and is unfairly influencing our children to align with everything Green including the party. The Department of Education must be held accountable and uphold this common sense standard. Due to the Green Party link, the 'Green Ribbon Schools' program; must be eliminated to protect free thought and our form of government.

The Department of Education ought to issue a public announcement explaining they are eliminating this program because they cannot align with one party, including the Green Party.

Quick reminder: The 1972 'Blueprint for Survival' was first published in 'The Ecologist' magazine, which was founded by 'Blueprint' co-author Edward Goldsmith. 'The Ecologist' magazine is credited with igniting the environmental movement and the 'Blueprint' is credited for the founding of the Green Party. The political ideology behind the Green movement and Green Party stem from the 'Blueprint' and these allies have been advancing the same political agenda for decades.

Where did the idea for 'Green Ribbon Schools' come from? According to a report from the Earth Day Network, dated April 26, 2011:

> **"Earth Day Network Coalition Scores Green Ribbon Schools Program Victory!**

Following are a few excerpts from that Earth Day Network report:

> "The U.S. Department of Education launched the "Green Ribbon Schools" award program on April 26, 2011. The program is **the first time the federal government has launched a comprehensive green schools**

initiative which **has tremendous implications for schools across the country…"**

"The Green Ribbon Schools program represents an incredible milestone for the health and sustainability of our nation's schools**, and we applaud the Department of Education's visionary leadership** in building one of the foundations of the green economy**."**

"We look forward to the announcement of the first winners of the Green Ribbon Schools program on Earth Day 2012."

Earth Day Network
Source: http://www.earthday.org

This announcement indicates the federal government has teamed-up with the Greens to push the Education for Sustainability agenda into schools nationwide. The headline, "Earth Day Network Coalition Scores Green Ribbon Schools Program Victory!" suggests announcing the winners on Earth Day is a victory, because it aligns the 'Green Ribbon Schools' program and the Department of Education with Earth Day in a big way.

Presenting a government award to schools and children for being the 'Greenest' and presenting that award on Earth Day, turns this presentation into a celebration of everything Earth Day stands for, from being Green and celebrating the earth to the political goals they advocate.

In addition, the Earth Day Network endorses the Earth Charter and is also an Earth Charter Partner. The goals of the Earth Charter mirror Green Party goals so the Earth Day Network also supports that agenda. The Department of Education has tied public education to the Earth Day Network, which has pledged to support the Earth Charter as international law over the US Constitution.

The Earth Day Network is also a major player in the Education for Sustainability movement so it is a good time to remember what US Secretary of Education Arne Duncan said in a letter to "Attendees at the UNESCO World Conference on Education for Sustainable Development" in March 2009. Secretary Duncan stated:

"President Obama also intends to make our country one of the leaders in responding to global climate change. Our goal is to ensure that we use some alternative sources of electricity, and we aim to reduce our greenhouse gas emissions.

These major changes require educating our people – both students and adults – about the importance of environmental sustainability

and training our people in this developing field. **We intend to do everything in our power to encourage education for sustainability**."

Source: http://www2.ed.gov/about/inits/ed/internationaled/unesco-letter.pdf)
(Bold emphasis added)

The Department of Education has announced they, along with President Obama, "intend to do everything in our power to encourage education for sustainability". Since the Earth Charter is an Education for Sustainability training tool, does that mean the Department of Education will be pushing the Earth Charter into our schools?

The Department of Education ought to also announce they will no longer be supporting Education for Sustainability programs until all concerns about this movement's political agenda and advocacy of Green Party ideology in the classroom are addressed.

5

Enslave or Empower?

Education has long been used by communist governments as a political weapon to train children, through the curriculum, to have nothing but a communist mindset to enslave them for a lifetime.

> "Education is a weapon whose effects depend on who holds it in his hands and at whom it is aimed."
>
> Joseph Stalin
> Russian Prime Minister (1879-1953)

In this case, the weapon is Education for Sustainability and it is aimed straight at destroying our culture, religion, society, economy and form of government. Public education is being used by the Greens to indoctrinate our children in an attempt to take-down this magnificent nation.

As unbelievable as it may sound, the agenda of the Education for Sustainability movement not only aligns with Green Party goals and communism, but the objectives and implementation scheme parallels Lenin's 'people-control' plan. Following is a revealing look at what the goals of the Father of Communism were, and how he imposed those goals.

> "**Lenin** made a perverse reading of the Enlightenment View of Man as modeling clay and **sought to create a new model of human nature and behavior through social engineering** of the most radical kind**. ...** "Bolshevism was the most audacious attempt in history **to subject the entire life of a country to a master plan**" writes Richard Pipes at the end of his 2 volume history of the revolution."
>
> Time Magazine
> April 13, 1998

Lenin's basic goals were to:

- create a **new model** of **human nature**
- create a **new model** of **human behavior**
- do this through **social engineering**
- **subject the entire life of a country to a master plan**

Social engineering is a method to change behavior through brainwashing, political indoctrination and radical training programs.

The basic goals of the Education for Sustainability movement are to:

- create a **new mindset, change beliefs, thinking and values**
- create new culture, society, economy, government, **change behavior**
- do this through public education and **social engineering**
- **subject the entire life of our country to the Green's master plan** by imposing the Green Party definition of sustainability in schools and communities nationwide

The following statements, by Anthony Cortese, confirm the objectives of the Education for Sustainability movement align with the social engineering and 'people-control' mindset of Lenin.

> "US Senator John Kerry and I started Second Nature eight years ago because **we felt that we needed a massive change in mindset**.
>
> And **we needed to work on higher education because higher education trains all the professionals in society** and the people who are leading all of our institutions, **all the future K-12 teachers. They train all, and also set-the-kids-up for our framework for learning**..."
>
> Anthony Cortese, Second Nature
> Sustainability & Ethics
> Oregon Sustainability Forum - September 2001

> "What would transformational change look like? According to Cortese, **it would reflect a complete shift in thinking, values and action.** ..."
>
> Oregon State University
> Sustainability News – November 2002

> **"Our most stalwart concept,** the one that we hold forth for future leaders in the Education for Sustainability movement, **is that the entire education experience must change behavior."**
>
> "By reinforcing the concept that **the educational experience of all students must be aligned with the principles of sustainability**, we help ensure the content of learning embraces interdisciplinary systems thinking to address environmentally sustainable action ..."
>
> Second Nature - Vision & Philosophy
> Source: http://www.secondnature.org

Like Lenin, the Education for Sustainability movement is using the classroom to socially engineer the beliefs, values and behaviors of children. The statement, "all students must be aligned with the principles of sustainability" means standardizing the beliefs of all students. Since Green Party goals and Education for Sustainability goals align, it follows that students will be trained to adopt the Green definition of sustainability which mirrors communism.

The concept of sustainability is presented as a new way to save the earth and take care of people, which touches our hearts. These are the emotional hooks to ensnare students and adults into supporting the Green agenda. The fact that Green goals for sustainability mirror communism or that ruthless crimes, like the murder of innocent people, occurred under communist rule, is not part of the 'sustainability' sales pitch. We need to remind our children that communist dictators rule with an iron fist not a loving hand. It all comes down to moral character and without a moral compass to guide a government; innocent people will get hurt again and again.

For decades political activists have used environmental education and topics like endangered species, social justice, environmental justice and global warming to Green student's opinions. These students were caught in the Green 'line of fire' so to speak, and they need time to digest this new information and realize they were targeted for political gain. We need to focus our energy on expelling Education for Sustainability programs, not arguing with our compatriots. We need to correct policy not people. Moral character and understanding are essential traits for all leaders who truly care about people and want to help people.

We need to look past the promise of a better world and understand what the Green definition of sustainability means.

Strategy to Impose Communism

> "A better and peaceful world is possible – a world where people and nature come before profits. That's' socialism. That's our vision. We are the Communist Party of the USA"
>
> Communist Party USA
> Source: http://www.cpusa.org

The Communist Party calls for socialism because it sounds less threatening than the real goal which is dictatorial communist rule. How is the concept of sustainability being used to implement a communist agenda? A good example is the joint call of the Education for Sustainability movement, the Earth Charter and the Green Party to redistribute the wealth and share all resources equally. The following Green Party statement reflects this ideology.

"Green communities are supported by the implementation of land trusts, intentional communities, shared ownership, and other alternatives to traditional individual land and property ownership."

Green Party Program 1990-1991 (page 7)

Green alternatives to individual land ownership are steps to abolish the right of individuals to own land and establish community or government control of the land base. The Greens, like the Communist Party, intend to eliminate private property ownership. A revealing look at how communism is imposed is found in the following statement from the Young Communist League.

"**Socialism is the society that will pave the way for a communist society by setting a foundation of co-operation and sharing of all things in common.** Communism is the realization of these goals."

Young Communist League
Source: http://www.yclcpusa.org

The imposition of communism begins with "setting a foundation of co-operation and sharing of all things in common". The goals of the Education for Sustainability movement parallel this plan. The following statement is from a 2001 article titled 'Education for a Sustainable Future: Accelerating the Transition to Sustainability' by Anthony Cortese and William McDonough.

"Envisioning a Sustainable Future let us imagine... a society in which all present and future humans are healthy and have their basic needs met. **What if everyone had fair and equitable access to the Earth's resources**, a decent quality of life, and celebrated cultural diversity."

Anthony Cortese, President, Second Nature
William McDonough, FAIA, Chairman,
Second Nature Board of Directors
Source: secondnature.org/Resources.html

To accelerate the transition to a sustainable society, the leaders of the Education for Sustainability movement advocate everyone have "equitable access to the Earth's resources". This statement by Cortese and McDonough lays the "foundation for co-operation and sharing of all things in common" which, as the Young Communist League pointed out, paves the way for communism. The goal of "equitable access to the Earth's resources" also trains students, America's future voters, to support an end to private property rights.

Another Education for Sustainability theme designed to align students with the idea of switching to a 'cooperative society where all things are shared in common' is the 'man is part of nature' philosophy of the Green Party. The goals laid out by Cortese and McDonough also parallel the 14th goal of the 'Humanist Manifesto'. On page 288 of Corliss Lamont's book, the 'Philosophy of Humanism', it states:

"**Fourteenth**: The humanists are firmly convinced that existing acquisitive and profit-motivated society has shown itself to be inadequate and that a **radical change in methods, controls and motives must be instituted.**

A socialized and co-operative economic order must **be established** to the end that the **equitable distribution** of the means of life be possible. The goal of humanism is a free and universal society in which people voluntarily and intelligently co-operate for the common good.

Humanists demand a shared life in a shared world."

Education for Sustainability is not an unbiased study program and the goal for everyone to have "fair and equitable access to the Earth's resources", also matches the following Green Party goal.

"... all persons have the right and opportunity **to benefit equally from the resources afforded us by society and the environment..."**

Green Party Program 2000
Ten Key Values: #2, Social Justice

Another direct link between the Green Party and Education for Sustainability is systems thinking. Systems thinking and the idea man is part of nature are core themes of the Education for Sustainability movement and the philosophical base of the Green Party. The following statement reflects the Green's systems thinking mindset.

"The Earth and its natural systems cannot be owned; they are to be respected and cared for in accordance with ecological principles."

Green Party Platform 1990-1991
Economics (page 8)

This is a systems thinking worldview. The Greens, like communists, oppose private property ownership. The use of systems thinking is another sly way to train our children to oppose private property ownership and adopt the Green position that the earth cannot be owned. The elusive goal of sustainability is a smokescreen to conceal this communist objective.

A common denominator of the Education for Sustainability movement, the Green Party and the Earth Charter is systems thinking because 'systems thinking' is THE TOOL to instill a Green mindset.

Training America's youth to adopt a Green mindset is the key to changing our culture, religion, society, economy, and form of government.

The Green mindset matches the following form of government.

"The theory of the Communists may be summed up in a single sentence: Abolition of private property."

Communist Manifesto
Karl Marx & Frederick Engels

The plan is to use fear of environmental ruin and the pretense of creating a sustainable future to trick students and the American people into accepting that government must take control of all the natural resources, including private property, in order to save the earth.

Education for Sustainability is not a lesson plan or an elective course but an all encompassing political indoctrination program designed to replace our culture, religion, society, economy and form of government with Green Communism or something just like it.

Political Objectives: Not Wishful Thinking

The goals for a sustainable future, described by Cortese and McDonough in the previous excerpt from the article, "Education for a Sustainable Future: Accelerating the Transition to Sustainability", represent clearly defined political objectives not wishful thinking. Once again, those political objectives include:

- **all humans have their basic needs met**
- **everyone has fair and equitable access to the Earth's resources**

Imposing these goals would require the power to control the Earth's resources and the power to distribute the resources based on whatever amount was deemed adequate to meet the basic needs of all people. Lenin issued a similar call for communism with the slogan "Peace, Bread and Land for All", which was the prelude to total government control. Lenin, Cortese, McDonough and the Education for Sustainability movement are on the same political page.

The Education for Sustainability movement is advocating centralized control of America's resources to train students to accept a new form of government that would enforce this agenda. One cannot provide equitable access to the Earth's resources without controlling the Earth's resources, which include land, water, mineral, food and all other forms of wealth.

The following statement is from the 1972 book 'Ecology' by Gus Hall. Hall was the Chairman of the Communist Party USA from 1959 to 2000. In this statement, Hall outlines the Communist Party position on resources, which aligns with the goals of the Education for Sustainability movement.

"Socialism corrects the basic flaw of capitalism. It sets human society on a new path. **The means of production, factories, mines and mills**

become the property of the people. They operate and produce only to fulfill human needs. They are not motivated by profits. **This is the foundation for a new set of priorities, for new values...What is involved is a conflict of values."**

Gus Hall
Chairman,Communist Party USA (1959-2000)

The goals of the Communist Party include:

- control of the Earth's resources
- use resources to meet basic needs
- change American's values
- establish new priorities and new values
- replace our form of government

The goals of the Greens and Education for Sustainability include:

- changing our economy
- providing equal access to the Earth's resources
- controlling or distributing the Earth's resources to meet basic needs
- changing student's thinking, values and behavior
- changing our form of government

The Green mindset is a communist mindset. The Communist Party promotes socialism but communist control is the end game. The following Green Party goals are worth reviewing because the goals of the Education for Sustainability movement parallel these goals and if not checked, our children will be trained to adopt this mindset.

"all persons have the right and opportunity to benefit equally from the resources afforded us by society and the environment..."

Green Party Program 2000
Ten Key Values: #2, Social Justice

"The Earth and its natural systems cannot be owned ..."

Green Party Platform 1990-1991
Economics (page 8)

The Earth Charter is also aligned with these Green Party goals and is being used to instill this mindset in our children. The Earth Charter states:

"**Promote the equitable distribution of wealth** within nations and among nations."

America operates on freedom. We are all free to explore opportunities but we are not guaranteed success or equal access to the Earth's resources. Equal access to the resources of the earth means many things, including equal access to the land and to what is on the land. Equal access to the Earth's resources would also include the resources on private property. Private property ownership is a cornerstone of America's freedom foundation.

We need to help our children understand that the Greens and the Education for Sustainability movement are pushing communism, which is a system of government that has proven harmful to both people and the environment. What would life under communism be like?

Not long ago, an older woman called in during a talk radio program. We had been talking about the communist agenda hidden behind the Green movement. She explained that she had grown up in Russia under communism before moving to the United States. She was concerned about the goals of the environmental movement. She shared a story about living in Russia. When she was a child her family had a plum tree in the front yard and they would eagerly watch the plums ripen. She said they would get excited about having plum pudding and plum jam, but as soon as the plums were ripe, the government came and picked all the plums. All they had were the plums that were left on the ground.

Not a happy picture but a vivid picture of what equitable access to the Earth's resources looks like in real life and, what that level of government control would be like.

A much happier story would be based on private property ownership and freedom where the family that took care of that plum tree was in charge of the fruit and could enjoy their bounty. After picking the fruit they could make enough jam to put on the shelf, give away as gifts or sell and buy things they needed. Life under communism would not be the same as the life of freedom we enjoy.

One of the planned outcomes of Education for Sustainability is to diminish the value of individual success. The general message is, leave your dreams behind and adopt a lifestyle of scarcity to avoid planetary ruin. Every child has unlimited potential and ought to be free to pursue their destiny. Students should not have to put up with Green Party politics, deception and planned discouragement in the classroom.

We need to help our children understand why freedom and private property ownership is a healthier choice for them and for the environment.

"And it is no accident that **the very worst environmental tragedies were created by communist governments, in which the power of the state completely overwhelms the capabilities of the individual steward."**

Al Gore
Earth in the Balance

For the past several years the Greens have hailed communist Cuba as a role model for sustainability. Well, Castro deflated that bubble. The following excerpt is from a September 9, 2010 article titled "Fidel Castro casts doubt on 'Cuban model" by the CNN Wire Staff, which stated:

"... Fidel Castro told a visiting American journalist that the "Cuban model" no longer works; an apparent admission of failings in the communist economic model introduced by his revolution more than 50 years ago.

"The Cuban model doesn't even work for us anymore," Castro told Jeffrey Goldberg of 'The Atlantic' in an interview last week."

Source:http://www.cnn.com/2010/WORLD/americas/09/08/cuba.castro.communism/index.html?iref=allsearch

Students need to be aware of this confession by Castro, because the Greens have equated life in this communist country to their goal of sustainability, which as Castro pointed out, doesn't work.

Although Education for Sustainability has been presented as non-partisan, it is clear the goals of this political movement are rooted in Green Party goals which mirror communism. The Communist Party promotes socialism and it is helpful to note the Green Party and the Socialist Party are basically one in the same.

"In 1998, the Oregon Green and Socialist Parties merged into the Pacific Green Party."

Common Dreams
Progressive Newswire May 3, 2002
Source: http://www.commondreams.org

Understanding the Greens, socialists, communists and progressives have come together under the banner of the Green movement enables us to make what are now critical distinctions between legitimate environmental concerns and steps to impose Green Communism. These groups and individuals have the right to free speech and to promote their ideas all day long in the marketplace but not in our schools.

An example of how a public institution is highlighting communism is found in a 2012 Spring term course description from Portland State, which states:

"Revolutionary Marxism: Theory and Practice

The onset of the Arab Spring, revolts in European capitals against austerity, and **the emergence of the Occupy Wall Street here in the US have made the need for understanding revolutionary political theories more urgent than ever.**

This course is designed to introduce students to the basic concepts of Marxist thought with an emphasis on the practical applications of Marxist Theory in local political struggle."

We will focus on four major areas throughout the semester including the Fundamentals of Marxist Theory, Marxism and Oppression, **Revolutionary Practice, and The Future of Socialism."**

Source:http:www.sa.pdx.edu/soc/footnote.cfm?id=23&dcode=IST %20&term=02&year=2012

Academic freedom allows ample room to discuss different ideas. This course outline indicates there will be "an emphasis on the practical applications of Marxist Theory in local political struggle". This suggests the course will emphasize how to apply Marxist theories to local issues, which would make this a training course not a theoretical discussion. Does this course represent the highest and best use of our tax dollars?

The misuse of public education to indoctrinate students to adopt a socialist or communist mindset is a major problem and an urgent issue of national importance. The following excerpt is from a December 15, 2009 National Association of Scholars article titled, 'Guided by a Red Star: Ed Schools Bring Frankincense to the Cradle of Marxism' by Ashley Thorne.

"While it is appropriate to study the now discredited but historically important ideas of Marxism in political science, philosophy, and economics courses, education schools have no need for radical ideology.

Ed schools should be preparing teachers to train the minds of the next generation, not to arm them with socialist politics. To do so cheats both future teachers and their future students out of the sound, unbiased education they deserve."

Source:http://www.nas.org/articles/Guided_by_A_Red_Star_Ed_Schools_Bring_Frankinense_to_the_Cradle_of_Marxism

The trend of using the classroom to push this political mindset appears to be part of the Education for Sustainability plan to use education as a tool to change our form of government. The following statements are from a 1996 interview with Anthony Cortese, where he outlined the plan to use education as a tool to change the mindset of teachers and students so "they will go out and advocate different government policies". Cortese said:

"There's a huge problem with the 3,500 colleges and universities in the country and the 126 medical schools – **we need to change the mindset of the teachers and students there**. Those who graduate from these institutions are the future teachers, doctors, government administrators, legislators and business people. **If we can educate them to act in a different way, then they will go out and advocate different government policies."**

"But **the most important reason we chose to work at the college and university level is because that is where the future teachers are being trained.**

In the next decade, approximately 50% to 70% of today's teachers will be retiring. So **it is a great opportunity to train teachers who will then integrate the environmental perspective into what they teach, right from the beginning."**

Anthony Cortese, CEO, Second Nature
Conservation Matters Magazine - Spring 1996
Source: http://www.clf.org/../CM/archive.htm

When we break-it-down and add-it-up the goals of this movement are to:

- target and change the mindset of teachers and students
- train future doctors, government administrators, legislators and business people to act differently so they will advocate and support different government policies
- integrate environmental ideas into lesson plans, how teachers teach
- change the cultural, religious, social, economic and political structure of our nation

Since 1996 the Education for Sustainability movement has orchestrated the implementation of this political indoctrination scheme into our schools and forced this agenda on teachers, on students and on innocent little children.

Political Side Effects

We have learned to read about the side effects of any medication before taking it because the side effects can be more dangerous than the original ailment. The same concept applies to Education for Sustainability and the entire 'go Green' prescription that we've been given to save the earth. There are serious side effects of this Green prescription and that matters, because our children are getting a huge dose of Green politics every day. The way to remedy this problem is to expel Education for Sustainability programs immediately.

Forcing students to conform to sustainability goals is a sneaky way to condition students to think inside a little Green box. If the Greens get their way, students will think inside that box for the rest of their lives. Education for Sustainability is a tool to produce mass conformity and nationwide submission to the Green agenda. Sustainability is a great sounding idea as long as no one mentions that the goals mirror communism. When we take a quick look at what the Greens and the Education for Sustainability movement are promoting in the name of sustainability, the alignment with Lenin's game plan is evident.

Lenin and Communism	**Greens and Education for Sustainability**
• Intolerant one way Red thinking	• Intolerant one way Green thinking
• One party, the Communist Party	• Promoting one party, the Green Party
• Peace Bread and Land for All	• Equal access to earth's resources for all
• Redistributed the wealth	• Planning to redistribute the wealth
• Planned communist society	• Planned Green or sustainable society
• Used education to train children to adopt Communist Party goals	• Using education to train children to adopt Green Party, Earth Charter goals

Lenin promised all things to all people with 'Peace, Bread and Land for All'. The Education for Sustainability movement is using the same promise that sustainability means all people will have 'equitable access to the Earth's resources'. This is a trap we must recognize and help our children avoid.

Another part of the Green ambush is the warm sounding idea of sustainable, self-sufficient, cooperative communities. How could these ideas be used to impose communism or change our form of government? In the following statement, Lenin, the Father of Communism, reveals how he organized the population into cooperative societies, which automatically became socialist societies, then communist societies.

> "The only task that remains is to organize the population into cooperative societies, with most of the population organized in cooperatives, socialism will achieve its aim automatically...the system of civilized cooperatives is the system of socialism"
>
> Lenin

This is the same strategy outlined by the Young Communist League. If Education for Sustainability is allowed to become the new mission of public education, America's children will be trained to adopt the Green definition of a sustainable lifestyle, which includes the creation of sustainable, cooperative, self-sufficient communities. This is the method to impose communism.

The Anti-Parent Component

The long arm of the Greens extends beyond the classroom because the Greens are serious about indoctrinating our children and use every opportunity to Green their hearts and minds. A clear example is found in a children's book on global warming which promotes Green activism. On page 100 of the Scholastic book, the 'Down to Earth Guide to Global Warming, it defines Green as:

> "green - Also known as "going green"; the adoption of a sustainable lifestyle that respects the environment while actively working to curb our carbon footprint and, leave the world better than we found it."
>
> The Down-to-Earth Guide to Global Warming
> Laurie David and Cambria Gordon

Young readers get the message, everything Green is good. This message empowers children to 'play adult' by making what ought to be an adult decision to adopt a sustainable lifestyle or to curb their carbon footprint. Empowering children to 'play adult' is a key part of training them to eat Green, live Green, worship Green, and vote Green in the future.

Children are being manipulated to form opinions on political issues based on feelings not fact. For instance, movies like the Lorax; a scary tale about the last tree seed on the face of the earth, enhances children's fear of environmental ruin in real life. A big part of the promotion of this movie was giving away a 'free pack of tree seeds' for children to plant. The tree seed give away is how the Greens made the story seem real. Encouraging children to go plant trees also promoted Green activism as a way to avoid that fearful future.

Mixing fantasy, fear and Green politics in children's entertainment is another form of eco-child abuse and another form of political indoctrination. The Green's political strategy is to completely saturate America's children with being Green until their ability to think beyond being Green is gone.

Children have no frame of reference to make adult decisions and that is why parents are in charge or ought to be in charge. We do not allow children to drive cars because they do not have the life experience or emotional capacity to cope with that level of responsibility. We do not allow children to perform brain surgery or vote for the same reason.

Following is a sad example of an anti-parent, youth empowerment, Green message.

"There are some things about our world that you know that older people don't know."

Al Gore
Inauguration speech to 12 year olds and teens
Source: Glenn Beck program, February 4, 2009

The following excerpt is from the comments Glenn Beck posted regarding Al Gore's speech and remarks to students:

"I'm trying to think where else this has been done. Soviet Russia, Nazi Germany, Mussolini's Italy. In fact, the Nazis took an extra step. Not only did they indoctrinate the kids and tell them you're probably right, you know but your parents don't; in fact, here's the next step: Why don't you tell us what your parents are telling you. Are we having the new Hitler youth? Is that what this is? The new Hitler youth? I'm sorry, that's so politically incorrect. The new green guard. Man your station, 12-year-olds, your parents just don't know."

Glenn Beck

Setting children up to think that they know more than their parents is a copycat strategy to drive a wedge in the family and devalue the parent-child relationship. Treating children like adults flatters their egos and empowers children to expect their parents to treat them like adults. Green teachers encourage children to go home and tell their parents what to think. If parents do not share the Green opinion, the child has been set up to ignore their parents and enabled to turn to Green teachers, instead of family, for guidance. Training children away from their parents and into the political ranks of the Greens is the name of this game. An example of how the Greens operate is found in the book 'Captain-Eco' co-authored by the former Chairman of the Green Party Jonathan Porritt. The story of 'Captain Eco' includes the following message:

"Here's the picture, in a nutshell. Your planet's in serious trouble - from pollution, toxic waste and the loss of forest, farmland and fresh water...."

"Your parents and Grandparents have made a mess of looking after the earth. They may deny it, but they're little more than thieves. And they're stealing your future from under your noses."

Captain Eco-And the Fate of the Earth 1991
Jonathon Porritt - Ellis Nadler

The story of 'Captain Eco' is based around a cartoon character that comes from the soul of the earth to teach children how to save the planet. The story begins with a letter explaining to the reader that children took over in the 1990's and forced political leaders to support the Green movement. This is a prime example of how fear of environmental ruin is used to train children away from their parents and into the Green camp. Telling emotionally charged tales which assign real life blame to a child's parents and grandparents is intended to trigger frustration and anger toward the child's family.

Is the objective to actually turn children away from their parents? Yes. The 'Captain Eco' message reflects a long term strategy. On January 10, 1963 a list of 45 Communist Party goals from the book "The Naked Communist" by Cleon Skousen, were entered into the Congressional Record. According to an article Skousen wrote for the December 1996 issue of "The American's Bulletin', his research into the communist agenda began "during his 16 year term of service with the FBI". Two of the 45 goals the Communist Party has been working on since 1963 are:

> 17. Get control of the schools. Use them as transmission belts for socialism and current Communist propaganda. Soften the curriculum. Get control of teachers' associations. Put the party line in textbooks.
>
> 41. Emphasize the need to raise children away from the negative influence of parents. Attribute prejudices, mental blocks and retarding of children to suppressive influence of parents.

The goals of the Education for Sustainability movement certainly reflect taking control of our schools and using the curriculum to advocate communist ideas. The Green's youth empowerment strategy is intended to give children permission to dismiss their parent's intelligence and values. The purpose of youth empowerment is to make being Green seem more important than anything else, including love of family. Why? Traditional values stand in the way of the Education for Sustainability movement's goal to change America's culture, religion, society, economy and form of government. Destroying family ties is a deliberate part of the GREEN-BOT process. An insight into the Green Party position on parental rights and youth empowerment follows:

> "Youth Rights ... We must ensure they have an upbringing that allows them to take their place as functioning, productive, and self-actualized members of their community."
>
> "Youth are not the property of their parents or guardians, but are under their care and guidance."
>
> Green Party Platform 2004
> Social Justice (page 23)
> Source: http://www.GP.ORG

Most parents do not consider their children property, but rather wonderful little people they love and have the great pleasure of sharing their lives with; which includes instilling the values that will guide their children to a happy life. This Green Party statement indicates children do not belong to their parents. If children do not belong to their parents, who do they belong to? The Green Party statement reflects the Communist Party view outlined in goal #41. In addition, the Green idea that youth "take their place as functioning, productive and self-actualized members of their community" fits the youth empowerment strategy.

Cubs Don't Hunt

If the Greens had any respect for natural law, they would show respect for the parent-child relationship. Natural law does not put babies in charge of parents. Like lions and cubs; lions do not send tiny cubs out into the wilderness to hunt for food because tiny cubs are not capable of hunting and because they would probably be killed. Cubs are disciplined by their parents to stay within certain boundaries until they have learned all the necessary survival skills to safely venture out into a dangerous world. Training children to take a position of authority over their parents is unhealthy and backwards.

If the Greens had any respect for natural law and were not just recruiting and using children to produce a voting block; they would not pit children against their parents. Greening students and Greening our schools also includes the following short list of subtle steps which pit children against their parents:

- walk or ride their bikes to school to lower their carbon footprint
- eat less meat or become a vegetarian to save the earth
- hug or touch a tree

"When was the last time you touched a tree?" is a question from a nature and spirituality section of a school booklet on sustainable living. Although we can all appreciate the splendor of trees, the purpose of this question is to introduce students to the idea of equating sustainability to earth-based spirituality.

Forming a personal relationship with a tree is a Green Party or deep ecology mindset. Unless students realize one of the goals of the Education for Sustainability movement is to change their religious beliefs, they could fall prey to adopting the Green definition of a sustainable lifestyle, without realizing it is headed toward earth-based spirituality and Humanism.

This short list helps to demonstrate how the Greens have changed the role of public education. Is pressuring children to ride their bike to school, instead of letting their parents drive them, the purpose of public education? No. The decision to allow a child to ride their bike to school is a safety issue and a parent's choice, not a school's decision. The same applies to a decision to become a vegetarian or form a relationship with a tree.

Most teachers are dedicated individuals who chose education as a career to help students learn skills, not to advance the Green agenda. These teachers can help return our schools to safe havens of learning. The following statement provides a revealing look at how the communist model of education compares to where we are with the Green invasion of America's schools.

> **"Teachers in the United States refrain from interjecting political bias in their classroom work,** and would be severely criticized if they used their teaching to promote personal political views."
>
> **"In the USSR, however, only one point of view—Marxism-Leninism—is permitted, and teachers are expected to present it to their pupils.** For this reason, even sentences used to teach principles of grammar, word problems in arithmetic and many others, all serve to reinforce Communist ideology..."
>
> Communism: What It Is and How It Works
> Schlesinger and Blustain (1964)

This distinction between two different approaches to education helps us to understand how the Greens have used the environmental cause to gradually change our standard of education to the point; it is on the verge of matching the Soviet model of political indoctrination.

If the environmental movement had declared their affiliation with the Green Party up-front (in the 70's or 80's) the American people would have taken action to ensure the professional teaching standard described in the first paragraph of the above quotation, remained intact. Instead, the Greens have used the environmental cause to conceal politically indoctrinating students. Unfortunately, the second paragraph describes the Education for Sustainability agenda. What would it mean if this program became the new mission of public education?

- only the Green point of view will be presented to students
- teachers will present the Green agenda in every subject, every day
- Green Party ideology will be reinforced, preschool through college

The outcome of this level of indoctrination would be an end to free thought as we know it and a shift to single party rule. Other methods to politicize education include:

- make it popular for students to wear the Green label in school
- orchestrate student activism in support of the Green agenda

- use students love of the great outdoors to embed Green ideology
- recognize and reward students for Green activism
- empower students with idea that it is up to them to save the earth
- empower children to think they know more than their parents

This general outline, with the exception of the word Green, represents some of the same manipulative tactics used to build the Hitler Youth. Hitler used education as a political hammer to instill student loyalty to the Nazi cause and pretty much nothing else. Parents did not realize what was happening until it was too late and they had lost their children to that political movement.

> **"When an opponent declares, 'I will not come over to your side, ' I calmly say, "Your child belongs to us already...**
>
> What are you? You will pass on. **Your descendants, however, now stand in the new camp. In a short time they will know nothing else but this new community."**
>
> Adolf Hitler
> The Rise and Fall of the Third Reich

If not checked, our children will learn to stand in a new all-Green camp and will "know nothing else" but the new Green community. It is also important to remember that Hitler used the idea that the earth was a living organism, as a way to get people to abandon traditional beliefs and help save the sacred soil. This decade, the Greens are using the same trick, that the earth is a living organism or a living being, Gaia or Mother Earth.

The Greens are also using a 'man is part of nature' Humanist idea to get students to abandon traditional religious beliefs. Hindsight is always 20-20. When God was no longer the reference point, moral atrocities occurred under Hitler's reign of terror.

Removing Education for Sustainability programs from America's schools is one of the most important duties of our time. The Greens know that little Green activists will grow up to be big Green activists and Green voters.

If a child reaches for a hot burner or steps toward a rattlesnake, we do not hesitate to do whatever it takes to make sure that child doesn't get hurt. The same is true regarding Education for Sustainability. We must protect our children from this harmful political movement.

Relinquish the Belief in God

How is the Education for Sustainability movement using the classroom to instill the worldview of the Green Party in our children?

> We have to understand that **we are an integral part of nature** and that we are **co-evolving with other species** in the biosphere."
>
> Anthony Cortese, Second Nature
> Leveraging Change: The Role of the University in a Sustainable Future
> MIT panel: Alliance for Global Sustainability - Cambridge, MA, January 2000
> Source:http://www.secondnature.org/history/writings/speeches/leveraging_change.htm

This is the mindset that the Education for Sustainability movement is training America's children to adopt. We all understand we are part of nature to a certain extent but the radical agenda attached to this movement reflects the spiritual agenda of the Green Party. The following statements, which outline the Green's spiritual agenda, are from the 1989 Green Party program.

> **"As human beings, we are struggling for meaning and purpose in a world that has reduced Earth and her creatures** to markets and commodities ..."
>
> **"Green spirituality is an attitude,** a state of being, **a way of celebrating and being in relationship with Earth."**
>
> **"Green politics and spirituality;** means that we are caregivers to Mother Earth recognizing our rootedness in nature's web of life of which **we humans are but one part**. It is recognizing that **Mother Earth gives us far more than we give her."**
>
> Green Party Program 1989 (page 39)
>
> **"The adoption of a new world view** that values the integrity of all life forms **is a necessary and integral part** of diverting the Earth from the destructive course on which we have placed it.
>
> **Adoption of such an approach entails the relinquishment of the dominating world view by Western cultures."**
>
> **"Ecological wisdom** teaches us to view ourselves as **part of nature rather than as on top of it or dominating it**."
>
> Green Party Program 1989 (page 20)

The dominating worldview the Greens are referring to, in the spiritual sense, is the belief in God. The Green's used the word 'relinquish' to describe their spiritual and political objectives. Relinquish means to abandon, forsake or give up. The goal is to get Western cultures, like ours, to give-up our belief in God.

The Green Party and the Education for Sustainability movement share the same worldview and the same political objective to change America's religious beliefs. The strategy to change our worldview was also laid out in the 1989 Green Party program, which, once again, states:

> "Ecological wisdom teaches us to view ourselves as part of nature rather than as on top of it or dominating it." — Bible states we have dominion over everything on the earth

This Green Party statement clarifies the worldview the Greens intend to impose and the worldview the Greens intend to eliminate.

- The worldview the Greens intend to impose is that man is part of nature

- The worldview the Green's intend to eliminate is that man was given dominion over nature and charged with being a good steward

The crux of the Green's strategy is to claim:

- the Western worldview or belief in God is to blame for environmental ruin
- believing in God is a detriment to the environment
- a new worldview is necessary to save the earth
- if students give-up the belief in God 'they' can save the earth

Education for Sustainability is a plan to destroy the fundamental belief that God created heaven and earth and charged man with being a good steward.

The Green Party worldview is a core theme of the Education for Sustainability movement and this worldview is being taught as curriculum in many of our schools. The Greens slipped this mindset into the curriculum by pretending students were learning about 'ecological wisdom' when they are actually being indoctrinated to adopt the Green Party worldview. The environmental cause is the decoy to advance an anti-God communist agenda.

The Greens are also using the captive audience situation the classroom provides to convince younger students to adopt Green beliefs by:

- tapping into a child's heartfelt love of God's creation

- emphasizing the urgent need for children to help save creation

- shifting children's spiritual focus from Creator to creation

- empowering children to adopt an earth-based or Humanist worldview
- pressuring children to go Green and relinquish their belief in God

The following statement, by Education for Sustainability leader David Orr, confirms the Green's spiritual focus.

> "...That in the end; honor the mystery of creation and celebrate the mystery of creation without having to dominate it or change it or re-engineer it, but learn to celebrate it. That's your work. That's my work. THAT is the great work of our time."
>
> David Orr
> Professor Environmental Studies and Politics
> Speech: Ecological Literacy
> Oregon Sustainability Forum September 6, 2001
> Transcript (page 18)

The Earth Charter is the tool to impose the international agenda of the Green Party. When we review what Gorbachev said about the Earth Charter in 1997 and realize the Earth Charter is now a major part of the Education for Sustainability movement, the agenda of this movement is easier to see.

> "My hope is that this charter **will be a kind of 'Ten Commandments', a 'Sermon on the Mount' that provides a guide for human behavior** toward the environment in the next century and beyond".
>
> Mikhail Gorbachev
> Los Angeles Times, May 1997

The Greens are selling 'Ocean front property in Arizona'

Over the years the Greens have used one assertion after another to justify their demands for radical change as a step to save the earth. All this time those assertions, including the call to make Education for Sustainability the new mission of public education, were steps to facilitate changing our culture, religion, society, economy and form of government.

The new book **"Exploring Synergies between Faith Values and Education for Sustainable Development"** from UNESCO, the UNESCO Chair on Education for Sustainable Development and the Earth Charter and UPEACE was released in 2012. The book presents multiple views regarding the spiritual aspects of Education for Sustainability and, although the usual disclaimers are used, the underlying message is consistent with the Green agenda.

One of the editors of this book is Richard Clugston; a member of the Earth Charter International Council and the coordinator of the Earth Charter Scholarship Project at Florida Gulf Coast University.

The segment Clugston wrote for this book highlights the message of Tu Weiming. Weiming called for a 'comprehensive spiritual humanism' in the last segment. The following statements, from Weiming's closing remarks, are a real eye opener.

> "The time is ripe for us to rethink the human in the 21st century. **We are in need of a comprehensive spiritual humanism** that is capable of integrating the four inseparable dimensions of human flourishing: self, community, Earth, and Heaven. As Ewert Cousins **wisely remarked, the Earth is our prophet**.
>
> **Those who are musical to the sound of the Earth will guide us on to a new path of survival.** Furthermore, **there is a great deal that humans seasoned in a modernistic mentality can learn from indigenous traditions.**
>
> Actually**, all spiritual traditions must undergo a profound transformation** to respond to the new human condition occasioned by the contemporary ecological crisis.
>
> **No religious leader can afford to focus on the sacredness of the Kingdom of God at the expense of the secular world** or the loftiness of the Pure Land at the expense of This Shore, the "red dust."
>
> The cultivation of a spirit of caring for the earth is widely recognized as a universal principle of global citizenship.
>
> Therefore, **it is imperative that all citizens of the world** take part in an ongoing dialogue among civilizations to **facilitate this vision."**
>
> Exploring Synergies between Faith Values and Education for Sustainable Development, Section: Ecological Implications of Confucian Humanism by Tu Weiming (page 81)
> Source:http://www.earthcharterinaction.org/invent/images/uploads/Feb_2_2012.pdf

A recap of the final message of this Education for Sustainability book follows:

- **we need a comprehensive spiritual humanism**
- **the Earth is our prophet**
- the sound of **the Earth will guide us on a new path** of survival

- **humans** seasoned in a modernistic mentality **can learn from indigenous traditions**

- **No religious leader can afford to focus on the sacredness of the Kingdom of God**

- **it is imperative all citizens of the world facilitate this vision**

A dialogue to facilitate the idea of Humanism is not just starting, Education for Sustainability programs are already advocating this mindset in our schools. These ideas appear on the very last page of the book because this is the message, that those who compiled this book want people to remember. And, then there is this statement:

> **"No religious leader can afford to focus on the sacredness of the Kingdom of God at the expense of the secular world ..."**

This is an important message or it would not be included in the new UNESCO and Earth Charter book on faith and Education for Sustainable Development. The statement infers that religious leaders and anyone else who is focused on the sacredness of the Kingdom of God is somehow a threat to the earth, at the expense of the secular world. The general meaning of the word secular is a worldview devoid of God.

This statement, combined with the other ideas in the last paragraphs of the book, infers that those who 'do not' believe in God will take better care of the earth and, that adopting an earth-based worldview, where 'the Earth is our prophet' is necessary to survive.

Since this is an Education for Sustainability or Sustainable Development theme book, it follows that the book is designed to promote certain messages and preferred beliefs. The inference those who believe in God might harm the earth is intended to steer students toward the earth-based crowd. The Green Party objective, to get people to relinquish their belief in God, is evident. This is a mind control game. The end justifies the means strategy is to just 'make something up and then pretend that it's true'. The Green's assertion that believing in the Kingdom God is an environmental threat, makes as much sense as the assertion, forks make people fat.

Looking at this from a different angle; over 90% of the American people believe in God. Should a tiny secular minority be allowed to use public education and our tax dollars, to train America's children to worship the earth, at the expense of the Kingdom of God? The saying 'sometimes a shepherd tends the flock but sometimes has to fight off the wolves' comes to mind.

Headhunters and Cannibals

As used in this context, the promotion of indigenous traditions or tribal customs shows no respect for those who believe in the Kingdom of God. From a political standpoint, the Green's are also pushing students and adults to adopt an earth-based or tribal worldview as a strategy to denounce God and pave the way for communism. The list of 45 communist goals, entered into the Congressional Record on January 10, 1963 from the book "The Naked Communist" by FBI veteran Cleon Skousen, is an invaluable reference to see through the Green's propaganda. Two more goals from that list follow:

> 27. **Infiltrate the churches** and **replace revealed religion with "social" religion. Discredit the Bible and emphasize the need for intellectual maturity which does not need a "religious crutch."**
>
> 28. **Eliminate prayer or any phase of religious expression in the schools** on the ground that it violates the principle of "separation of church and state."

The 1963 Communist goals included replacing 'revealed religion with social religion', discrediting 'the Bible' and eliminating the praise of God, which is America's foundational and moral base, from our schools. Well, where are we? We have tolerated steps to impose these goals to weaken America's moral base. Education for Sustainability and Gorbachev's Earth Charter, which he hails as a 'New Ten Commandments', are now being used to train our children to adopt Green Party beliefs to replace America's religious base and form of government.

The American standard of politically neutral, or Party neutral, public education is an essential safeguard to free thought, individual freedom and the democratic process. Education for Sustainability is replacing that standard with a politically biased agenda. An example of how students are treated, and feel about this treatment, is from a report about Oregon State University (OSU).

> "The university's emphasis on tolerance does not extend to Christians, said Joel Klein" ... "In academia there's a bias against evangelicals" he said "I've had a world religions class where I was told my beliefs were wrong"
>
> "Faith Under Fire" (at OSU)
> Gazette Times - February 12, 2005

Although unfair and unacceptable this type of harassment in the classroom is common. Ridicule is a tool to change student's beliefs. Why would a student attending a public institution in America be told their belief in God was wrong? Oregon State University was already working with Second Nature in 2002 and is known for advocating sustainability on campus. As we know, the Earth

Charter is an Education for Sustainability training tool. The Earth Charter fine print sheds light on this issue as the stated objectives include:

> "Advance the **study of ecological sustainability** and promote the open exchange and wide application of the knowledge acquired."
>
> "**Recognize and preserve the** traditional knowledge and **spiritual wisdom** in all cultures **that contribute to environmental protection** and human well-being."
>
> Earth Charter (page 3, section 8)
> Source: http://www.earthcharterinaction.org

If we read between the lines, an important goal emerges. The second statement indicates that one of the goals of the Earth Charter is to have the authority to decide what 'spiritual wisdom' does or does not "contribute to environmental protection". This also indicates the Earth Charter wants the power of law to decide what religious wisdom, or religion is allowed.

If God's word automatically fell into the category of a 'spiritual wisdom' deemed worth preserving, why would the Greens and Gorbachev, the co-author of the Earth Charter, insist on returning to the belief that man is part of nature or Humanism?

A stated purpose of Education for Sustainability is to change America's religious beliefs. The Greens intend to force their beliefs on the American people by using Education for Sustainability to train our children to adopt Green Party and Earth Charter principles as their faith base. Again, Education for Sustainability is rooted in Green Party ideology. It is vital we understand sustainability and systems thinking are tools to indoctrinate students to embrace the anti-God worldview of the Greens. Green Party ideology includes a broad scope of earth-based beliefs, from the worship of Mother Earth and Her creation, to deep ecology and Humanism. Greens refer to God as a 'sky God'.

Promoting earth-based wisdom or tribal beliefs in the classroom as a tangible solution to environmental concerns blurs the deliberate plan to change America's religious base and deeply held belief in God. It is also worth noting that civilization moved past the headhunters, cannibals and other earth-based tribal customs some time ago. Respect for the spiritual beliefs of others is one thing but Education for Sustainability is not about respect; it is a calculated plan to erase the belief in God from the hearts and minds of America's children and replace it with Green Party beliefs. One of the leading Green Party organizers, Charlene Spretnak, described the core concepts of Green Party ideology in the following statements.

> "**The core concepts are sustainability and interrelatedness**. In fact one could say that **human systems are sustainable to the extent they**

reflect the fact of interrelatedness: the dynamics of Nature arching and stretching **through the cycles of her** permutations, the dynamics of humans interacting, deftly or brutally, with the rest of Nature, the dynamics of **the person interacting with a system and that system with others."**

The Spiritual Dimension of Green Politics (page 22-23)

Although the Greens indicated in the early 1980's that they did not consider themselves to be Humanist, times change. The Earth Charter, which reflects the Humanist mindset, was part of the Green Party platform in 2000; recognized as the ethical base of the Green Party in 2001 and still part of the Green Party platform in 2010.

The Earth Charter, UNESCO book on Education for Sustainability and faith covers multiple ideas, but the final thought in the book hits the real objective, which is world Humanism. The last statements in the book, which infers that all those focused on the sacredness of the Kingdom of God might be a threat to the earth, is a lot like the con artist trying to sell 'ocean front property in Arizona'. That kind of scam only works if people accept what the con artist 'says' is true, instead of trusting in what they 'know' to be true.

"It is for freedom that Christ has set us free. Stand firm then and do not let yourselves be burdened again by a yoke of slavery."

Galatians 5:1

America's founding principles are based on a strong and fundamental belief in God. Our forefathers understood that moral character was an essential ingredient to the success of a free people and a free nation. References to the Lord were included in America's founding documents and evident in the timeless wisdom of the founding fathers. The belief in God is part of our history, our culture, our lives and our strength as a nation. It all comes down to moral character and understanding where moral character comes from.

"If we ever forget we are one nation under God, then we will be a nation gone under."

Ronald Reagan
Prayer Breakfast 1984

We all cherish free thought and the right to our individual beliefs. We have long operated on a 'live and let live' philosophy out of respect for the rights of others. That said, the Greens have gone too far. We cannot allow the Green movement to continue to use our schools and our tax dollars to turn our children against 'God and Country' under the pretense of creating a sustainable future or saving the earth.

6

Multi-Faceted Line of Attack

Approximately 89% of America's children attend public schools. Education for Sustainability is a vehicle to take control of public education and standardize or 'Green' the personal and political beliefs of our children to control 89% of the future vote. Education for Sustainability is a Green Party indoctrination program to foster single party rule. If we choose freedom for our children and for ourselves, we must take our schools back now. How are the Greens using the concept of sustainability to standardize children's beliefs and behaviors?

Invasion of the Lunch Box

Training children to think and act the same begins by intimidating little ones to conform to Green demands in multiple areas, including passing judgment on their lunch. A prime example of how this works is found in a sustainability quiz called "Sustainability: A view for Kids" from the Sustainable Oregon Schools Initiative. Part of that quiz follows. Please grab a pencil and answer the following four questions.

"When I bring my lunch, I bring:

a. a homemade sandwich
b. a prepackaged lunch meal.

My mom says we are out of milk, I:

a. suggest that we walk the half mile to the store to get some.
b. stay home and watch TV, she'll drive over to get some.

We stopped at the farmer's market last Sunday,I

a. couldn't wait to leave so we could go to the store and buy some mangos.
b. was thrilled to find some local apples.

When I get old enough to buy my own car, I want to get:

a. the biggest, fastest car I can afford.
b. a hybrid or other fuel efficient vehicle."

The answers to each of these questions follow. The behavior the Sustainable Oregon Schools Initiative is training students to adopt is clear and the justification for that behavior is stated in the (parentheses) after each answer.

- The answer to what kind of lunch is sustainable is:
  homemade (Less waste)

- The answer to driving or walking to the store for milk is:
  walk (Driving will require fossil fuel and produces greenhouse gases. Plus, walking is good exercise.)

- The answer to what kind of fruit to select is:
  eat local food (Local produce requires less transportation, and the farmer might receive more money for apples than wholesale. This keeps the farmer in business.)

- The answer to what kind of car to drive is:
  hybrid (Hybrid vehicles burn less fossil fuel and generate lower emissions than conventional cars. Alternative fuel vehicles are also good sustainable alternatives."

Source: http://www.sustainableschools.org 3/2/07
Source:http://web.archive.org/web/20100816214957/http://sustainableschools.org/documents/Sustainability%20for%20kids%20070302.pdf

The issue of concern is not if we personally agree or disagree with these answers, but rather that this quiz trains students 'what' to think not 'how' to think individually. There are only two answers to choose from and only one correct answer. There is zero room for free thought or individual choice. Children either accept the Green answer or fail the test. This is not education but political indoctrination, which is not the purpose or the role of public education in America. This quiz is a prime example of how children are being manipulated and trained to be GREEN-BOTS.

This politically charged quiz also pits children against parents and others who believe in liberty. What if a child's parents drive an SUV or just happen to like mangos? America's children are being led to believe that there is no longer room for their dreams or personal choices. The Green message is, they must conform and others must conform. This quiz also advances the Green agenda by convincing children to go home and 'beg or tell' their parents to adopt the sustainable lifestyle dictated in class.

This lesson shows how the concept of sustainability and fear of environmental ruin are used to train our children to accept Green control of their lives and, to believe their survival depends on the American people accepting this kind of control over their lives. This kind of lesson can also create anger toward those who do not conform to Green demands as non-compliance is ridiculed. These lessons are designed to change values and behavior. Social engineering, political indoctrination and brainwashing are all methods to change the way people think. Many tactics in the Education for Sustainability arsenal align with the components of brainwashing such as:

- one choice only answers
- goal to change students beliefs and behavior
- make the ideology of one political party the focus of public education
- use avoiding environmental ruin to create personal stress
- use sustainability to standardize goals and values

Following is a comparison between Webster's definition of brainwashing and the goals of Education for Sustainability.

Brainwashing:	**Education for Sustainability:**
✔ change attitudes or alter beliefs	✔ change thinking, values, actions
✔ controlled, systematic indoctrination	✔ instill sustainability goals from preschool through university
✔ based on repetition	✔ instill Green goals in every subject
✔ psychological-stress or confusion	✔ nonstop fear of environmental ruin

Communist leaders make it a habit to use education to brainwash students to support the Communist Party and control the population. Education for Sustainability is aligning students with the agenda of the Green Party which mirrors communism. It appears all that has changed is the name of the political party; it has gone from Red to Green. The following statement by Mikhail Gorbachev is from a 1994 interview regarding his involvement in the Green movement. Gorbachev's goal to radically change what people think suggests why Education for Sustainability is one of the Earth Charter's top priorities.

> "A revolution has to take place in people's minds..."
>
> Mikhail Gorbachev
> From Red to Green, Audubon, 1994

Indoctrination is the plan. Since 1994, Gorbachev's Earth Charter has, thanks to the assistance of the Green movement, become a major part of the

Education for Sustainability agenda and is already being used in many of our schools.

Many schools on the following list may not realize that Earth Charter goals parallel Green Party goals, but that is no excuse. The endorsement of the Earth Charter by these institutions equates to using our tax dollars to advocate international law over the US Constitution, which is another major reason to get Education for Sustainability and the Earth Charter out of America's schools now. How many of our schools and departments have already aligned with the Earth Charter? The Earth Charter Initiative's list of endorsers includes the following colleges and universities:

Antioch College

Bellevue Community College

College of the Atlantic

College of St. Benedict, St. John's University Environmental Studies Program

Michigan State University

North Shore Community College

Lakeland College

Marygrove College

University - Vermont Law School

University - Yale University School of Forestry & Environmental Studies

University of California, Santa Cruz Environmental Studies

University of California, Santa Cruz Recreation Department

University of Connecticut

Oklahoma City University

University of Louisville Center for Environmental Education

University of Maine Cooperative Extension

University of Maryland Baltimore County

University of Mississippi

Northwestern University

Pacifica Graduate Institute

Philadelphia University, Office of Spiritual Development

Prescott College

Pitzer College

Radford University

University of Redlands

Seattle University

Unity College

University of South Carolina, Sustainable Universities Initiative

University of South Florida, Equal Opportunity and Diversity

University of South Florida, Manatee Community College Ecology Club

Saint Mary's College

University of Texas - Houston, School of Public Health

University of the District of Columbia

University of the Pacific

Vassar College

University of Vermont

University of Washington

University of Wisconsin Oshkosh

Source:http://www.earthcharterinaction.org/content/catagories/Country/United States#

Our public schools are not supposed to be used, by any one political group, to indoctrinate America's children to support any one political party. The radical agenda of the Education for Sustainability movement, and alignment of that agenda with the goals of the Green Party and the Earth Charter, ought to be grounds to immediately expel this program. Academic freedom does not extend to brainwashing students behind closed doors.

Double Crossed

Education for Sustainability and the Earth Charter are vehicles to smuggle Green Party ideology into our schools. The book 'Earth Rising' by Philip Shabecoff, published in 2000, confirms the plan to advance Green politics through public education. The purpose of the book 'Earth Rising' was to outline the future agenda of the Green movement based on Shabecoff's interviews with multiple key leaders in the Green movement.

The spokesperson for the Green Party was interviewed right along with the leaders of the major environmental groups and the Education for Sustainability movement. The Green Party spokesperson was included in these interviews because the Green Party and Green movement are aligned and work together.

A few Green leaders Shabecoff interviewed follow:

• Green Party spokesperson	John Resenbrink
• Second Nature	Anthony Cortese
• Professor	David Orr
• Earth Day	Denis Hayes
• National Wildlife Federation	Mark Van Putten
• Friends of the Earth	Brent Blackwelder
• Natural Resource Defense Council	John Adams
• Environmental Defense Fund	Fred Krupp
• World Resource Institute	Jonathan Lash
• National Religious Partnership for the Environment	Paul Gorman
• The Wilderness Society	William Meadows
• ALF-CIO, Environmental Liaison	Jane Perkins
• Sierra Club	Carl Pope
• League of Conservation Voters	Deb Callahan
• National Environmental Trust	Phillip Clapp
• World Wildlife Fund	Katherine Fuller
• Native Forest Council	Tim Hermach
• Land Trust Alliance	Jean Hocker
• Southwest Network for Environmental and Economic Justice	Richard Moore

Following are this author's summary of the Green movement's future agenda, which are based on the conclusions Shafecoff laid out in 2000, after he interviewed the leaders of the Green movement.

- Use public education (preschool, K-12 and college) to shape children's beliefs and inculcate Green values

- Focus on science, guide projects and use the results

- Reform education; get on school boards to control standards and curriculum, including college and university boards

- Use support for the environmental cause to change America's political, social and economic systems

- Get churches to embrace a new theology (a new spirituality)

- Use sustainability, change economy, fulfill human needs

- Use American's support for the environmental cause to build the Green Party and elect Green Party candidates

In the following statement, Shabecoff outlined a key piece of the Green Party agenda and cements the point with a quote from Green Party spokesperson John Resenbrink, stating:

> "He concluded that the current political system will not be able to address our ecological problems, and therefore, "we need a new constellation of power".

Resenbrink's statement indicates the Green Party strategy was to assert that we must change our political system in order to save the environment. The Education for Sustainability movement also plans to change our government system and is using the environmental cause as the excuse to train students to embrace the Earth Charter as their guide to a sustainable future.

Resenbrink's assertion, that our political system cannot address ecological concerns and therefore we need a new one, is groundless and unreasonable but what if America's children are trained to believe that? The Education for Sustainability movement is training students to believe that notion by presenting the Earth Charter as a necessary alternative to our current system. If our children are indoctrinated to adopt the Earth Charter throughout school they will grow-up and, as planned, support the ratification of the Earth Charter as law over the US Constitution or, simply obey the Earth Charter as law even if it's not ratified.

We can turn this ship around if we work together and take immediate and decisive action to stop the political indoctrination of America's children. This is one of the most important duties of our time. A quick look at what Shabecoff wrote about Anthony Cortese in 2000, combined with the updated information in this book, shows the Greens have hijacked public education and are promoting Green Party goals camouflaged as Education for Sustainability. Shabecoff wrote:

> "Anthony Cortese, president of Second Nature, a Boston based organization dedicated to inculcating the importance of "education for sustainability" in professionals in higher education ...contended:
>
> **"The current educational system, Cortese said, reinforces "the deep cultural belief that humans are separate from nature.** ..."
>
> "... **Cortese is trying to persuade school administrators ... to ... integrate ecological and environmental material into every element of their curricula**".

Earth Rising - 2000 (page 70-71)

America's support for the environmental cause has been severely abused. Education for Sustainability, which includes the Earth Charter, is on track to become the primary focus of all learning and practice in America's schools. If not checked, our children will be trained to support the international agenda of the Greens and become enemies of our culture, religion, society, economy and form of government.

To paraphrase Lenin, 'give us your child for 8 years and it will be a communist forever' and that's what's going on here. Our public schools and our tax dollars are being used by the Greens, to brainwash our children to adopt the communist agenda of the Green Party and to manufacture GREEN-BOTS who will submit to Green Communism and help impose that agenda on the American people.

> "Freedom is a fragile thing and is never more than one generation away from extinction. It is not ours by inheritance; it must be fought for and defended constantly by each generation, for it comes only once to a people. Those who have known freedom and then lost it have never known it again."
>
> Ronald Reagan

Freedom is on the line. We need to rethink where we are, as a nation and as individuals, regarding just how far out of whack things have gotten due to the demands of the Green movement. Removing this politically biased program from our schools is an urgent issue of local, state and national concern. If we allow Education for Sustainability to align America's children with the Green Party agenda, we will all wind-up living under Green Communism. Training students to eat Green, live Green, worship Green and vote Green is not cute. This dictatorial training program puts free thought, individual freedom and our form of government at risk.

It is important to understand that Education for Sustainability legislation has been passed, but it is also important to know legislation can be overturned. Our political representatives were probably not informed that Education for Sustainability was rooted in Green Party ideology, or that the international Earth Charter was part of the package, when they cast their vote. The following statement, from a Second Nature 2011 report, 'Education for Sustainability Blueprint', confirms the name of the legislation that was passed and the involvement of the US Department of Education.

> "Sustainability Education was recognized in federal law for the first time with the creation of the University Sustainability Program in Higher Education Opportunity Act, followed by the Sustainability Education Summit: Citizenship and Career Pathways for a Green Economy hosted by the U.S. Department of Education in September of 2010."
>
> Source: http://www.secondnature.org/efsblueprint/efs-blueprint.pdf

Core Team

Anthony Cortese and Professor David Orr are part of the core team advancing the agenda of the Education for Sustainability movement. Professor Orr serves on the Boards of multiple organizations involved in the Education for Sustainability movement, including a group called the Bioneers. David Orr and Anthony Cortese were featured speakers at the 2011 Bioneers conference. The mission of the Bioneers is to, among other things, advance progressive politics. The Bioneers Creation Story states:

> "The conference has always provided an explicit orientation toward broadly progressive views..."

Source: http://www.bioneers.org/about/the-bioneer-creation -story
(or) the Board: http://www.bioneers.org/about/board-of-directors

According to David Orr's speaker biography for the National Council for Science and the Environment Conference, held January 18, 2012, Orr also serves as a Board member for the following organizations:

- Second Nature
- The Rocky Mountain Institute
- The Center for Ecoliteracy
- The Center for the Respect of Life and the Environment (CRLE)

Source: http://www.environmentandsecurity.org/topics/view/76252

Professor Orr is a Board member for the Center for Respect of Life and the Environment or CRLE. It is important to note that CRLE is one of the leading Earth Charter partner groups and organized one of the first Earth Charter meetings in the United States in 1996. Richard Clugston is the Executive Director of both CRLE and the Earth Charter US.

Clugston also serves on the international Earth Charter Council and is the former Executive Director of the University Leaders for a Sustainable Future, another Education for Sustainability group committed to pushing the Earth Charter into our schools. The University Leaders for a Sustainable Future also works with Second Nature. There is a consistent crossover of the groups and individuals pushing Education for Sustainability into our schools. It is important to understand the political background of a few key players.

David Orr is a Professor of Environmental Studies and Politics at Oberlin College. The 2008, Winter Edition of the 'Earth Island Journal' featured an article, "Conversation: David Orr discusses ecological instruction in the 21st century". An excerpt from that article follows:

"Since the 1992 publication of his influential book Ecological Literacy, **David Orr has been among the leading thinkers of the US environmental movement."**

Source:http://www.earthisland.org/journal/index.php/eij/article/conversation/

David Orr is also a member of the Obama Administration's National Advisory Committee for the Presidential Climate Action Project. Another member of that committee is Van Jones.

Source: http://www.climateactionproject.com/advisory.php

Van Jones is the co-founder of 'Green for All' and a former advisor to the White House Council on Environmental Quality. Jones controversial political background is important to understand. A March 1, 2010 WorldNetDaily article "Catch a falling czar's astounding comment..." by Aaron Klein, included the following statements:

"Jones resigned in September from his post as advisor to the White House Council on Environmental Quality after it was exposed **he founded a communist revolutionary organization..."**

"...Jones previously stated **his advocacy for green jobs was part of a broader movement to destroy the U.S. capitalist system**."

Klein wrote, "In a 2005 Uprising Radio interview, Jones talked about using "green" jobs to bring down the capitalist system". Klein then revealed the following quotation from Van Jones.

"Inside that minimum demand was a very radical kernel that eventually meant that **from 1964 to 1968 complete revolution was on the table for this country**,' he said. **"And I think that this green movement has to pursue those same steps** and stages."

Source: http://www.wnd.com

Klein pointed out that "Jones previously stated his advocacy for green jobs was part of a larger movement to destroy the capitalist system" and then he linked Jones revolutionary goals to the Green movement. These facts are important. Jones is considered a leader in the Green movement or he would not have been selected to serve on the White House Council on Environmental Quality. When Jones had to resign from the White House Council on Environmental Quality, due to his ties to communism, he received national media attention. Jones ties to communism are well known.

Where is Jones now? He is in a teaching and leadership position with the Bioneers, a leading group in the Education for Sustainability movement. David

Orr serves on the Bioneer's Board. Jones is one of the top 3 instructors featured in the "Teaching Bioneers" program, right along with David Orr.

Source: http://www.bioneers.org/programs/education/teaching-bioneers

The timeless saying 'birds of a feather flock together' comes to mind. The Bioneers are a self-identified group of progressives that are working directly with Second Nature to advance the agenda of the Education for Sustainability movement.

Source: http:www.bioneers.org/programs/education/second-nature

The political agenda of the Greens and progressives align. Progressive is just a softer term for communism. Following are 2 lists of prominent groups working directly with Second Nature to advance Education for Sustainability goals:

- Campaign for Environmental Literacy
- National Wildlife Federation
- Earth Day Network
- American Association of Community Colleges

Source: http://www.secondnature.org/policy/policy_partnerships.html

- American Council on Renewable Energy
- American Indian Higher Education Consortium
- American Meteorological Society
- Association for the Advancement of Sustainability in Higher Education
- Au Sable Institute of Environmental Studies
- Bioneers
- Campaign for Environmental Literacy
- Clinton Foundation
- ecoAmerica
- Environmental Defense Fund
- STARS Founding Partner
- United Negro College Fund (UNCF)
- US Conference of Mayors
- US Green Building Council (USGBC)
- US Partnership for Education for Sustainable Development

Source: http://www.secondnature.org/Partners.html

One of Second Nature's Partner groups is the Clinton Foundation. An interesting look back at the 1990 Winter Edition of 'InCONTEXT' magazine, which featured the following, letter to the editor, from Governor Bill Clinton:

> "Thank you for sending me a copy of your recent issue of InCONTEXT. I enjoyed the article featuring Norman Fleishman on 'Redefining Entertainment'. His behind the scenes work has educated many Hollywood writers about the important social and environmental issues that are increasingly the concern of the 'middle'. **I wish you continued success**

in your goal to make the major cultural shifts our world is now experiencing to be as graceful and as positive as possible."

Bill Clinton
Governor of Arkansas

What major cultural shifts was Bill Clinton aware of or anticipating in 1990? Of interest, Anthony Cortese served on the 'President's Council on Sustainable Development' established by President Clinton in 1993. Cortese outlined the Education for Sustainability movement's plan, to change our culture, religion, society, economy and political structure or form of government, in 1996. Today, the Clinton Foundation is one of Second Nature's Partners helping to implement this agenda.

Systems Thinking: Weapon to Change, Control, Destroy

The concept of systems thinking is not new but the Greens are using this concept as a strategic political weapon to train students to apply the Green way of thinking to every aspect of their lives. The strategy is to:

- target the roughly 89% of America's children that attend public school
- use systems thinking in every subject to embed Green beliefs and values
- produce mass support for change in multiple areas, all at the same time
- harness 89% of the future vote

The Education for Sustainability movement is pushing systems thinking as the new focus of learning, in every discipline, to immerse students in sustainability goals so they cannot escape GREEN-BOT programming.

"By reinforcing the concept that **the educational experience of all students must be aligned with the principles of sustainability**, we help ensure **the content of learning embraces interdisciplinary systems thinking** to address environmentally sustainable action ..."

Second Nature - Vision & Philosophy
Source: http://www.secondnature.org

The idea that "all students must be aligned with the principles of sustainability" and, that the "content of learning" must embrace systems thinking is the plan to use every subject, everyday to reinforce systems thinking to align students with Green goals for sustainability. This is an indoctrination plan; pure and simple. This change in the role of public education and curriculum; is how the Greens plan to indoctrinate "all students" at every grade level, in cities and towns across America, to adopt the Green alternative to our culture, religion, economy and form of government.

Over the last 40 years the message of the 1972 'Blueprint for Survival' has been updated and expanded to advance the goals of the Green movement and the Green Party. One of the main goals of the 'Blueprint for Survival' was to develop a 'new philosophy of life' for a stable or sustainable society. The following quotation from the 'Blueprint' includes a reference to God but that is misleading. Believing in God is a philosophy of life. The 'Blueprint' called for a new belief that was "properly scientific" which sounds like Humanism.

> "In other words, there must be a fusion between our religion and the rest of our culture, since there is no valid distinction between the laws of God and Nature, and Man must live by them no less than any other creature.
>
> **Such a belief must be central to the philosophy of the stable society and must permeate all our thinking.** Indeed it is the only one which is properly scientific, and science must address itself much more vigorously to the problems of **co-operating with the rest of Nature, rather than seeking to control it."**
>
> Blueprint for Survival - 1972 (#349)

Sure enough, forty years later the Greens are pushing systems thinking and Humanism as a new philosophy of life for a sustainable society. Those with a heart for God already understand the responsibility of dominion and what being a good steward entails. One of the primary objectives of Education for Sustainability, as Second Nature pointed out, is to ensure "all students" are aligned with sustainability goals and systems thinking. This also aligns all students with the core philosophy of the Green Party.

The following statement, from the book 'Green Politics' by Green Party organizers, Capra and Spretnak, indicates 'systems thinking' opposes the Western worldview that the natural world has an order where man is a step above the animal kingdom.

> **"Western culture has been dominated for several hundred years by a conceptualization** of our bodies, the body politic and **the natural world as hierarchically arranged..."** - a - "... **systems view** involves looking at the world in terms of relationships and integration"...
>
> Green Politics - 1986
> Fritjof Capra and Charlene Spretnak

To clarify the systems thinking worldview, the authors of 'Green Politics' used the following quotation from Green Party spokesperson and philosophy professor, Manon Maren-Griesbach's book, the 'Philosophy of the Greens':

> **"...let yourself be guided by the meaning of ecology, that everything is interwoven, there is no such thing as first or second**. ... "

> "The emphasis is on relations and interconnections – in Gregory Bateson's words, "**the pattern which connects the crab to the lobster and the orchid to the primrose and all four of the them to me – is the foundation of Green thought and being, whether it is called grassroots democracy** or something else. **This consciousness is simply there in the Greens...**"
>
> **"We define ecological politics** as those measures that understand **human beings and our environment as being part of nature.** ... "

The core philosophy of the Green Party is systems thinking. Again, just how important is the systems thinking, man is part of nature, theme to the Education for Sustainability movement?

> **"All students would understand that we are an integral part of nature.**"
>
> Anthony Cortese, Second Nature
> Speech: Education for a Sustainable Future
> Oregon Sustainability Forum - September 6, 2001
> Transcript (page 10)

This is the worldview of the Green Party. Teaching systems thinking in every subject is the way to teach Humanism as curriculum, and instill a 'Green over God' mindset all day long. This is the strategy to subvert America's moral base and open the door to Green Communism.

We need to keep in mind that when the Greens started invading our classrooms, many of today's adults were children or teens that were unfairly influenced by Green teachers to embrace a communist mindset. Our young people need time to understand what the Greens did. In the meantime, they have a right, as we do, to freedom of speech. Freedom of speech must be protected by all, for all. Our focus needs to be on getting Education for Sustainability programs out of our schools.

Formula to Impose Change

The foundation of Education for Sustainability is a systems thinking formula that considers the relationship between society, economy and the environment in the decision making process. This 'sustainability' formula is a key part of the strategy to impose the agenda of this movement, including changing our economic system to a Green economy. This formula stems from the 1972 'Blueprint for Survival', co-authored by systems thinker Edward Goldsmith; a Founding Father of the Green Party. Green Party ideology and systems thinking are inseparable.

The following statement could easily be used to describe the Education for Sustainability formula.

> "...Ideally" - "...ecology and economics should not be in conflict: **ecology should provide the approach, the framework for an understanding of the interrelationships of social and environmental systems ..."**
>
> **"One of our long-term goals, therefore, must be to unite economics and ecology."**
>
> Blueprint for Survival
> Towards the stable society: strategy for change (#243 - 244)

This concept became the formula and strategy of the Green Party. Green Party spokesperson, John Resenbrink, confirmed the Green Party policy of uniting the concepts of ecology, economy and society in following statement:

> **"The Green Policy of uniting the concepts of ecology and economy and applying the principle of sustainability to society as a whole"** ... "adds community as an integral feature of the good life."
>
> John Resenbrink
> The Greens and the Politics of Transformation - 1992

The plan to align environmental and economic decisions with the Green Party definition of sustainability and then impose the Green definition of sustainability agenda on society as a whole is the political strategy to impose the agenda of the Green Party. Education for Sustainability is based on the same formula and strategy to impose their idea of sustainability on students and the American people.

> **"To achieve sustainability, a school, government, or any other entity must appreciate the interdependence of environment, economy and society."**
>
> Sustainable Oregon Schools Initiative – 2007
> Source: http://www.sustainableschools.org

The base formula of the Education for Sustainability movement is a Green Party formula, political strategy and policy. The Education for Sustainability agenda also parallels the following ideas from the 'Blueprint':

- a systems thinking approach
- unite social, environment and economic decisions
- tie decisions to the goal of creating a sustainable society
- tie the decision-making process to a set of limitations

- use set of limitations to train people to stay within boundaries
- use education as an indoctrination tool to force political change
- indoctrinate students to conform and fit in a planned society

The Education for Sustainability movement has promoted the idea of creating a sustainable society and systems thinking mindset as a critical part of saving the earth. However, since the concepts and goals of the Education for Sustainability movement, parallel the agenda of the Green Party, it is more than likely that Education for Sustainability is a tool to impose the political agenda of the international Greens.

The Green movement's network of groups; which includes environmental groups, Green Party affiliates, Earth Charter endorsers and Education for Sustainability advocates, are pushing these programs into our schools. Seemingly innocent environmental education programs have been steadily expanded in scope to justify the Education for Sustainability agenda and call to make this political indoctrination program the new mission of public education.

What we have witnessed over the past 40 years is the advancement of goals laid out in the 'Blueprint for Survival', including the idea of creating a sustainable society and using education as a tool to help accomplish that political objective. The following statement is from the introduction of the 'Blueprint for Survival'.

> **"Our task is to create a society which is sustainable** ..."
>
> Blueprint for Survival
> Introduction: the need for change (#166)
> Source: http://www.theecologist.info/page33.html

One of the main sections in the 'Blueprint for Survival' is "Toward the stable society: strategy for change". The following statement confirms the 'Blueprint's' reference to a 'stable society' and a 'sustainable society' go hand in glove.

> **"Towards the stable society: strategy for change** - the second section of A Blueprint for Survival occupied all of The Ecologist Vol. 2 No. 1, January 1972. **It sets out the essential steps towards building a stable and sustainable society.**
>
> Source: http://www.theecologist.info/page32.html

Again, 'The Ecologist' magazine, which first published the 'Blueprint for Survival', is recognized for igniting the environmental movement. The founder of the 'Ecologist Magazine' co-authored the 'Blueprint', which is also recognized for inspiring the founding and agenda of the international Green Parties.

The Green movement's demand to create a sustainable society is not based on a spontaneous response to environmental concerns but on implementing a political agenda laid out in 1972. We are dealing with a political movement not an environmental movement. The Green movement is using the environmental cause and the idea of sustainability to camouflage imposing the agenda of the Green Party and the Earth Charter in America and in America's schools.

The following statement from Second Nature confirms the political agenda of the Education for Sustainability movement is not about the "environmental problems per se" but about using education to correct the problem of how our society, business, economic and political system is designed.

> "**We do not have environmental problems per se** - we have negative environmental consequences **of the way we have designed our business, social, economic, and political systems**."
>
> Second Nature - Mission Statement
> Source: http://www.secondnature.org

According to the author's of the 'Blueprint' one of the most important strategies to impose their agenda was to use education to 'inculcate' (instill, beat, hammer or indoctrinate) students so they were 'fitted' to live in the society planned by the authors. This is where the concept of Education for Sustainability originated. Agenda item number 276 in the 'Blueprint' states:

> "It is self-evident that **no amount of legislative, administrative or industrial change** will create **stable communities if the individuals who are meant to comprise them are not fitted for them.**
>
> **As soon as the best means of inculcating the values of the stable society have been agreed upon, they should be incorporated into our educational systems.**
>
> Indeed, **it may not be until the generation of 40-50 year olds have been educated in these values** (so that as far as possible everybody up to the age of 50 understands them) **that stable communities will achieve sufficient acceptance for them** to be permanently useful."
>
> "Towards the stable society: strategy for change"
> Source: http://www.theecologist.info/page32.html

The Education for Sustainability movement appears to be the answer to the call "As soon as the best means of inculcating the values of a stable society have been agreed upon, they should be incorporated into our educational systems".

"And **humans are guided by a whole set of beliefs and values, and those come from culture, from religion, from social, economic, and political structure. We need to change all of those."**

Anthony Cortese, Second Nature
Conservation Matters Magazine - Spring 1996
Conservation Law Foundation Publication
Source: http://www.clf.org/../CM/archive.htm

Education for Sustainability is the vehicle and the agreed upon values are Green Party values which mirror communism. The Green Party also advocates advancing Green Party values through education.

"**We advocate a diverse system of education that would** introduce children early to the wonders of the Great School (Nature), and would **cultivate the wisdom of eco-education, eco-economics, eco-politics, and eco-culture."**

Green Party Platform 2004 (page 17)

Using the classroom to train children to adopt an eco-culture, eco-economy and Green or eco-politics sounds just like the Education for Sustainability plan to use education to politically indoctrinate children to adopt a Green culture, Green economy, Green spirituality and a new Green political system.

A Sustainable Lifestyle

When the Greens talk about a sustainable society, what kind of lifestyle do they have in mind? What did the co-author of the 'Blueprint for Survival' Edward Goldsmith, consider a sustainable lifestyle? A December 16, 2006 article in the 'Telegraph Magazine' titled, "Eco-hero – Edward Goldsmith" by Annabel Freyberg provides a glimpse:

"...Goldsmith remained for more than a decade, leading a "highly ecological life – **no car, no heating, a composting lavatory**, which lost me a lot of friends as it never worked properly ..."

Source: http://www.edwardgoldsmith.org/938/eco-hero-edward-goldsmith/

Another article, titled "Edward Goldsmith: Environmentalist who founded the 'Ecology' magazine and championed the green movement" was featured in the 'The Independent' in October 2009. The author of the article, David McKittrick, attributes the following statement to Goldsmith:

"I spent a lot of time in Africa, in tribal societies," he explained. **"One thing I became convinced of was that these were the only truly 'sustainable' societies I had ever seen.**

Source: http://www.independent.co.uk/

According to Goldsmith, the man "who championed the green movement", a truly sustainable society would resemble a tribal lifestyle or life in a hut in an African village. Does Goldsmith's idea of a sustainable society in any way reflect the Green's definition of a sustainable lifestyle? Is there any connection between Goldsmith's 'no car, no heat and a composting lavatory' lifestyle and the goals of the Education for Sustainability movement?

A few of the goals listed in Second Nature's report, "Visions of Sustainability 2050" by Anthony Cortese, follow. As you read this list of objectives, please consider what it would mean to reduce the consumption of food, water and energy in the United States by 75%.

- **consumption has been reduced by 75%** in the industrialized world
- **fossil fuels and materials in the economy is reduced by 75%.**
- Strong, healthy, culturally diverse and environmentally **sustainable local communities are the goal of economic and social policy.**
- ... inner cities have been revitalized to make business and jobs accessible to inner city residents by **public transportation, bicycling or walking.**
- **The United Nations** has been reconstituted to be more democratic and to be the **chief peacekeeper and advocate for a just and sustainable world.**
- The **world population is stabilized** at a level that is within the short and long term carrying capacity of the earth's finite resources.
- **International governance** has been reformed ... **Defers environmental decisions to environmental treaties.**
- The gap between the richest 20% of the population and the poorest has dropped from 70:1 to 7:1.
- The global climate has re-stabilized to the level it was at in 1950. This has happened through **a 75% reduction in fossil fuels** and a 50% increase in forested land worldwide.

Source: http://www.secondnature.org/pdf/snwritings/articles/2050SustVision.pdf

These are political not educational objectives. Education for Sustainability is a plan to train America's children to accept this entire agenda and Green control of their lives. This plan is not sitting on a shelf until 2050; the Greens and the Education for Sustainability movement are working to impose this agenda now.

Below is a short list of the 2050 Education for Sustainability goals, followed by a comment (in parenthesis) regarding additional points to consider.

- reduce consumption by 75%
  (consumption includes food, water, energy, gas, materials)

- sustainable communities are the goal of economic and social policy
  (change or enact policies to impose the Green agenda locally)

- reduce fossil fuel use by 75%
  (push walking, biking and public transportation to reduce gas and automobile use as steps to limit personal mobility)

- the United Nations is world peacekeeper
  (UN rather than America's experts in charge of American's safety)

- defer environmental decisions to international treaties
  (loss of sovereignty, legal standing or protection of US Constitution)

Although the 'vision of a sustainable future' is presented in a gentle light, these goals reflect loss of personal freedom and national sovereignty. The current push for sustainable communities also happens to match the following goals in the 1989 Green Party program under 'Land Use' (page 9) and the 1990-1991 Green Party program under 'Habitats'(page 24):

> "**Human habitats must be designed or redesigned** so that they are built with energy efficiency in mind, on a human scale, with integrated land uses.
>
> **Such integrated land uses should provide, for example, ready access between home and work, a local supply of food,** ready access to natural areas, **and a de-emphasis on individualized motorized transport.**
>
> Human habitats should be connected to each other by a system of ecologically responsible **mass transit**."

The Green movement is using the concept of sustainability to implement the agenda of the Green Party. The Education for Sustainability goal to reduce fossil fuel use by 75% goes hand in glove with the Green Party goal to get us out of our cars and into mass transit. The aim is to control transportation and limit personal mobility.

Other steps toward reducing fossil fuel use by 75% include playing the 'survival card' over and over so students will believe that they must walk, bike or use public transportation to save the earth. The Greens are using the classroom to train students to accept restricted mobility, prepare for a nearly car-less society and submit to a Green controlled life.

Another strategy to reduce fossil fuel use by 75% involves putting American businesses that provide these natural resources out of business. If the Greens are successful, we would be dependent on foreign oil. Gas makes America tick. Almost everything we do depends on gas, from the trucks that transport our food, to farmer's tractors that help produce our food, to airplanes, boats, motorcycles, school buses, emergency vehicles, police cars and the family vehicle.

Each and every one of these businesses, services and activities require gas to operate. The Education for Sustainability plan to reduce our gas consumption by 75% would disrupt, alter or stop most of these activities. The Greens recently attempted to use the sand lizard to shut-down oil wells in Texas, but were not successful. One of the bragging points in Second Nature's, 2011 'Education for Sustainability Blueprint', a progress report on their success, includes the following statement:

> **"The Energy Action Coalition has effectively stopped 130 proposed new coal plants."**
>
> Source: http://www.secondnature.org/efsblueprint/efs-blueprint.pdf

The issue of concern is not a debate about the merits or disadvantages of new or old coal plants. The issue is the role of public education. Public education was not intended to be used as a tool by a political movement to put certain businesses, out of business, or to put a political party in power.

As earlier stated, the plan to reduce fossil fuel use by 75% is not on a shelf. Arnold Schwarzenegger, a leading Green advocate, has called for the termination of fossil fuel use. In a March 2, 2011 report, **"Schwarzenegger calls for fossil fuel termination"**, author Phil McKenna stated:

> "In a free-wheeling address the former Mr. Universe and Hollywood superstar electrified an audience of the nation's leading energy innovators calling on them to **"subvert the status quo" and "overthrow the old energy order".**
>
> Source:http://www.newscientist.com/blogs/onepercent/2011/03/schwarzenegger-calls-for-fossi-1.html

We all support energy innovation but this is a death sentence for an industry we depend on. The Green goal to get people out of their cars and into mass transit is not a spontaneous solution to an environmental concern. This is the execution of a plan, laid out in the 1972 that has since been modernized and expanded by the Greens. The following statement, which outlines the goals for sustainable, self sufficient communities, is #271 in the 'Blueprint for Survival'.

"From there, **the progressive imposition of restrictions on private transport and the stimulation of public transport so that it could provide a fast, efficient and flexible alternative would be a matter of course." ...**

"In the long term, however, decentralization will bring a diminished demand for mobility itself. As Stephen Boyden has pointed out [7], **people use their cars for four main reasons: to go to work, to go to the countryside, to visit friends and relations**, and to show off.

In the stable society, however, each community will provide its own jobs, there will be countryside around it, **most friends and relations will be within it,** and there will be much more reliable and satisfying ways of showing off."

Blueprint for Survival:
Towards the stable society: strategy for change
Source: http://www.theecologist.info/page32.html

What we are seeing is the implementation of an agenda laid out decades ago in the document that inspired the Green Party platform. The Green movement and the Green Party, plus a group of elitists, are implementing a communist agenda under the guise of environmental protection.

NCEP: Naturally Creative Earth Politics

Multiple facts from multiple sources have confirmed the alliance of the Green Party and the Earth Charter and how the goals of the Education for Sustainability movement parallel the goals of these groups. Another confirmation comes from a political coalition, proposed around 2003, called 'Naturally Creative Earth Politics' or NCEP. The four groups in the Naturally Creative Earth Politics Coalition, a coalition of "New Progressives" are:

- Green Party of the US
- Earth Charter Initiative
- Cultural Creatives
- Project Nature Connect

The outline of the Naturally Creative Earth Politics proposal follows:

1. "The target demographic will be the Cultural Creatives. The core values and ideals of Cultural Creatives are given in this short questionnaire.

2. **The federally recognized political party will be the Green Party of the US.** The core values of the Green Party are listed in the Ten Key Values statement.

3. **The foundational organizing document and principles** - the Declaration of Interdependence - **will be the Earth Charter.**

4. **The process to use for the educational** and healing **shift in consciousness needed to bring it all to fruition will be the Natural Systems Thinking Process** (NSTP) developed by Project Nature Connect."

Source: http://www.reststop.net/NCEP/Purpose.html

There it is. Clear as a bell. The Green Party US and the Earth Charter are not only philosophically aligned; they are working together. The Greens understand this alliance but how many Americans understand the Education for Sustainability movement is using the Earth Charter in multiple schools to train our children to align with the Green Party and the Earth Charter agenda?

The NCEP proposal refers to the Earth Charter as a 'Declaration of Interdependence'. The Greens are using this play on words to infer that the Declaration of Independence is old-hat and that the Earth Charter is a safe replacement. The strategy is to use the familiar sounding language of the Declaration of Independence to make the Earth Charter sound safe, when it actually represents a threat to our form of government and personal freedom.

It is vitally important we understand the last strategic objective in the NCEP proposal. This statement reveals that the Greens recognize 'systems thinking' is THE political TOOL to change our way of thinking so we will accept the imposition of the Green Party and Earth Charter agenda. Training the American people, and our children, to adopt a systems thinking mindset would not only prevent objections to the imposition of Green Communism, it would lay out the welcome mat.

The NCEP plan is to use systems thinking to impose a shift in consciousness or a new mindset. This sounds just like the plan to impose a 'new philosophy of life' called for in the 1972 'Blueprint for Survival'. This also sounds like Gorbachev's plan to create a revolution in our minds. This also sounds like the plan to use Education for Sustainability to impose a 'massive change in mindset' on students and the American people.

The American people have been led to believe that the Green movement is non-partisan. The Naturally Creative Earth Politics Coalition confirms the Green Party and the Earth Charter share the same agenda and work together. Since most of the leading organizations in the Green movement, including Education for Sustainability groups, have endorsed the Earth Charter, it is clear the

Green movement supports the communist agenda of the Green Party and the Earth Charter and, is imposing that agenda on the American people.

The Greens have kept these political links off the public radar to stay invisible so they can continue to use the environmental cause to implement the goals of the Green Party and the Earth Charter piece by piece, undetected. The Green movement's constant push for students and the American people to 'go Green' and to Green everything in our lives, is a deliberate plan to 'Green the American mind'. The Green label is part of a mental conditioning process to train students, as well as the American people, to accept all the Green directives to save the earth without realizing those directives are to implement Green Communism, not save the earth.

The NCEP Coalition confirms the Green Party and the Earth Charter are essentially the same. The Green Party is advancing the agenda of the international Earth Charter. The use of the Earth Charter; as a training guide by the Education for Sustainability movement equals training America's children to adopt the goals of the Green Party and foster single party rule.

Again, the strategy revealed in the NCEP Coalition is that SYSTEMS THINKING is THE TOOL to impose the agenda of the Green Party and the Earth Charter. The core theme of the Education for Sustainability movement is systems thinking.

Beyond the need to get these programs out of our schools, we need to help our children understand, that the Green label stands for political indoctrination, communism and oppression, not a healthy environment.

The following charts illustrate how the agenda of the Education for Sustainability movement aligns with the political agenda of the Green Party.

Education for Sustainability is a harmful political indoctrination and training program.

The Education for Sustainability movement is using public education to align students with the agenda of the Green Party.

EDUCATION FOR SUSTAINABILITY

1996: Political Agenda Defined

"And humans are guided by a whole set of beliefs and values, and those come from culture, from religion, from social, economic, and political structure. We need to change all of those."

— Anthony Cortese, CEO Second Nature
Interview about Education and Sustainability
Conservation Matters – 1996

Political Strategy: Indoctrinate Students

"Most people are focusing on policy issues, how to change the politics in Washington ...when, in fact ... if we're talking about sustainability in the long term, we've got to change the way we think because it's the only way we'll change our behavior. Now, higher education is important for all levels of education because it prepares most of the professionals who develop, lead, manage, teach, work in, and influence society's institutions in K through 12 education."

— Anthony Cortese, Second Nature
Oregon Sustainability Forum - 2001

Earth Charter: Training Tool

The Earth Charter has been selected as a guide to teach Education for Sustainability principles and is being used in multiple schools to train students to adopt Earth Charter goals; including ratification as international law, which would supplant the US Constitution.

GREEN PARTY

1972: Political Agenda Outlined

"Such a movement cannot hope to succeed unless it has previously formulated a new philosophy of life ... and a precise and comprehensive program for bringing about the sort of society in which it can be implemented."

— Blueprint for Survival 1972 (Preface)
Inspired founding of the Green Party

Political Strategy: Indoctrinate Students

"It is self-evident that no amount of legislative, administrative or industrial change will create stable communities if the individuals who are meant to comprise them are not fitted for them. As soon as the best means of inculcating the values of the stable society have been agreed upon, they should be incorporated into our educational systems."

— Blueprint for Survival 1972

Earth Charter: Ethical Base

The goals of the international Earth Charter mirror Green Party goals and communism. The Earth Charter is part of the Green Party platform. The Green Party and the Earth Charter are 2 of the 4 political groups in the NCEP Coalition of New Progressives.

Education for Sustainability

Formula and Strategy: To Impose Political Change

Education for Sustainability is based on a formula of uniting social, economic and environmental decisions as a strategy to impose their idea of a sustainable society.

"To achieve sustainability, a school, government, or any other entity must appreciate the interdependence of environment, economy and society."

— Sustainable Oregon Schools Initiative 2007

Sustainability Goals: Vehicle to Impose Green Political Agenda

"We do not have environmental problems per se, we have negative environmental consequences of the way we have designed our business, social, economic, and political systems."

— Second Nature, Mission Statement

"Education seeks to provide ... spiritual emancipation" .... "The sustainability transition is in effect a social and political revolution that hopefully can take place through peace and understanding."

— O'Riordan, T. (1994) Education for the sustainability transition. (UNESCO booklet)

Training Program: Change Thinking, Values and Behavior

"Our most stalwart concept, the one that we hold forth for future leaders in the Education for Sustainability movement, is that the entire education experience must change behavior."

— Second Nature, Vision & Philosophy

Green Party

Formula and Strategy: To Impose Political Change

1972 'Blueprint for Survival' outlined a formula to unite social, economic and environmental decisions as a strategy to impose their idea of a sustainable society.

"One of our long-term goals, therefore, must be to unite economics and ecology" .... "ecology should provide the approach, the framework for an understanding of the interrelationships of social and environmental systems..."

— Blueprint for Survival
Inspired founding of the Green Party

Sustainability Goals: Vehicle to Impose Green Party Agenda

"The Green Policy of uniting the concepts of ecology and economy and applying the principle of sustainability to society as a whole" ...

"...sustainability is a central and guiding philosophy for action by private and public persons..."

— John Resenbrink, Green Party spokesperson
The Greens and the Politics of Transformation

Political Strategy: Change Thinking, Values and Behavior

"Such a movement cannot hope to succeed unless it has previously formulated a new philosophy of life" ... "and a precise and comprehensive program for bringing about the sort of society in which it can be implemented."

— Blueprint for Survival (Preface)

Education for Sustainability

Systems Thinking: Tool to Impose Green's Earth-based Worldview

"By reinforcing the concept that the educational experience of all students must be aligned with the principles of sustainability, we help ensure the content of learning embraces interdisciplinary systems thinking to address environmentally sustainable action ..."

— Second Nature - Vision & Philosophy

"...Now, this shift in world view is not going to come easy, you know, because it means a change in thinking, values and action." ... "Change in mind set requires a sustained, long-term effort to transform education at all levels."

— Anthony Cortese, Second Nature
Education for a Sustainable Future
Oregon Sustainability Forum - 2001

Man is Part of Nature Mindset: Embed Earth-based Worldview

"All students would understand that we are an integral part of nature."

— Anthony Cortese, Second Nature
Oregon Sustainability Forum, 2001

Equitable Access: Private Property?

"Let us imagine a society that has all present and future humans healthy and where they have their basic needs met, have fair and equitable access to Earth's resources."

— Anthony Cortese, Second Nature
Leveraging Change: The Role of the University in a Sustainable Future - 2000

Green Party

Systems Thinking: Green's Earth-based – Humanist Worldview

"The emphasis is on relations and interconnections – in Gregory Bateson's words, "the pattern which connects the crab to the lobster and the lobster to the orchid to the primrose, and all four of them to me – is the foundation of Green thought and being..."

— Manon Maren-Griesbach -
The Philosophy of the Greens
Green Politics – 1986 by Capra & Spretnak

"The core concepts are sustainability and interrelatedness." ... "the person interacting with a system and that system with others."

— The Spiritual Dimension of Green Politics – by Spretnak

Man is Part of Nature Mindset: Relinquish Belief in God

"The adoption of a new world view that values the integrity of all life forms is necessary" .... "Adaption of such an approach entails the relinquishment of the dominating world view by Western cultures. Ecological wisdom teaches us to view ourselves as part of nature rather than as on top of it or dominating it."

— Green Party Program 1989 (page 20)

Communism: No Private Property

"The Earth and its natural systems cannot be owned ..."

— Green Party Platform 1990-1991

A Free America or A Green America?

Our forefathers gave their lives to give us our freedom. Now, it is our watch and we have a problem to solve. For generations, Americans across this great nation have enjoyed the privilege of free thought and endeavored to preserve this basic freedom. Maintaining the standard of a politically neutral or Party neutral public education has always been an essential safeguard. The Green movement has violated this standard and the public trust. Education for Sustainability is rooted in Green Party ideology and free thought is at risk.

How many students realize the purpose of Education for Sustainability is to change their beliefs, manage their behavior, direct their views and use them to change America's culture, religion, society, economy and form of government? How many Americans realize this agenda is being pushed into our schools and forced on the children we love?

Our number ONE priority must be to expel Education for Sustainability programs, including the Earth Charter, from our schools. We cannot allow the Greens to divert our attention from this priority issue. Green leaders understand, if they can indoctrinate and control America's children, they can control America's future. This is why Education for Sustainability is a top priority for Gorbachev.

> "However, **we founders and supporters should consider our mission accomplished only when the Earth Charter is universally adopted** by the international community."
>
> Mikhail Gorbachev
> Preface: The Earth Charter in Action
> The Third Pillar of Sustainable Development (2005)
> Source:http://www.earthcharterinaction.org/invent/images/uploads/ENG-Gorbachev.pdf

Based on this directive from Gorbachev, the Greens intend to impose the Earth Charter plan to enslave the American people and our children, no matter how long it takes ... unless we stop the political movement that is imposing the Earth Charter plan in America.

That political movement is the Green movement. Today's Green movement stands for the political indoctrination of our children and the imposition of Green Communism, not a healthy environment.

We do not have to give-up our goal of a healthy environment to reject the political agenda of the Green movement, which includes the political symbolism that defines this movement, which is the 'Green' label. Stopping the political indoctrination of our children requires removing the political symbol of the Green movement (the 'Green' label) from our schools and elsewhere.

7

Training for Treason

In 2001 Anthony Cortese and Professor David Orr were featured speakers at the Oregon Sustainability Forum, a Sustainable Northwest event. Professor Orr's activist background is impressive. Orr is recognized as one of the 'leading thinkers of the US environmental movement', is a member of the Obama Administration's National Advisory Committee for the Presidential Climate Action Project and is recognized for his leadership role in the Education for Sustainability movement. Professor Orr is an experienced player in the national political arena.

During his speech at the Oregon Sustainability Forum, Orr clarified the political agenda of the Education for Sustainability movement. Excerpts from Orr's speech follow; Professor Orr said:

> **"So I want to talk about education** and I want to talk about education in the broadest possible sense of the word. We confuse schooling, which happens in schools, with education which is a lifelong process. And we've got a lot of work to do. **Education has to reach out to an entire citizenry and that's what you're about, that's what I'm about."**
> (page 8 paragraph 2)

> **"We've got to begin to change the way we think**. **This is a crisis in every way to how we think**." - "And the last item here, **we often forget**; **the political challenge**. That's why I like the "Three E" approach to this**.** **We've got to begin to think about equity, and justice, and, fairness, the distribution of wealth within and between societies** and within and between generations, and also within and between us and other life forms."
> (page 8 paragraph 4 and 6)

> **"And here it is, I think, the political challenge. That's the electoral map,** from the election of the year 2000, and the red is George Bush country and the blue or the gray are Al Gore and Ralph Nader country. They won the real estate. ..."
> (page 9 paragraph 2)

> **"Environmental education:** What we do in education, and every bit of education is environmental education; by what we include, by what we exclude. It's all part of the same thing. **We teach people they're part of or a-part from the natural world. So what we do in education – all of it is environmental education."** (page 13 paragraph 7, page 14 paragraph 1)

"The leverage potential for higher education is huge. I don't know anybody that's worked harder on this point than Tony Cortese and the organization, Second Nature, which I'm pleased to be a Board member on."

(page 14 paragraph 2)

"So how do we teach sustainability? How do we engage people in this transformation? Well, what I'm doing is the worst possible way to do it. **The real way to do it is to engage people in solving problems.** I don't want to go into this slide in great detail, just in the interests of time, but **at the environmental studies program at Oberlin College, we've done a couple of things. One is we engaged about 250 students in the design of a building –** I'll show you in just a few minutes. So we took architecture and made pedagogy out of it. And then **we are also now engaging students...**even Goodstein and other people out here are doing, and beginning **to think through our role in climatic change."**

(page 14 paragraph 5)

"The public is ready for a positive kind of environmentalism." - "And we can do that in ways that attract people, so that electro-map changes dramatically. It's not just blue versus red, but it becomes solidly Green everywhere." (page 15 paragraph 2)

"...It's green design. It's sustainable agriculture. It's regenerative forestry. It's urban ecological planning. It's a whole series of things that all of you are engaged in. **THIS is the great work of our time. There is none other. It isn't to make the economy grow. It is not to defeat fascist or communists, or anything of the kind."**

(page 18 paragraph 2)

"This involves – Going back to my map of the United States – This involves a political transformation." - "...**Now we fought a revolution** over remote tyranny, except at that time it was George The Third. Now it's us. **There has to be a political transformation in this country. In the same way, that there was in the generation from 1750 to 1790."**

(page 18 paragraph 3)

David Orr -**Professor of Environmental Studies and Politics**
Speech: Ecological Literacy – Transcript (19 pages)
Oregon Sustainability Forum - September 6, 2001

David Orr's praise for Anthony Cortese and close involvement with Second Nature indicates these leaders in the Education for Sustainability movement know exactly what this program is for, where it is headed and how to get there.

Orr said, "There has to be a political transformation in this country. In the same way, that there was in the generation from 1750 to 1790." In this statement, Orr ties the goal of political transformation to revolution and basically calls for the overthrow of our form of government "in the same way" that occurred when this nation was formed.

The Declaration of Independence severed ties with Great Britain in 1776 and after the revolutionary war; steps to establish our form of government and the United States Constitution took place from 1787 to 1789, according to the Cato Institute. These dates fit the time frame for Orr's reference.

Achieving "political transformation in this country" in that "same way" suggests a revolutionary overthrow of our government to establish a new form of government in the United States. Orr's call for a new form of government aligns with the Education for Sustainability agenda laid out by Cortese in 1996, which included changing our "political structure" or form of government.

Professor Orr is a national spokesperson for the Education for Sustainability movement and these statements reflect the pulse, direction and strategy of this political movement. Orr's politically charged message and call to action informed educators and activists about the purpose of environmental education, Ecological Literacy and Education for Sustainability programs. Ecological Literacy, or ecological wisdom, as the Green Party calls it, is a key part of the indoctrination process. Another point Orr made regarding the political purpose behind these programs follows:

> **"So how do we teach sustainability? How do we engage people in this transformation?** Well, what I'm doing is the worst possible way to do it. **The real way to do it is to engage people in solving problems.**

This statement also indicates the purpose of teaching sustainability is to engage students and others in implementing the transformation agenda. It follows, that the transformation agenda includes Orr's call for a political transformation.

The Education for Sustainability movement is training students to be against our form of government and to support a revolutionary transformation to a different form of government by Greening the map, or other means. Needless to say this political agenda does not belong in America's schools. Education for Sustainability programs also connect being Green with voting Green. Another point Orr made we need to pay close attention to follows.

> "The public is ready for a positive kind of environmentalism. ... And we can do that in ways that attract people, **so that electro-map changes dramatically.**
>
> **It's not just blue versus red, but it becomes solidly Green everywhere."**

Orr's call to Green the electoral map confirms there is a political agenda behind the Education for Sustainability movement or a speech about 'Ecological

Literacy' would not include a call to Green the electoral map or for "a political transformation in this country."

Orr did not suggest voting for any blue or red candidates. He said turn the electoral map "solidly Green everywhere." There is only one political party associated with the color Green and the electoral map, and that is the Green Party.

This is no small deal. The call to Green the electoral map by Professor Orr, who is one of the highest ranking leaders in the Education for Sustainability movement, is a solid confirmation that the Education for Sustainability movement is a political front to indoctrinate America's children to align with the Green Party.

Orr's directive to Green the map also verifies the plan is to use this program to train students to vote Green as another way to trigger the planned "political transformation" of our nation. If the electoral map was solidly Green everywhere that political transformation would look like single party rule; a Green Party dictatorship and Green Communism. The harmful purpose behind Education for Sustainability includes:

- indoctrinate students of all ages to align with the Green Party
- foster an overthrow of our government and shift to Green Communism
- produce a nation of GREEN-BOTS to vote for a solid Green electoral map

David Orr is a Board member for some of the top organizations in the Education for Sustainability movement, including Second Nature, the Center for Respect of Life and Environment and the Center for Ecoliteracy. All these groups have endorsed the Earth Charter, which is directly aligned with the Green Party agenda. How early is the Education for Sustainability movement starting their GREEN-BOT training programs?

Targeting the Kindergarten Vote

In 2005, the Bioneers conference featured an 'Educator's Forum' presented by the Center for Ecoliteracy. The Bioneers conference program described the purpose of the 'Educator's Forum' in the following promotional statement:

> **"Educator's Forum: Educating Our Children For a Sustainable World. When we realize that kindergarteners will vote in twelve short years the impact education has on the future of our world snaps into focus."**

Luckily, **learning communities are transforming the nature of education by modeling sustainable principles** based on place and community connectivity.

Join the Center for Ecoliteracy and the Bioneers Youth Initiative for an interactive forum **to explore the role of educators in changing the world."**

Source: http://www.bioneers.org/conference/program05.php (or) http://web.archive.org/web/20051123044507/http://www.bioneers.org/conference/program05.php

The purpose of this 'Educator's Forum', which was presented by one of the leading Education for Sustainability groups, exposes the plan to use education to indoctrinate innocent little children to obey sustainability rules and think Green so they will vote Green when they grow-up. The outline of this session suggests the plan is to:

- target kindergartners because they will vote in 12 short years
- use education and all 12 years to train students to vote Green
- use Education for Sustainability to standardize student's beliefs
- recruit teachers to help indoctrinate children and change the world
- indoctrinate America's children to take control of America's future

The title of this 'Educator's Forum' was misleading; a more accurate description would have been to call it a "Brainwasher's Forum".

It is worth repeating that David Orr serves on the Bioneers and the Center for Ecoliteracy Boards, because Orr's 2001 call to Green the electoral map ties right in to the 2005 forum to target the Kindergarten Vote. Yes, Orr was serving on the Center for Ecoliteracy's Board of Directors when the 'Educator's Forum' to target the 'Kindergarten Vote' took place. Orr was also a featured speaker at that 2005 Bioneers conference, along with Fritjof Capra, the co-founder and Chairman of the Board for the Center for Ecoliteracy.

It is hard to imagine that with David Orr's participation as a Board member with the Center for Ecoliteracy, and as a featured speaker at this conference along with Fritjof Capra, that he was not aware of the aims of the 'Educators Forum' presented by his affiliate organization. Affiliations are important. The Center for Ecoliteracy's Fritjof Capra is a well known Green Party organizer and co-author of the 1986 book 'Green Politics'.

Source:http://web.archive.org/web/20050524073608/http://www.ecoliteracy.org/about/board.html

The idea of this topic for an 'Educators Forum' and, that it was presented by a leading Education for Sustainability group, indicates leaders of this political movement believe it is acceptable to use the classroom to politically indoctrinate kindergartners to be future Green voters. The strategy is to Green the schools, Green the students and Green the electoral map.

Orr's call to Green the electoral map plus the focus on the impact education can have on the future because "kindergartners will vote in 12 years" snaps the plan to use education to politically indoctrinate our children into focus. Targeting kindergartners for political gain reflects the mindset of dictators not educators.

Training For Treason

The harmful agenda behind the Education for Sustainability movement includes deceiving students and the American people by using this program to:

- target our innocent children for political gain
- train our precious children to be GREEN-BOTS
- gain access to 89% of the future vote
- push 'go Green' campaigns to mask politically indoctrinating students
- diminish the value of individual success
- put free thought and individual freedom at risk
- train students to align with Green Party goals for a sustainable lifestyle
- foster single party rule, use students to Green the electoral map
- erode America's moral base, use systems thinking to instill Humanism
- train students to align with the international Earth Charter as law
- impose Green economy, unite social, economic, environmental decisions
- use systems thinking to foster an end to private property ownership
- use systems thinking to change our culture, society and economy
- erode America's founding principles including basic freedoms
- advocate the overthrow of our form of government

- train students of all ages to conform and adopt Green Communism
- train America's children to be enemies of the United States of America

The Education for Sustainability movement is waging psychological warfare in the classroom to impose the agenda of the Green movement, the Green Party and the international Earth Charter.

The following statement is an excerpt from the Constitution of the United States of America, Article III. Section. 3:

> **"Treason against the United States shall consist** only in levying War against them, **or in adhering to their Enemies, giving them Aid and Comfort.** No Person shall be convicted of Treason unless on the Testimony of two Witnesses to the same overt Act, or on Confession in open Court."

Which of the following actions, directly associated with the Education for Sustainability movement, reflects aiding or comforting an Enemy of the United States?

- endorsing the Earth Charter with a commitment to "support the implementation of Earth Charter principles with an international legally binding instrument" which is a law
- supporting the Earth Charter as "a common standard by which the conduct of all individuals, organizations, businesses, governments, and transnational institutions is to be guided and assessed."
- promoting the Earth Charter in our schools and using it as a training guide to align our children with Earth Charter principles
- using public education to undermine America's founding principles, including the US Constitution, by training students of all ages to adopt an agenda that mirrors Green Party goals and communism.

The Green movement is using Education for Sustainability to train America's children to be actively engaged in a revolutionary political agenda that is clearly an enemy of our form of government and therefore, an enemy of the United States of America. Education for Sustainability is 'Training for Treason'.

If we do not protect America's founding principles, including our moral base, and ensure those values are passed on to America's children, everything else we do will be for naught.

We must step between our children and the Education for Sustainability movement and stop the indoctrination. 'Training for Treason' is the resource to:

- understand the scope of Education for Sustainability
- help expel this program and protect the children we love
- recognize the implementation of this political agenda
- identify this program in schools or districts
- take action and help others understand

With each passing day more of our children are trained to be GREEN-BOTS. Stopping the misuse of public education to politically indoctrinate our children is one of the most important issues of our time. Our children are in harms' way and this is a call to action.

Now it is up to you.

PS: You can help stop the political indoctrination of America's children. For more information on the movement to expel Education for Sustainability and return our schools to safe havens of learning, please see the following page.

We Choose Freedom

May the spirit and legacy, of the land of the free and home of the brave, live on.

What groups in the Green movement have endorsed the Earth Charter and made a commitment to advance this political agenda in your area? For a state by state list of Earth Charter endorsers see the Appendix.

One of the first things you can do to help is to stop using the 'Green' label and help others understand; you support a healthy environment but do not support the political agenda of the Green movement and Education for Sustainability. Encourage others to do the same. In addition, you can respectfully advise your political representatives on the local, state and national level, that you request their assistance to expel this political indoctrination program from your schools. It is vital to know their position on this issue before casting your vote.

Holly Swanson is the founder and director of the following campaigns and spearheading a national movement to expel Education for Sustainability programs and return our schools to safe havens of learning.

OPERATION GREEN OUT!

Operation Green Out! is a national citizens campaign formed to get Green politics out in the open and out of America's schools.

We Choose FREEDOM

In a broader sense 'We Choose Freedom' takes into account all aspects of the political indoctrination of America's children. The mission of 'We Choose Freedom' is to 'uphold and pass on' America's founding principles of freedom.

For more information, including what you can do to help, please contact:

Address: P.O. Box 2645, White City, OR 97503 Voice: 541-830-1446

Email: wechoosefreedom@earthlink.net (or) greenout@earthlink.net

Book order line: **1-877-715-5481**

'Training for Treason' by Holly Swanson $20.00 plus shipping & handling

'Set Up & Sold Out' by Holly Swanson $20.00 plus shipping & handling

Appendix

Earth Charter Endorsers in the United States as of October 10, 2008

According to the Earth Charter endorsers list, the Orion Society and Orion Grassroots Network, represent 871 organizations that have endorsed the Earth Charter. Groups in the 2008 Orion Society Grassroots Network are indentified in this list of Earth Charter endorsers with an *

Alabama

Community Earth Network	Mobile	Alabama
Nature-Connect.net & Nature-Connect.com	Birmingham	Alabama
Southern Sustainable Agriculture Working Group (SAWG)*		Alabama
States Council of Lassaira and New Albion	Anniston	Alabama
Wild South - AL Office*		Alabama
WildLaw*		Alabama

Alaska

64th Parallel International	Anchorage	Alaska
Alaska Boreal Forest Council		Alaska
Alaska Center for the Environment		Alaska
Alaska Community Action on Toxics		Alaska
Alaska Conservation Foundation*		Alaska
Alaska Initiative for Community Engagement*		Alaska
Alaska Pacific Univ. Outdoor & Env. Educational Program*		Alaska
Alaska Wildlife Alliance*		Alaska
Bear Necessities Coalition*		Alaska
Calypso Farm and Ecology Center	Fairbanks	Alaska
Center for Alaskan Coastal Studies*		Alaska
Copper River Watershed Project		Alaska
Discovery Southeast		Alaska
Eastern Kenai Peninsula Enviro	Seward	Alaska
Explorers for Humanity	Anchorage	Alaska
Eyak Preservation Council*		Alaska
Friends of Glacier Bay		Alaska
Southeast Alaska Land Trust		Alaska
The Healing Light	Anchorage	Alaska
The Island Institute*		Alaska
Noyes Slough Action Committee*		Alaska
Prince William Sound Science Center*		Alaska
Sitka Conservation Council*		Alaska
Southeast Alaska Conservation Council*		Alaska
Southeast Alaska Land Trust*		Alaska
Trustees for Alaska*		Alaska
Wrangell Mountains Center*		Alaska
Yukon River Drainage Fisheries Association*		Alaska

Arizona

Ancient Pathways*		Arizona
Arcosanti*		Arizona
Arizona Live Arts Network (AZLAN)	Prescott	Arizona
Arizona Wilderness Coalition*		Arizona
Arizona-Sonora Desert Museum*		Arizona
Border Ecology Project		Arizona
Cascabel Hermitage Association*		Arizona
Center for Biological Diversity		Arizona
Center for Native and Urban Wildlife*		Arizona
Center for Partnership Studies		Arizona
Center for Sustainable Environments*		Arizona
Coalition for Interfaith & Intercultural Knowledge & Action		Arizona
Dawn SouthWest	Tucson	Arizona
Development Center for Appropriate Technology		Arizona
Dunbar/Spring Organic Community Garden		Arizona
Environmental Education Exchange*		Arizona
Franciscan	Phoenix	Arizona
Friends of the Santa Cruz River		Arizona
Global Straw Bale Network		Arizona
Grand Canyon Association*		Arizona
Grand Canyon Trust		Arizona
Grand Canyon Wildlands Council		Arizona
Interfaith Dialogue Institute		Arizona
International Dark-Sky Association*		Arizona
Local to Global Justice*		Arizona
Milagro Cohousing Community		Arizona
Personal Touch Enterprises	Glendale	Arizona
Phoenix Zoo	Phoenix	Arizona
Prescott College	Prescott	Arizona
Prescott Creeks Preservation Association	Prescott	Arizona
Reptile Research*		Arizona
Silverbell Trading	Tucson	Arizona
Sky Island Alliance		Arizona
Society for Ecological Restoration International*		Arizona
SolFest Southwest		Arizona
Terrain.org*		Arizona
Tree of Life Foundation*		Arizona
Voices: Community Stories Past & Present	Tucson	Arizona
Windspirit Community	Winkleman	Arizona
Women Builders		Arizona

Arkansas

AR Center for the Study of Integrative Medicine		Arkansas
Arkansas Earth Day Foundation		Arkansas
Heifer International*		Arkansas
Limbertwig Press*		Arkansas
Newton County Wildlife Association		Arkansas

California

Academy For Future Science	Los Gatos	California
Acorn Group, the		California
Acterra: Action for a Sustainable Earth	San Francisco	California
Action for Nature		California
Action Coalition for Global Change	San Francisco	California
Adina for Life Inc.	San Francisco	California
Agricultural Land-Based Training Association (ALBA)	Salinas	California
Akira Studios	Bybee	California
Albion River Watershed Protection Association	Elk	California
Alliance for Democracy, Mendocino Coast Chapter	Fort Bragg	California
American Land Conservancy* National Office	San Francisco	California
American River Conservancy		California
Americorps Watershed Stewards Project*		California
Antioch New England Institute*	Antioch	California
Antioch University Los Angeles,Grad Programs Education		California
Asia Maritime Foundation	San Francisco	California
Asian Pacific Environmental Network		California
Association for Environmental & Outdoor Education*		California
Association of Waldorf Schools of North America	Fair Oaks	California
Association of World Citizens	San Francisco	California
Atomic Mirror, the	Port Hueneme	California
Auto-Free Orange County		California
Awakened Woman Occidental		California
Be Do Have Software, Inc.	San Jose	California
Big Sur Land Trust		California
Bikestation Coalition		California
Boojurn Institute for Experiential Education*		California
Bucklin Law Firm	West Hills	California
Business Alliance for Local Living Economics*		California
California Certified Organic Farmers*		California
California Chaparral Field Institute*		California
California Indian Basketweavers Association*		California
California Safe Schools*		California
California Trout*		California
Californians for Western Wilderness*		California
Cal Poly State University		California
California Wildlife Defenders		California
Camelot Leadership Company	Novato	California
Canada Goose Project		California
CANARYCLUB.ORG	Santa Rosa	California
Cardinal Newman High School	Santa Rosa	California
The Celidon Foundation*		California
Center for Creative Inquiry*		California
Center for Ecoliteracy		California
Center for Transformation Ecology	Fairfax	California
Center for Urban Agriculture at Fairview Gardens		California
Spiritual Alliance for Earth (SAFE)	Oakland	California
Chapman Ranch School	Mt. Baldy	California
Citizens for Peaceful Resolutions	Ventura	California
City Slicker Farms*		California
City of Berkeley	Berkeley	California

Close to Home*		California
Cloud Forest Institute	Ukiah	California
Community Environmental Council		California
Community Forestry International*		California
Community Learning Services*		California
Companions of the Way	Salinas	California
Concern America	Santa Ana	California
Consumer Change*		California
CRSP Los Angeles Eco-Village*		California
Cunningham Marsh Preservation Committee		California
Damien High School Amnesty International Club		California
Democracy Unlimited of Humboldt County*		California
Desert Protective Council*		California
Dominican Sisters of San Rafael	San Rafael	California
Earth Care International	San Diego	California
Earth Colony	Los Angeles	California
Earth Island Institute & Brower Youth Awards*		California
Earth Partners	Jackson	California
EarthAlive Films	San Geronimo	California
Earthcapades	Pacifica	California
EarthLight Magazine	Oakland	California
Earthville Network	Oakland	California
East Bay Conservation Corps*		California
Ecocity Builders	Oakland	California
Ecology Center	Berkeley	California
Ecology Center at Pitzer College		California
Ecology Center	Berkeley	California
Ecopalooza Green Living Network		California
El Dorado Nature Center		California
Elk Grove Community Food Bank Services*		California
Environmental Volunteers*		California
Environmental Commons	Gualala	California
Environmental Movement, the	San Francisco	California
Evolutionary Management	San Diego	California
Evolutionary Ventures	Larkspur	California
Exploring a Sense of Place*		California
Fallbrook Land Conservancy		California
Fellowship of Humanity	Oakland	California
Food First/Institute for Food & Development Policy*		California
Forest Issues Group		California
Foundation for Conscious Evolution	Santa Barbara	California
Foundation for Global Community	Palo Alto	California
Friends of ECOS*		California
Friends of the Estuary at Morro Bay	Morro Bay	California
Friends of the River		California
Friends of San Francisco Estuary*		California
Friends, Artists & Neighbors of Elkhorn Slough*		California
Gaea Center		California
Garden Project	San Francisco	California
GetVegan		California
Global Citizen Center*		California
Global Environment Project Institute		California
Global Exchange		California

Global Green USA	Santa Monica	California
Global Oneness Project*		California
Global Options Consulting, & Calif.St.Univ.	Playa del Rey	California
Global Security Institute		California
Globe & Sierra Nevada Alliance	Fresno	California
GOLDENEAGLEVIDEO	Santa Barbara	California
Golden Gate Raptor Observatory*		California
Goodhumans		California
Green Earth Foundation	Sonoma	California
Green Fire - 7 Generations Ministry	Nevada City	California
Greenminds	Oakland	California
Green for All*		California
Gualala Municipal Advisory Council (GMAC)	Mendocino County	California
greenmuseum.org*		California
Guided Discoveries*		California
Health Care Without Harm*		California
Hemp Collaborative	BIG BEAR	California
Hidden Villa*		California
Homeless Garden Project		California
Husbandry Institute*		California
Inland Empire Conservation Corps	San Bernardino	California
Institute of Classical Homeopathy*		California
Interdependent Project	Cedar Ridge	California
International Development Exchange (IDEX)	San Francisco	California
International Process Network, the		California
International Rescue Committee*		California
Island Mountain Institute for Sustainable Agriculture*		California
Keep the Sespe Wild		California
Kern Valley River Council		California
Kevin Rafferty Executive Consulting	Murrieta	California
Leadership Institute for Ecology and the Economy*		California
Leamanpotential Foundation	Berkeley	California
Lemmon Foundation	San Francisco	California
Literacy for Environmental Justice*		California
Living Systems Design	Burlingame	California
Local Economy*		California
Los Angeles Eco-Village/CRSP		California
Marin Agricultural Land Trust*		California
Mattole Restoration Council		California
Meedan*		California
Midland School*		California
Milenio	San Francisco	California
Millennium People's Assembly Network MPAN		California
Mojave Moon Marketing & Entertainment, Inc.	Beverly Hills	California
Mono Lake Community		California
Morning Light Sangha		California
Napa Valley Peace Table	Napa	California
Nation 12	Santa fe Springs	California
National Writing Project*		California
National Capital Institute*		California
Nectar & Flame Consulting	Albany	California
New College of California*		California
New College of California – North Bay Campus*		California

North Coast Demonstration Garden	Mendocino	California
Northcoast Regional Land Trust*		California
Nova Media	San Rafael	California
Nuclear Age Peace Foundation	Santa Barbara	California
Ocean Conservation Research*		California
Oikonos - Ecosystem Knowledge*		California
OneLife Institute*		California
One Love Vibrations Foundation	Malibu	California
One World Inc. California		California
Open Space Alliance	Santa Cruz	California
OrganicAthlete*		California
Organic Bouquet	San Rafael	California
Pachamama Alliance, the	San Francisco	California
Pacific Environment*		California
Pacifica Graduate Institute	Santa Barbara	California
Pantheist Awareness Network	Visalia	California
Passionfish*		California
Peace Earth Action with Creative Ethics (PEACE) Ashram	Danville	California
Peacemaker Community	Santa Barbara	California
Peaceways/Young General Assembly	San Mateo	California
Pesticide Action Network North America*		California
Petaluma Progressives	Petaluma	California
Pitzer College	Claremont	California
Placer Nature Center	Rocklin	California
PlanetAura	Los Angeles	California
Planet Drum Foundation*		California
Population Coalition	Redlands	California
Presbyterians for Restoring Creation*		California
Preschoolers for Peace	Santa Cruz	California
Programa Star/Eco Station	Culver City	California
Project Great Futures*		California
Reality for Life-ReL	San Anselmo	California
RealTechWriters	San Francisco	California
Redwood Valley Outdoor Education Project*		California
Regeneration Project & Interfaith Power & Light*		California
Regeneration Project [Env. Ministry Grace Cathedral]	San Francisco	California
Religious Science Center of San Luis Obispo	San Luis Obispo	California
Restore Hetch Hetchy	Yosemite	California
Return of the Natives Restoration Education Project*		California
Riekes Center Nature Stufies Program*		California
Rising Leaf Watershed Arts		California
River of Words	Carmel	California
Riverhill Farm*		California
Rock Creek Press	Ukiah	California
Rockwood Leadership Program*		California
Rose Foundation for Communities and the Environment		California
Sacred Ecology Center	Santa Ana	California
Sacred Indigenous Youth Education Circle	Lytle Creek	California
Saint Francis Region		California
San Francisco Presbytery Peacemaking Task Force	Oakland	California
San Joaquin Outdoor School*		California
Santa Sabina Center	San Rafael	California
Santa Monica Baykeeper*		California

Save the Redwoods League*		California
School of Lost Borders	Big Pine	California
SCRAP Gallery*		California
Seven Generations Circle (Global Renaissance Alliance)	Santa Cruz	California
Shaping A Life By Hand	San Simeon	California
Shifting Baselines Ocean Media Project*		California
Sierra Business Council*		California
Sierra Club of the United States, the	San Francisco	California
Sierra Friends Center*		California
Sierra Nevada Alliance*		California
Sisters of Saint Joseph of Orange	Orange	California
Sisters of St. Joseph of Carondelet	Los Angeles	California
Sisters of the Holy Family	San Jose	California
Skyline Harvest	Camptonville	California
Slide Ranch*		California
Smith River Project		California
Soka Gakkai International-California	San Francisco	California
SOLASDANA		California
Soul to Spirit	Fremont	California
South Yuba River Citizens League*		California
South Fork Trinity River Land Conservancy		California
Spirit Rising Productions	San Francisco	California
Stanford University, Earth Sciences*		California
State of the World Forum	San Francisco	California
St, Joseph's Social Service Centre	Venice	California
St. Mary FaithJustice Ministry	Gilroy	California
Surfrider Foundation		California
Sustainable Exchange & Dharma Ridge	Los Gatos	California
Sustainable Futures Project	San Francisco	California
Sustainable Mill Valley		California
Sustainable Monterey County*		California
Sustainable Works	Santa Monica	California
Sustainable World Coalition		California
Synergia Learning Ventures*		California
Tahoe-Baikai Instiitute*		California
Teleosis Institute		California
The Seven Hills School	Walnut Creek	California
Theological Roundtable: Eco. Ethics &Spirituality GTU	Berkeley	California
Three Circles Center*		California
The Trust for Public land*		California
Transformation 2000 Network -Yr 2020 Vision Initiative	Del Mar	California
Transformation of Education	San Jose	California
Transportation Research Assoc., Inc	San Luis Obispo	California
TreePeople		California
UC Berkeley	Berkeley	California
UC Santa Cruz Recreation Department*		California
University of California Santa Cruz Environmental Studies		California
University of London	Los Angeles	California
University of Redlands	Redlands	California
University of the Pacific	Stockton	California
Antioch New England Grad. School Dept. of Clinical Psyc,	Antioch	California
Antioch Los Angeles Grad. Program in Education	Antioch	California
Antioch Los Angeles, Grad. Programs in Education	Marina del Rey	California

University - Antioch Seattle B.A. Program	Antioch	California
University - Antioch Seattle Center for Programs	Antioch	California
University - Antioch Seattle Center for Creative Change	Antioch	California
University - Ecology Center at Pitzer College		California
University - Environmental Field Program Antioch Coll	Antioch	California
Urban Creek Council		California
Urban Tilth*		California
Ursa Minor Arts & Media	San Rafael	California
Ventana Wilderness Alliance:Bellarmine Prep		California
Ventura Charter School of Arts and Global Education	Ventura	California
Vertical Landscape	San Francisco	California
Waste Free Lunches*		California
The Watershed Project*		California
Watershed Institute		California
Wetlands Action Network		California
Wetlands Action Plan		California
WhyAfrica	Hayward	California
Wild Farm Alliance*		California
Wild Rose House of Taste	Gilroy	California
WILDCOAST		California
Wildwoods Foundation, the	Los Angeles	California
Women for a Better World*		California
Women of Vision and Action	Walnut Creek	California
WomenRise	Santa Cruz	California
Women's Environmental Network*		California
World Festival of Sacred Music	Los Angeles	California
World Pantheist Movement USA		California
World Peace Flag Organization		California
www.worldpeaceflag.com	Marina del Rey	California
Yosemite Institute		California
Youth in Focus*		California
Zap Electric Bikes and Scooters	Milpitas	California

Colorado

Animas Conservancy	Durango	Colorado
Animas Valley Institute*		Colorado
Aspen Center for Environmental Studies*		Colorado
Atlas Arckology*		Colorado
Bear Creek Watershed Association		Colorado
Big City Mountaineers*		Colorado
Blue River Watershed*		Colorado
Booher	La Veta	Colorado
Catamount Institute*		Colorado
Center for Native Ecosystems*		Colorado
Center for ReSource Conservation	Boulder	Colorado
Challenge Aspen*		Colorado
Coalition for the Upper South Platte*		Colorado
Colorado Environmental Coalition*		Colorado
Colorado Foundation for Water Education*		Colorado
Colorado Grizzly Project		Colorado
Colorado Mountain Club		Colorado
Colorado People's Environmental & Economic Network		Colorado

Colorado Mountain Club*		Colorado
Colorado Rivers Alliance		Colorado
Colorado Watershed Network		Colorado
Colorado Wild*		Colorado
Creole West Productions	Fort Collins	Colorado
Cure Organic Farm*		Colorado
Deer Hill Foundation		Colorado
Denver Urban Gardens		Colorado
Durango Nature Studies*		Colorado
Earth Web Project	La Veta	Colorado
Earthlinks		Colorado
EcoCycle*		Colorado
Envirofest		Colorado
Fort Lewis College Environmental Center*		Colorado
Fresh Market Company		Colorado
Global Explorers		Colorado
Gloria Barron Prize for Young Heroes*		Colorado
Global Response	Boulder	Colorado
Gore Range Natural Science School*		Colorado
Great Old Broads for Wilderness		Colorado
Greenway and Nature Center of Pueblo		Colorado
Grounds for Learning		Colorado
High Country Citizens' Alliance		Colorado
High Country News*		Colorado
High Desert Foods*		Colorado
High Plains Environmental Center		Colorado
Institute of Taoist Education and Acupuncture, Inc.	Louisville	Colorado
Leopold Education Project – CO		Colorado
Living Law Institute, the	Snowmass	Colorado
Men's Leadership Alliance*		Colorado
Mile High Business Alliance*		Colorado
Mile High Youth Corps - Ameri Corps		Colorado
Mothers Acting Up*		Colorado
Mountain Classic Mortgages		Colorado
Mountain Park Environmental Center		Colorado
Naropa University Environmental Studies Program*		Colorado
National Coalition of American Nuns	Denver	Colorado
Office for Resource Efficiency*		Colorado
Open World Foundation for a Sustainable Future	Boulder	Colorado
Outdoor Leadership Training Seminars	Denver	Colorado
Plains Conservation Center*		Colorado
Primal Echo, LLC	Boulder	Colorado
Prison Dharma Network	Boulder	Colorado
Rock the Earth Director, Colorado		Colorado
Rocky Mountain Institute*		Colorado
Rocky Mountain Peace and Justice Center	Denver	Colorado
San Juan Citizens Alliance*		Colorado
San Juan Field School*		Colorado
San Juan Mountains Association*		Colorado
San Miguel County	Tellurid	Colorado
Sinapu Boulder,		Colorado
Social Concern Office of Catholic Diocese Jefferson City	Jefferson	Colorado
Sopris Foundation*		Colorado

Soul Journey 2000	Boulder	Colorado
Stoneworks		Colorado
South Platte Park*		Colorado
Southern Rockies Ecosystem Project*		Colorado
The Temple of Gaia	Boulder	Colorado
Thorne Ecological Institute*		Colorado
Town of Crested Butte, Colorado	Crested Butte	Colorado
Trinity Foundation	Boulder	Colorado
Western Hardrock Watershed Team*		Colorado
Western Resource Advocates*		Colorado
Western Slope Environmental Council		Colorado
Wild Bear Center for Nature Discovery*		Colorado
The WILD Foundation*		Colorado
The Wilderness Land Trust*		Colorado
Wilderness Workshop*		Colorado
Work for Progress*		Colorado

Connecticut

Natchaug River Alliance Chaplin,		Connecticut
Bacon Academy Community Activism Class*		Connecticut
Berkshire-Litchfield Environmental Council*		Connecticut
Better Days Alliance	Higganum	Connecticut
Central Connecticut State University		Connecticut
Chubby Bunny Farm*		Connecticut
Connecticut Farmland Trust*		Connecticut
Connecticut Fund for the Environment*		Connecticut
Connecticut Conference, United Church of Christ	Hartford	Connecticut
Connecticut RiverFest		Connecticut
CT Regional of Sisters of Merc (335 Members and Assoc	West Hartford	Connecticut
Cultural Creatives in Action		Connecticut
Denison Pequotsepos Nature Center		Connecticut
Diamond Lake Trust	Glastonbury	Connecticut
Earth Rise Initiatives		Connecticut
East Haven Land Trust	East Haven	Connecticut
E.O. Smith High School		Connecticut
Farmington River Watershed Association*		Connecticut
Flamig Farm Inc		Connecticut
Forest Hill Farm*		Connecticut
Friends of Ambler Farm*		Connecticut
Friends of Animals*		Connecticut
Friends of Ash Creek		Connecticut
GaiaQuest*		Connecticut
Highstead*		Connecticut
Hockanum River Watershed Association		Connecticut
Integrated Day Charter School	Norwich	Connecticut
Interreligious Eco-Justice Network*		Connecticut
It Takes a Village to Raise a Child	Ellington	Connecticut
LUCITA	Milford	Connecticut
Mercy Ecology Institute	Madison	Connecticut
Natural Science Society	West Hartford	Connecticut
Naubesatuck Watershed Council		Connecticut
New Canaan Nature Center*		Connecticut

New Haven Ecology Project*		Connecticut
Northeast Organic Farming Association*		Connecticut
Ocean View Foundation		Connecticut
Oxford Trust Land	Oxford	Connecticut
Pollution Extermination Group Inc.	Naugatuck	Connecticut
Pomperaug River Watershed Council*		Connecticut
Shine a Light for Peace	Shelton	Connecticut
Sisters of Mercy NH Region II		Connecticut
Stamford Land Conservation Trust		Connecticut
Study Circles Resource Center*		Connecticut
Suffield Outdoor Leadership Opportunities*		Connecticut
Tobacco Valley Resource Group		Connecticut
Trinity Conference Center*		Connecticut
Trinity Episcopal Church		Connecticut
UNA	North Haven	Connecticut
University of Connecticut		Connecticut
University of Mississippi	Oxford	Connecticut
West Haven Watersheds Association		Connecticut
Wildlife in Crisis	Weston	Connecticut
Yale University School of Forestry & Environmental Studies		Connecticut
Earth Charter Community of the Lower Valley, Inc	Moodus	Connecticut
Integrated Day Charter School	Norwich	Connecticut

Delaware

Spiralcat Innovations	Newark	Delaware
Tetra Tech, Inc.	Christiana	Delaware
World Federalist Association	Wilmington	Delaware

District of Columbia – Washington, D.C.

Alaska Coalition*
Alaska Rainforest Campaign*
American Anthropology Association (AAA)
American Lands Alliance*
Appalachia Clean Streams Program*
Campaign for America's Wilderness*
Casey Trees Endowment Fund*
Center for Food Safety
Center for Respect of Life and Environment - CRLE
Center for Science in the Public Interest*
Center for Visionary Leadership
Citizens for Global Solutions
Coalition for Smarter Growth*
Congregation of the Sisters of St. Joseph of Peace
Container Recycling Institute*
Discovery Creek children's Museum of
Earth Charter USA*
Earth Policy Institute*
Environmental Film Festival in the Nation's Capital*
Gaea Foundation Resource Center for Activism & Arts*
Green Media Toolshed*
Greenpeace*

Georgetown University, Department of English
Global Bridge Productions
Green Homes Now LLC
Humane Society of the United States, the
ISAR: Resources for Environmental Activists*
Justice, Peace and Integrity of Creation (JPIC)
Marine Fish Conservation Network*
Maryknoll Office for Global Concerns -Ossining, N.Y.
Maryknoll Sisters
Mountain Institute
National Conference for Community and Justice (NCCJ)
National Council of Churches Eco-Justice Programs*
Next Step: Samaritan Ministry of Greater Washington*
North American Assoc. Environmental Education NAAEE
The ONE Campaign*
Parents for Nontoxic Alternatives*
Physicians for Social Responsibility
Population Connection*
Power Shift*
Rensselaer Student Pugwash Washington Office
Roosevelt Institution – DC Office*
Sierra Club Action Fund*
Solar Electric Light Fund*
Surface Transportation Policy Project*
Throwplace.com*
TransGlobal Ventures, Inc.
University of the District of Columbia
University Leaders for a Sustainable Future - ULSF
University of Washington
University - Georgetown University Dept of English
US Conference of Mayors
Wallace Global Fund
The Washington Center for Internships*
Washington Parks & People*
World Federation of Engineering Organizations (WFEO)
World Resources Institute
Worldwatch Institute*
Yahara Preparative Mtg of the Religious Soc of Friends (Quaker)

Florida

Algae Biofuels, LLC	Palm Bay	Florida
Apache Fog Studio	Tampa	Florida
Association of Cymry Wiccae		Florida
Aubrey A Garcia World Reformers Group	Panama City	Florida
Back-Rubs To Go.org	Lutz	Florida
Bee Haven Farm*		Florida
Bigelow Laboratory for Ocean sciences	Key West	Florida
Bowie Urban Planners		Florida
Brooker Creek Preserve Environmental Education Center*		Florida
Caribbean Conservation Corporation*		Florida
Catalytic Services		Florida
Center for Earth Jurisprudence*		Florida

Center for Environmental & Sustainability Education*		Florida
Champion Tree Project International	Lake Worth	Florida
Citizens of Earth	Tampa	Florida
Common Ground for Conservation	Miami	Florida
Conservancy of Southwest Florida*		Florida
Conservancy of the Wild Heart		Florida
Conservation Trust for Florida*		Florida
COXPOTS	Dunnellon	Florida
Darlynn's Darlins*		Florida
Earth Charter of Sanibel*		Florida
Earth Charter USA Community Initiatives –Office	Tampa	Florida
Earth Learning*		Florida
Eckerd College Earth Society		Florida
ECOSanibel (Earth Charter of Sanibel)		Florida
Ecotourism Development, Inc.	Jupiter	Florida
ECO-Action, Inc.	Orlando	Florida
EEI Recycling	St. Petersburg	Florida
Felburn Foundation	Yankeetown	Florida
First United Church (UCC) of Tampa	Tampa	Florida
Florida Cannabis Action Network	Tampa	Florida
Florida Coalition for Peace & Justice	Graham	Florida
Florida Environmental Health Association	Jacksonville	Florida
Florida Green Party		Florida
Florida Gulf Coast University	Jacksonville	Florida
Florida League of Cities, Inc.	Tallahassee	Florida
Florida Panther Society*		Florida
Florida West Coast RC & D*		Florida
Future Life Progression Hypnotherapy	Miami Lakes	Florida
Grace Unlimited Inc.		Florida
Green Party of Florida	Sarasota	Florida
Green Party of Hillsborough county	Tampa	Florida
Green Sanctuary Committee;Unitarian Universalist Church	Tallahassee	Florida
Heart of the Earth		Florida
Institute for Regional Conservation*		Florida
Internal Insights	Tampa	Florida
Jefferson High School	Tampa	Florida
Love Foundation, Inc., the	Tampa	Florida
Lovearth.net	Siesta Key	Florida
Manatee Community College Ecology Club	North Port	Florida
Martin Foundation		Florida
Mother's Hip Connection Education Foundation	Tallahassee	Florida
National-Louis University	Clearwater	Florida
Natural Awakenings Tampa Bay Area	Tierra Verde	Florida
Nature Coast IONS	Homosassa	Florida
The Nature Conservancy Lake Wales Ridge Program*		Florida
Nature's Food Patch	Clearwater	Florida
New College	Sarasota	Florida
New World Society	Inverness	Florida
Nova Southeastern University*		Florida
Office of Justice and Peace, ST Augustine Diocese	Jacksonville	Florida
Ovalle Media Group Inc.	Miami	Florida
O.N.E.W.I.L.D.W.O.R.L.D. Â®		Florida
Peace Education International	Miami Beach	Florida

Pine Ridge Sanctuary		Florida
Presbyterians for Restoring Creation		Florida
Red Hills Writers Project*		Florida
Reef Relief	Key West	Florida
Riverwoods Field lab*		Florida
Sanibel –Captiva Conservation Foundation*		Florida
Sarasota County Green Party	Sarasota	Florida
Sarasota Green Connection	Sarasota	Florida
Sarasota Green Marketplace	Sarasota	Florida
Seacamp Association, Inc.*		Florida
SGI USA	Pompano Beach	Florida
Southwest Florida Water Management District*		Florida
Spiritual Realization Society	Clearwater	Florida
Stewarts of the St. Johns River		Florida
Sustainable Works, Green Team Project	Jacksonville	Florida
The American Board of Pathology	Tampa	Florida
The Healing Center of Dunedin	Dunedin	Florida
Total Success Coaching, Inc.	Tampa	Florida
Trout Lake Nature Center, Inc.		Florida
Univ. of So. Florida Manatee Comm. College Ecology Club		Florida
University of South Florida, Equal Opportunity& Diversity	Tampa	Florida
University - Eckerd College Earth Society	St Petersburg	Florida
Venus Project, the	Venus	Florida
Walkable Communities	Orlando	Florida
Wildlands Project*		Florida
Worden Farm & CSA*		Florida

Georgia

Beyond Grass	Atlanta	Georgia
Blue Heron Nature Preserve*		Georgia
Blue Ridge Outdoor Education Center		Georgia
Captain Planet Foundation	Atlanta	Georgia
Center for a Sustainable Coast*		Georgia
Chapel Hill Middle School	Decatur	Georgia
Chattahoochee Nature Center		Georgia
Chattooga Conservancy*		Georgia
Church of Y Tylwyth Teg - Welsh Tradition in America		Georgia
Dunwoody nature Center*		Georgia
Earth Share of Georgia		Georgia
Elachee Nature Center*		Georgia
Gardens for Peace	Atlanta	Georgia
The Georgia Conservancy*		Georgia
Georgia Forestwatch		Georgia
Georgians Against Nuclear Energy		Georgia
Georgia Peace and Justice Coalition		Georgia
Little Nancy Creek Watershed Alliance		Georgia
National Center for Human Rights Education	Atlanta	Georgia
Project South*		Georgia
Sapelo Foundation	Brunswick	Georgia
SE Alliance for Sustainable Development	Atlanta	Georgia
Sisters of St. Francis of Savannah	Savannah	Georgia
Sisters of St. Francis of Sylvania	Sylvania	Georgia

Southface*		Georgia
Tallahassee/South Georgia Chapter		Georgia
The Creators Gift 137		Georgia
The "United Multi-Media Consortium"	Alpharetta	Georgia

Hawaii

Bamboo Ridge Press*		Hawaii
Church of the Crossroads		Hawaii
Environment Hawaii*		Hawaii
GE Free Hawaii		Hawaii
Hague Appeal for Peace Pacific Forum	Honolulu	Hawaii
Halau Ku Mana Public Charter School	Honolulu	Hawaii
Hawaii Genetic Engineering Action Network		Hawaii
Hawai'i Institute for Human Rights	Kahului	Hawaii
The Hawaii Island Writers Association*		Hawaii
Historic Hawaii Foundation*		Hawaii
Iolani Peace Institute		Hawaii
The Kohala Center*		Hawaii
Maryknoll Sisters, Waianae	Waianae	Hawaii
Maui Peace Action		Hawaii
Maui Tomorrow*		Hawaii
Naalehu School Library		Hawaii
Naalehu Theatre & Museum*		Hawaii
Pacific Whale Foundation	Wailuku	Hawaii
Pacific Writers Connection*		Hawaii
Regenerations International Botanical Garden	Kapaa	Hawaii
TREE Hawaii		Hawaii

Idaho

Alliance for Wild Ethics	Victor	Idaho
Boise State University	Boise	Idaho
Committee for Idaho's High Desert		Idaho
Earthfire Institute*		Idaho
Sawtooth Science Institute*		Idaho
Snake River Alliance / Idaho's Nuclear Watchdog		Idaho
Sun Valley Trekking		Idaho
Western Watersheds Project*		Idaho
Wild Gift*		Idaho
Wolf Education and Research Center (WERC)*		Idaho
Wood River Land Trust*		Idaho

Illinois

American Assn. of University Women	Western Spgs	Illinois
Ames Educational Consultants	Oak Park	Illinois
Center for Neighborhood Technology		Illinois
Center for Sustainable Community	Stelle	Illinois
Center of Higher Development*		Illinois
Chicago Media Watch		Illinois
Conservation Design Forum	Elmhurst	Illinois
Council for a Parliament of the World's Religions	Chicago	Illinois

Department of History, Ill. State Univ.	Normal	Illinois
Douglas-Hart Nature Center*		Illinois
Ecology Action Center		Illinois
Evanston Interreligious Sustainability Circle		Illinois
Faith in Place	Chicago	Illinois
First Congregational Church Illinois		Illinois
Forest Park Nature Center*		Illinois
Grand Prairie Friends		Illinois
Green Earth Home Cleaning (SM)		Illinois
Green Party US	Chicago	Illinois
Harmony Creek Farms		Illinois
Illinois Student Environmental Network		Illinois
Inter-Natural Alinement		Illinois
Justice Peace & Integrity of Creation Wheaton Franciscans	Wheaton	Illinois
Knox College Environmental Studies Program*		Illinois
Kheperu em INU	Chicago	Illinois
Liberty Prairie Conservancy		Illinois
Loyola Student Environmental Alliance		Illinois
McHenry County Conservation District*		Illinois
McHenry County Defenders*		Illinois
Momentum Unlimited	Chicago	Illinois
The Nature Conservancy Illinois Chapter*		Illinois
Natural Tree Furniture	Rockford	Illinois
Nature in Legend and Story		Illinois
Neighborhood Law Office		Illinois
NeighborSpace*		Illinois
New Community Project*		Illinois
Northwestern University Evanston		Illinois
Oakdale Nature Preserve	Freeport	Illinois
Pod Country Club Hills		Illinois
Prairie Rivers Network	Champaign	Illinois
Principia College Biology & Natural Resource Dept.		Illinois
Recycled Energy Development*		Illinois
Regional Association of Concerned Environmentalists		Illinois
Rivers Project, Southern Illinois University		Illinois
The Road Less Traveled*		Illinois
Rogers Park Greens	Chicago	Illinois
Safe Tables Our Priority (S.T.O.P.)*		Illinois
Sageheart Alliance	Chicago	Illinois
School for New Learning/DePaul University	Chicago	Illinois
Severson Dells Education Foundation		Illinois
SGI-USA Mid America Region	Chicago	Illinois
Sisters of Mercy Justice Committee Chicago Reg. Comm.	Chicago	Illinois
Sisters of Mercy Northeast Justice Team		Illinois
Sisters of St. Joseph of La Grange	LaGrange Park	Illinois
Social Justice Network		Illinois
Southwest Chicago PADS*		Illinois
Students for Environmental Concerns		Illinois
The Light Weavers	Chicago	Illinois
University of Chicago Religion & Environment Initiative*		Illinois
University of Chicago Civic Knowledge Project*		Illinois
Wheaton Franciscan Sisters	Wheaton	Illinois

Indiana

Bradford Woods Outdoor Center*		Indiana
Campaign for Sustainable Economics	Indianapolis	Indiana
Central Indiana Land Trust*		Indiana
Church of the Earth Nation		Indiana
Community Sustainability Project*		Indiana
Congregation Justice Committee of Sisters of Holy Cross	Notre Dame	Indiana
Congregation of the Sisters of the Holy Cross, the		Indiana
Congregation Peace, Justice Comm. Sisters of Providence	St. Mary of the Woods	Indiana
Earlham Environmental Action Coalition	Richmond	Indiana
EcoPax*		Indiana
Elkhart Environmental Center*		Indiana
Environmental Education Association of Indiana		Indiana
Fiat Spiritus Community	Donaldson	Indiana
Heartwood Center for Health and Healing		Indiana
Holy Cross International Justice Office	Notre Dame	Indiana
Holy Cross Services Corporation	Notre Dame	Indiana
Hoosier Environmental Council*		Indiana
Indianapolis Museum of Art - Art & Nature Park*		Indiana
LCWR Region VII	St, Mary of the Woods	Indiana
Merry Lee Environmental Learning Center*		Indiana
Our Lady of Victory Missionary Sisters	Huntington	Indiana
Poor Handmaids of Jesus Christ	Donaldson	Indiana
Prairiewoods: Franciscan Spirituality Center		Indiana
Protect Our Rivers Now*		Indiana
Sherman & Company	Indianapolis	Indiana
Sisters of the Holy Cross	Notre Dame	Indiana
Spirit & Place Civic Festival*		Indiana
Protect Our Rivers Now!	Indianapolis	Indiana
Saint Mary's College	Notre Dame	Indiana
SHALOM Int'l Ntwk:Justice, Peace & Integrity of Creation	Notre Dame	Indiana
Sisters of Providence of	Saint Mary-of-the-Woods	Indiana
Sisters of Saint Francis	Mishawaka	Indiana
Sisters of St. Francis Oldenburg Indiana		Indiana
Sisters of the Holy Cross of Notre Dame	Notre Dame	Indiana
Spirit & Place Civic Festival		Indiana
Unitarian Universalist Church of Indianapolis		Indiana
United States Leadership of Sister of Notre Dame de Namur		Indiana
University - Saint Mary's College		Indiana
White Violet Center for Eco-Justice*		Indiana
Whitewater Valley Land Trust	Centerville	Indiana

Iowa

Center for Energy & Environmental Education*		Iowa
Congregation of the Humility of Mary	Davenport	Iowa
Dark Sky Initiative*		Iowa
Grinnell College Environmental Action Group, the		Iowa
Iowa Environmental Council	Des Moines	Iowa
Iowa Project on Place Studies*		Iowa
Leopold Center for Sustainable Agriculture*		Iowa

Mississippi River Birds & Biodiversity Observatory*		Iowa
National Catholic Rural Life Conference	Des Moines	Iowa
1000 Friends of Iowa*		Iowa
Practical Farmers of Iowa*		Iowa
Prairiewoods Franciscan Spirituality Center*		Iowa
School for Moral Courage	Iowa City	Iowa
Sisters of Charity of the Blessed Virgin Mary	Dubuque	Iowa
Sohodojo, Inc.*		Iowa
Standing by Words Center*		Iowa
Student Organic Farm		Iowa
University - Grinnell College Environmental Action Group	Grinnell	Iowa
University - Grinnell College Environmental Action Group,	Grinnell	Iowa
Women, Food & Agriculture Network*		Iowa

Kansas

Dillon Nature Center		Kansas
International Sisters Network	Overland Park	Kansas
Kansas Area Watershed Council		Kansas
Kansas City Center for Urban Agriculture*		Kansas
Kansas Green Party	Lawrence	Kansas
The Land Institute*		Kansas
Michoacan Reforestation Fund	Lawrence	Kansas
National Action Network, Kansas Chapter		Kansas
Pollution Posse Kansas Chapter		Kansas
Sierra Club Kansas Chapter Montgomery Country Group		Kansas

Kentucky

Appalachia Science in the Public Interest*		Kentucky
Appalshop*		Kentucky
Archdiocese of Louisville KY	Louisville	Kentucky
Bernheim Arboretum & Research Forest*		Kentucky
Center for Environmental Education at MSU*		Kentucky
Community Farm Alliance*		Kentucky
Daniel Carter Bearc Environmental Center*		Kentucky
Kentucky Resources Council, Inc.	Frankfort	Kentucky
KY Alliance Against Racist & political Repression*		Kentucky
The Mary E. Wharton Nature Sanctuary at Floracliff*		Kentucky
Parish Social Ministry, Catholic Charities Archidiocese	Louisville	Kentucky
Pennyrile Area Development District	Hopkinsville	Kentucky
Professional Porch Sitters	Louisville	Kentucky
Rural Center for Responsible Living	Burkesville	Kentucky
Sisters of Charity of Nazareth Earth Committee	Nazareth	Kentucky
Sisters of Charity of Nazareth Western Province Board		Kentucky
Sustainable Communities Network*		Kentucky
UK Appalachian Center		Kentucky
University of Louisville Center Environmental Education	Louisville	Kentucky
Waldorf School of Louisville*		Kentucky

Louisiana

American Design Technology, Inc.	New Orleans	Louisiana
Centenary College	Shreveport	Louisiana
Global Network for Justice	New Orleans	Louisiana
Gulf Restoration Network*		Louisiana
Louisiana Bucket Brigade*		Louisiana
New Orleans Public Schools	New Orleans	Louisiana
Ouachita Riverkeeper*		Louisiana
Parkway Partners*		Louisiana
School Sister of Notre Dame Assoc. Shreveport Chapter	Shreveport	Louisiana

Maine

Acadia National Park*		Maine
Adams Elementary School	Castine	Maine
Angel Farm	Damariscotta	Maine
Arising Arts	Scarborough	Maine
Audubon Expedition Institute*		Maine
Beehivve Design Collective*		Maine
Biodiversity Research Institute*		Maine
Blue Hill Co-op		Maine
Center for Cetacean Research and Conservation	Brunswick	Maine
Center for Ecological Living and Learning (CELL)*		Maine
Chaplaincy Institute of Maine		Maine
Chewonki Foundation, the	Wiscasset	Maine
Cobscook Community Learning Center*		Maine
College of the Atlantic	Bar Harbor	Maine
Dirigo Institute for Place Based Learning*		Maine
Dorr Museum of Natural History*		Maine
The Eleuthero Community*		Maine
Ferry Beach Ecology School		Maine
Global Awareness Project		Maine
The Good Life Center*		Maine
Great Harbor Maritime Museum*		Maine
Hancock County Locally Grown Foods Project		Maine
Hart-to-Hart Farm*		Maine
Healthy Aging Task Force*		Maine
Healthy Foods from Healthy Soils*		Maine
Independent Food Project*		Maine
International Institute for Humane Education		Maine
Island Institute	Rockland	Maine
Kants Hill School*		Maine
Maine Conservation Corps*		Maine
Maine Council of Churches, Env. Justice Program*		Maine
Maine Farmland Trust*		Maine
Maine Organic Farmers & Gardeners Association*		Maine
MaineShare*		Maine
Maine Solar Energy Association		Maine
Medomak Camp & Retreat Center*		Maine
MDI Water Quality Coalition	Mt. Desert	Maine
Morris Farm Trust	Wiscasset	Maine
Natural Resources Council of Maine*		Maine

New Hope Products Company, Inc.	Biddeford	Maine
Peace & Justice Center of Eastern Maine*		Maine
Penobscot River Restoration Trust*		Maine
Regulatory Assistance Project*		Maine
Sheepscot Valley Conservation Association		Maine
RESTORE: The North Woods*		Maine
Saddleback Institute*		Maine
Solar Energy Awareness Demonstration Seminars		Maine
Tanglewood 4H Camp & Learning Center*		Maine
The International Exchange Student News	Cape Porpoise	Maine
Unity College		Maine
University of Maine Cooperative Extension		Maine
University - College of the Atlantic	Bar Harbor	Maine
University - Unity College		Maine
Whole Health Center, the	Bar Harbor	Maine
Wolf Pine Farm		Maine

Maryland

1 Sky*		Maryland
Alliance for Childhood*		Maryland
American Hiking Society*		Maryland
Anacostia Watershed Society	Bladensburg	Maryland
Association of {Partners for Public Lands*		Maryland
Benedictine Sisters of Baltimore, Emmanuel Monastery	Baltimore	Maryland
Calvert Group, Ltd	Bethesda	Maryland
Center for a New American Dream*		Maryland
Chesapeake Bay Earth School*		Maryland
Chesapeake Bay Foundation*		Maryland
Chesapeake Climate Action Network*		Maryland
Chesapeake Wildlife Heritage*		Maryland
Church of the American Indian USA	W. Bethesda	Maryland
Clean Water Action-MD*		Maryland
Defenders of Wild Cumberland, Inc.		Maryland
Earth Community Center		Maryland
Eastern Shore Land Conservancy*		Maryland
Echo Hill Outdoor School*		Maryland
EcoResolve		Maryland
Emmanuel Monastery	Lutherville	Maryland
Environmental Concern Inc*		Maryland
Environmental Crisis Center	Baltimore	Maryland
Eyes of Paint Branch		Maryland
Fairhaven School*		Maryland
Global and Civic Responsibility	Towson	Maryland
Global Coalition for Peace		Maryland
Grassroots.org*		Maryland
Institute for Conservation Leadership*		Maryland
Institute Justice Team, Sisters of Mercy of the Americas	Silver Spring	Maryland
Irvine Nature Center*		Maryland
Jones Falls Watershed Association*		Maryland
Landon School Environmental Club		Maryland
Maryland Native Plant Society		Maryland
Nanticoke Watershed Alliance*		Maryland

National Assoc. for Equal Opportunity in Higher Education*		Maryland
National Board of Leadership Conf. Women Religious	Silver Spring	Maryland
Nuclear Information & Resource Service	Takoma Park	Maryland
Parks & People Foundation*		Maryland
Peace & Justice Committee of Protestant Lutheran Church		Maryland
Pickering Creek Audubon Center*		Maryland
Roots & Shoots Program, Jane Goodall Institute*		Maryland
Rudolf Steiner Institute*		Maryland
Shared Earth Foundation, the	Chestertown	Maryland
Sisters of Mercy of the Americas	Silver Spring	Maryland
Skills for the 21st Century	Bethesda	Maryland
Sultana Projects*		Maryland
University of Maryland Baltimore County	Baltimore	Maryland
Volunteer Maryland*		Maryland
Windstar Wildlife Institute		Maryland

Massachusetts

1-Blue Planet Foundation, Ltd.	Mashpee	Massachusetts
A.C.C.E.S.S. Art Corp International*		Massachusetts
Allen & Osborne, Inc	Plymouth	Massachusetts
Alliance for Democracy	Waltham	Massachusetts
Americorps Cape Cod*		Massachusetts
Animals for Intermediaries*		Massachusetts
Appalachian Mountain Club -Southern New England Office*		Massachusetts
Arkhom Inc.	Greenfield	Massachusetts
Au Sable Institute of Environmental Studies		Massachusetts
The BARKA Foundation*		Massachusetts
Berkshares, Inc.*		Massachusetts
Berkshire Environmental Action Team*		Massachusetts
Berkshire Grown		Massachusetts
The Berkshire Museum*		Massachusetts
Berkshire Taconic Community Foundation*		Massachusetts
Bidwell Illustration & Design		Massachusetts
Bikes Not Bombs*		Massachusetts
Black Mesa Weavers for Life and Land*		Massachusetts
Boston Area Gleaners, Inc.*		Massachusetts
Boston Research Center for the 21st Century	Cambridge	Massachusetts
Business Solutions	Boston	Massachusetts
Campaign for Environmental Literacy*		Massachusetts
Caretaker Farm*		Massachusetts
Center for Contemplative Mind in Society*		Massachusetts
Center for Ecological Technology		Massachusetts
Center for Psychology & Social Change	Cambridge	Massachusetts
CERES		Massachusetts
Charles River Watershed Association*		Massachusetts
Charles River Conservancy		Massachusetts
Clean Power Now*		Massachusetts
Clean Water Action - MA*		Massachusetts
Climate Crisis Coalition*		Massachusetts
Co-op Power*		Massachusetts
Community Involved in Sustaining Agriculture*		Massachusetts
Community Land Trust in the Southern Berkshires		Massachusetts

Congregation of St. Joseph	Boston	Massachusetts
Conservation Law Foundation*		Massachusetts
Conway School of Landscape Design*		Massachusetts
Cooperative Development Institute*		Massachusetts
Cougar Network*		Massachusetts
Counting Prayers*		Massachusetts
Cultural Survival*		Massachusetts
Cuvilly Arts and Earth Center	Ipswich	Massachusetts
Drumlin Farm Wildlife Sanctuary*		Massachusetts
Dump & Run*		Massachusetts
e inc.*		Massachusetts
Eagle Eye Institute*		Massachusetts
Earth Action	Amherst	Massachusetts
Earth Covenant Community	Cambridge	Massachusetts
earthstewards page on www.thoughtsnmemories.net	Ashfield	Massachusetts
Earthlands*		Massachusetts
Earthwatch Institute*		Massachusetts
Earthworks Boston*		Massachusetts
EcoLogic		Massachusetts
Ecologic development Fund*		Massachusetts
Ecological Landscaping Association*		Massachusetts
Ecowaters Project*		Massachusetts
Eel River Watershed Association	Plymouth	Massachusetts
E.F. Schumacher Society		Massachusetts
The FARM Institute*		Massachusetts
The Farm School*		Massachusetts
The Food Project*		Massachusetts
For the Planet	Newburyport	Massachusetts
Four Winds Farm*		Massachusetts
Garfield Foundation*		Massachusetts
The Gasoline Alley Foundation*		Massachusetts
The Global Classroom*		Massachusetts
Global InterAction	Boston	Massachusetts
Grassroots International*		Massachusetts
Great Barrington Land Conservancy*		Massachusetts
Great Barrington Rudolf Steiner School		Massachusetts
Green Berkshires, Inc.*		Massachusetts
Green Corps*		Massachusetts
Green Roundtable*		Massachusetts
GreenAgers*		Massachusetts
Growing Places Garden Project*		Massachusetts
Hands Across the River Coalition (H.A.R.C.)		Massachusetts
Haymarket Consulting Group		Massachusetts
Healthlink*		Massachusetts
Heirloom Harvest Community Farm & CSA*		Massachusetts
Hitchcock Center for the Environment		Massachusetts
Home, Inc.*		Massachusetts
Hoosic River Watershed Association		Massachusetts
Housatonic River Institute*		Massachusetts
International Physicians for the Prevention of Nuclear War		Massachusetts
In This Place / The Tracking Way Magazine*		Massachusetts
Indian Line Farm*		Massachusetts
Institute for Community Economics*		Massachusetts

Interlock Media*		Massachusetts
Investor's Real Estate Capital	Everett	Massachusetts
Lampson Brook Farm, CSA	Belchertown	Massachusetts
Land's Sake*		Massachusetts
Landmark Volunteers*		Massachusetts
Lawrence Grassroots Initiative		Massachusetts
Little Franciscans of Mary	Worcester	Massachusetts
Living Routes - Ecovillage Education		Massachusetts
Manomet Center for Conservation Sciences		Massachusetts
Maria Mitchell Association		Massachusetts
The Marion Institute*		Massachusetts
Marion Foundation	Marion	Massachusetts
Mass. Riverways Program*		Massachusetts
Massachusetts Climate Action Network*		Massachusetts
McVinney & Co	Brookline	Massachusetts
Montessori School of the Berkshires*		Massachusetts
Moon in the Pond Farm*		Massachusetts
Mount Grace Land Conservation Trust*		Massachusetts
Mt. Everett High School Aquaponics Program*		Massachusetts
Musketaquid Arts & Environment Program*		Massachusetts
Mystiv River Watershed Association*		Massachusetts
Nantucket Conservation Foundation*		Massachusetts
National Religious Partnership for the Environment*		Massachusetts
New England Wild Flower Society*		Massachusetts
New England Yearly Meeting of Friends (Quakers)	Worcester	Massachusetts
New Entry Sustainable Farming project*		Massachusetts
The New Franchise Institute*		Massachusetts
Northeast Wilderness Trust*		Massachusetts
North Shore Community College	Danvers	Massachusetts
Northfield Mount Hermon School	Mt. Hermon	Massachusetts
One Heart Arts	Northampton	Massachusetts
Organizers' Collaborative*		Massachusetts
Orion Grassroots Network (871 organizations)	Great Barrington	Massachusetts
Orion Magazine	Great Barrington	Massachusetts
Orion Society	Great Barrington	Massachusetts
Pascommuck Conservation Trust	Easthampton	Massachusetts
Pioneer Valley local First*		Massachusetts
Pioneer Valley Seed Collective	Conway	Massachusetts
Pioneer Valley Wetland Volunteers & Beaver Solutions Co.		Massachusetts
Polis-tics, Inc.	Gloucester	Massachusetts
Program on Corporations, Law & Democracy*		Massachusetts
Project Native*		Massachusetts
Project Word*		Massachusetts
Race Mountain Tree Services	Sheffield	Massachusetts
Rainbow Chiropractic		Massachusetts
Rainbow Solutions	Medford	Massachusetts
Red Tomato*		Massachusetts
Remineralize the Earth*		Massachusetts
RESTORE: The North Woods		Massachusetts
RideBuzz*		Massachusetts
Sacred Earth Network, Inc.	Petersham	Massachusetts
Sciencecorps	Lexington	Massachusetts
Second Nature	Boston	Massachusetts

Seeds of Solidarity Education Center	Orange	Massachusetts
Semester Intensive at Kripalu Center*		Massachusetts
Sheffield Land Trust*		Massachusetts
Silent Spring Institute*		Massachusetts
Sirius Community*		Massachusetts
Sisters of Charity Halifax	Wellesley Hill	Massachusetts
Soul of the Ark Institute for Env. Art & Educaiton*		Massachusetts
Southeastern Environmental Education Alliance*		Massachusetts
Stearns Farm CSA*		Massachusetts
Strategic Counsel on Corporate Accountability*		Massachusetts
Sustainable Peace Buliders	Amherst	Massachusetts
Tenemos Retreat Center	Shutesbury	Massachusetts
the creative union	Brewster	Massachusetts
The Latin American Inst for Ecological & Sus. Dev (ILDES)	Shutesbury	Massachusetts
The Soft Earth	Woods Hole	Massachusetts
The Stillpoint Foundation	Walpole	Massachusetts
the Thoreau Society*		Massachusetts
The Trustees for Reservations*		Massachusetts
United for a Fair Economy*		Massachusetts
The Unity Project	Dorchester	Massachusetts
Urban Ecology Institute*		Massachusetts
Timeless Architecture	Boston	Massachusetts
Traprock Peace Center	Deerfield	Massachusetts
Unitarian Universalist Association of Congregations		Massachusetts
Unitarian Universalists	Boston	Massachusetts
University - North Shore Community College		Massachusetts
Walden Woods Project	Lincoln	Massachusetts
Waltham Fields Community Farm*		Massachusetts
Wellspring House, Inc.	Gloucester	Massachusetts
WILD CARE, Inc.		Massachusetts
Williamstown Rural Lands Foundation*		Massachusetts
World Animal Net (WAN)	Boston	Massachusetts
World Forum for Peace & Global Education	Marlborough	Massachusetts
WorldSustain*		Massachusetts
YMCA Camp Burgess & Hayward*		Massachusetts
Youth Adventure Corps*		Massachusetts
Youth Employment Summit	Boston	Massachusetts
Youth Enrichment Services*		Massachusetts
Zen Peacemakers*		Massachusetts
Zoo New England		Massachusetts

Michigan

Adrian Dominican Sisters-Off. Global Mission, Justice & Peace	Adrian	Michigan
Au Sable Institute of Environmental Studies*		Michigan
Capital Area Audubon Society		Michigan
Care of Earth Committee of the Grand Rapids Dominican	Grand Rapids	Michigan
Center for Research in Integrative Learning and Teaching		Michigan
Central Lake Superior Watershed Partnership		Michigan
Church of Spiritual Truth		Michigan
Circle Pines Center*		Michigan
Community Farm	Bear Lake	Michigan
Earth Keeper Initiative*		Michigan

Eco Home Gear, LLC	Lake Angelus	Michigan
Environmental Earth Keepers	Lake Orion	Michigan
Friends of Manitou Arbor Ecovillage	Kalamazoo	Michigan
Gratiot Lake Conservancy*		Michigan
Great Lakes fishery Trust*		Michigan
Institute for Sustainable Living, Art & Natural Design (ISLAND)		Michigan
LandChoices*		Michigan
Leadership Conference Women Religious VII MI & IN		Michigan
Leelanau Historical Museum*		Michigan
Lizardkeeper	Flint	Michigan
Marygrove College	Detroit	Michigan
Michigan Environmental Council*		Michigan
Michigan Interfaith Coalition for Creation	Freeland	Michigan
Michigan State University	East Lansing	Michigan
Michigan State University RISE Program		Michigan
Michigan St. University, Univ. Committee for a Sust. Campus		Michigan
MorningStar Adventures, Inc.	LeRoy	Michigan
MorningStar Productions International		Michigan
Nazareth Center for Eco-Spirituality	Kalamazoo	Michigan
Religion, Ecology, Spirituality W. MI Env. Action Council	Grand Rapids	Michigan
SEE North*		Michigan
Seney Natural History Association*		Michigan
Sisters of Mercy -Americas Regional Community of Detroit	Farmington Hills	Michigan
Society for Nonprofit Organizations*		Michigan
Tip of the Mitt Watershed Council		Michigan
Turtle Island Project*		Michigan
Urban Options	East Lansing	Michigan
U.S.-Canada Great Lakes Islands Project	East Lansing	Michigan
Web Tracks	Grand Rapids	Michigan
Worlds Together Travel Network	Mason	Michigan

Minnesota

Alliance for Sustainability	Minneapolis	Minnesota
The American Bear Association*		Minnesota
American Public Information on the Environment	Northfield	Minnesota
Association of Waldorf Schools of North America*		Minnesota
Audubon Center of the North Woods*		Minnesota
Center for Earth Spirituality and Rural Ministry	Mankato	Minnesota
Charles A. and Anne Morrow Lindbergh Foundation, the	Minneapolis	Minnesota
Coalition for a Clean Minnesota River	New Ulm	Minnesota
College of St. Benedict - St. John's Univ. Env. Studies Prog.	St. Joseph	Minnesota
Flutterbyes Natural Child Care*		Minnesota
Friends of the Boundary Waters Wilderness		Minnesota
Green Crayon		Minnesota
Hartley Nature Center*		Minnesota
Harvest Moon		Minnesota
Healing Spirit Metropolitan Community Church	Rochester	Minnesota
Honor the Earth*		Minnesota
Institute for Agriculture and Trade Policy		Minnesota
Institute for Local Self-Reliance*		Minnesota
Intl Human Rights & Immigration Counseling Center (IHRICC)	Falcon Heights	Minnesota
Land Stewardship Project		Minnesota

Lee & Rose Warner Nature Center		Minnesota
The Leopold Education Project*		Minnesota
MinGei Center for Creation Spirituality, the	Cottage Grove	Minnesota
Minnesota Center for Environmental Advocacy		Minnesota
Minnesota Conservation Corps*		Minnesota
Minnesota Waldorf School*		Minnesota
Minnesota Zoo		Minnesota
Mississippi River Revival		Minnesota
Morning Earth*		Minnesota
North House Folk School*		Minnesota
Organic Consumers Association	Finland	Minnesota
River Bend Nature Center - Minnesota*		Minnesota
Rochester MN Franciscan	West St. Paul	Minnesota
Sarah's... an Oasis for Women	St. Paul	Minnesota
Sisters of St. Joseph of Corondelet - St.Paul Province	St. Paul	Minnesota
St. John's University Environmental Studies Program Dir	Collegeville	Minnesota
Sustainable Resources Center*		Minnesota
THE CIRCLE	Minneapolis	Minnesota
The Land Steward	White Bear Lake	Minnesota
The Manitou Project		Minnesota
Tod Drescher Architecture	Marine on St. Croix	Minnesota
Twin Cities Trout Unlimited*		Minnesota
Will Steger Foundation*		Minnesota
Women in the Wilderness*		Minnesota

Mississippi

Crow's Neck Environmental Education Center*		Mississippi
Miss. Dept of Wildlife, Fisheries & Parks*		Mississippi
Native Plant Regeneration Project*		Mississippi
Natural Resources Initiative of North Mississippi*		Mississippi
Strawberry Plains Audubon Center*		Mississippi

Missouri

Art from Recycled Materials/The Peace Project		Missouri
Colibri Urban Housing Collective		Missouri
Earth Share of Missouri*		Missouri
First Presbytarian Church of Kirkwood		Missouri
Franciscan Sisters of Mary		Missouri
GATEWAY VINCENTIAN VOLUNTEERS	St. Louis	Missouri
The Green Center*		Missouri
Green Earth Commercial Cleaning		Missouri
Harris-Stowe State University		Missouri
Inroads Ministry		Missouri
Intercommunity Environmental Council of Women Religious	St. Louis	Missouri
Loretto Earth Network		Missouri
Mid Rivers Ethical Society		Missouri
Open Space Council*		Missouri
Osceola, Missouri		Missouri
Penticostal Hollinness Churches	Springfield	Missouri
Sisters of Loretto	St. Louis	Missouri
Sisters of Loretto and Comembers	Saint Louis	Missouri

Sisters of Mercy of the Americas Reg. Community of St. Louis	Saint Louis	Missouri
Sisters of Saint Joseph of Carondelet	Saint Louis	Missouri
Sisters of St. Francis of Savannah, MO	Savannah	Missouri
Sisters of St. Joseph of Carondelet, Cong. Leadership Team	St. Louis	Missouri
Social and Environmental Concerns Committee	Kirkwood	Missouri
St. Clair County Missouri		Missouri

Montana

American Independent Business Alliance*		Montana
American Wildlands*		Montana
Common Ground Farm*		Montana
Corporation for the Northern Rockies*		Montana
De La Salle Blackfeet Middle School*		Montana
Environmental Studies Program, U Montana*		Montana
Friends of the Rocky Mountain Front	Choteau	Montana
Great Bear Foundation	Missoula	Montana
Greater Yellowstone Coalition*		Montana
Missoula Urban Demonstration (MUD) Project		Montana
Musicians United to Sustain the Environment		Montana
Montana Conservation Corps*		Montana
Montana Trout*		Montana
Montana Yellowstone Expeditions Foundation*		Montana
National Forest Protection Alliance*		Montana
Northwest Connections	Swan Valley	Montana
Park County Environmental Council	Livingston	Montana
Real Food Market & Deli	Helena	Montana
Rim Country Land Institute*		Montana
Spring Lake Park Habitat Restoration & Preservation Team		Montana
Sustainable Living Systems*		Montana
Sustainable Obtainable Solutions*		Montana
Walking in Beauty*		Montana
Wilderness Watch		Montana
Wildlands Center for Preventing Roads		Montana
Wild Rockies Field Instiitute*		Montana
Wilderness Watch*		Montana
Wildlands CPR*		Montana
Women's Opportunity & resource Development*		Montana
Women's Voices for the Earth		Montana
Yaak Valley Forest Council		Montana
Yellowstone to Yukon Conservation Initiative - USA*		Montana

Nebraska

Common Good Farm*		Nebraska
Grassland Foundation*		Nebraska
Green Prairie Foundation for Sustainability*		Nebraska
Maryknoll Affiliates	Omaha	Nebraska
Nebraska Green Party*		Nebraska
Nebraska sustainable Agriculture*		Nebraska
Platte Valley Unitarian Universalist Fellowship		Nebraska

Nevada

Citizen Alert*		Nevada
Clear Creek Watershed Council*		Nevada
Friends of the Red Rock Canyon		Nevada
Great Basin Institute*		Nevada
Great Basin Outdoor School*		Nevada
Lake Mead National Recreation Area*		Nevada
Nevada National Resource Education Council*		Nevada
Nevada Wilderness Project*		Nevada
Open Wisdom Institute	Las Vegas	Nevada
Park Run Management Company	Las Vegas	Nevada
Sierra Watershed Education Partnerships*		Nevada
The United Methodist Church	Reno	Nevada
Winnemucca Community Garden*		Nevada

New Hampshire

Advocates for the North Mill Pond*		New Hampshire
Antioch New England Graduate School	Jaffrey	New Hampshire
Antioch New England Grad School, Dept. of Clinical Psyc	Keene	New Hampshire
Antioch New England Grad. School, Dept. of Env. Studies	Keene	New Hampshire
Ashuelot Valley Environmental Observatory*		New Hampshire
Audobon Society of New Hampshire*		New Hampshire
Center for Place-Based Education*		New Hampshire
Cheshire Mediation		New Hampshire
Clean Air-Cool Planet*		New Hampshire
Daloz Mill and Farm BioCultural Center*		New Hampshire
Eco Art a la Carte*		New Hampshire
The Fells / Friends of John Hay Wildlife Refuge*		New Hampshire
Glen Brook*		New Hampshire
Greater Derry Humane Society, Inc.		New Hampshire
Harban Living Farm*		New Hampshire
High Mowing School		New Hampshire
Institute for Community and Environment		New Hampshire
Kroka Expeditions*		New Hampshire
Lucky Fish Communications	Derry	New Hampshire
Maryknoll Sisters, Maryknoll, NY	Concord	New Hampshire
Monadnock Institute of Nature Place & Culture	Rindge	New Hampshire
Mount Washington Observatory*		New Hampshire
Namaste Greenfire/Earthcore Affinity		New Hampshire
New Hamshire Federation of Humane Organizations		New Hampshire
Northern Forest Center	Concord	New Hampshire
NW Quarterly Meeting of the Religious Society of Friends	Marlborough	New Hampshire
Omniscopic Inc.		New Hampshire
Pegasus Foundation	Concord	New Hampshire
Project Laundry List	Portsmouth	New Hampshire
ReEnergizeUS*		New Hampshire
Sacred Fire Foundation*		New Hampshire
SAFE-New Hampshire*		New Hampshire
Second Wish Studio	Greenland	New Hampshire
Squam Lakes Natural Science Center*		New Hampshire
Stonewall Farm*		New Hampshire

The Student Conservation Association*		New Hampshire
Temple-Wilton Community Farm*		New Hampshire

New Jersey

Building Environmental Education Solutions		New Jersey
Campaign for Tobacco Free Kids	Hoboken	New Jersey
Cape Eleuthera Foundation*		New Jersey
Center for Conscious Living		New Jersey
Center House	Princeton	New Jersey
Cape Eleuthera Foundation*		New Jersey
Clifton Environmental Protection Commission*		New Jersey
Duke Farms Foundation*		New Jersey
Familycology Movement*		New Jersey
Felician Sisters of Lodi	Lodi	New Jersey
Forked River Mountain Coalition		New Jersey
Genesis Farm	Blairstown	New Jersey
GreenFaith*		New Jersey
Greenwood Gardens*		New Jersey
Hackensack Riverkeeper		New Jersey
Isles, Inc.*		New Jersey
Liberty Corner School		New Jersey
Missionary Sisters of the Immaculate Conception	Paterson	New Jersey
Morris Land Conservancy*		New Jersey
Natural Lands Trust*		New Jersey
Nature Center of Cape May	Cape May	New Jersey
New Jersey Audubon Society*		New Jersey
New Jersey School of Conservation*		New Jersey
No War No Warning*		New Jersey
NY/NJ Baykeeper*		New Jersey
Pequannock River Coalition		New Jersey
Picture Peace	Madison	New Jersey
Princeton Environmental Institute	Princeton	New Jersey
Sprout House	St. Chatham	New Jersey
Stony Brook-Millstone Watershed Association*		New Jersey
Sustainable Success LLC	Clementon	New Jersey
Teaneck Creek Conservancy		New Jersey
Terra Nova*		New Jersey
Township of Bedminster Environmental Commission*		New Jersey
Upper Raritan Watershed Association		New Jersey
Wisewoman Healing Ways	West Milford	New Jersey
WSOU 89.5 FM		New Jersey

New Mexico

Acoustic Ecology Institute*		New Mexico
Amigos Bravos: Friends of the Wild Rivers*		New Mexico
Artesia Clean & Beautiful		New Mexico
Art & Science Collaborations, Inc. (ASCI)		New Mexico
Bioneers & Collective Heritage Institute*		New Mexico
The Center for Seven Directions Practice*		New Mexico
Children & Nature Network*		New Mexico
Clear Light Books, Inc	Santa Fe	New Mexico

Coalition for the Valle Vidal*		New Mexico
EcoVersity		New Mexico
Environmental and Animal Rights Society	Santa Fe	New Mexico
Food Not Bombs*		New Mexico
The Forest Guild*		New Mexico
Global Environmental Response Team	Taos	New Mexico
HarvestH2O.com*		New Mexico
Healthy Housing Coalition, the	Cedar Crest	New Mexico
Healthy Land Conservancy*		New Mexico
Interhemispheric Resource Center		New Mexico
Los Alamos Study Group		New Mexico
Millennium Leadership Institute		New Mexico
National Indian Youth Leadership Project*		New Mexico
New Mexico Academy for Sciences and Mathematics	Santa Fe	New Mexico
New Mexico Environmental Law Center	Santa Fe	New Mexico
New Mexico wilderness Alliance*		New Mexico
Owl Mountain Retreat*		New Mexico
Project Crossroads		New Mexico
The Quivira Coalition*		New Mexico
Rivers & Birds*		New Mexico
River Source	Santa Fe	New Mexico
SEED Graduate Institute*		New Mexico
simpleChange*		New Mexico
Southwest Environment Center	Las Cruces	New Mexico
Southwest Organizing Project*		New Mexico
Tierra Madre		New Mexico
The Tracking Project*		New Mexico
Upper Gila Watershed Alliance*		New Mexico
Western Environmental Law Center –	Taos*	New Mexico
Western Voice		New Mexico
WildEarth Guardians*		New Mexico
Wild Resiliency Institute	Santa Fe	New Mexico
Yogaia	Santa Fe	New Mexico

New York

A Sustainable Future: CUNY CEPP*		New York
The Adirondack Council*		New York
Adirondack Mountain Club*		New York
Anarchist Action of Rochester	Rochester	New York
Apple Pond Farm & Renewable Energy Education Ctr*		New York
The Art and Nature Project*		New York
Asociacion por la Paz Intercontinental O.N.G.		New York
Aurora Group HEADQUARTERS	Smithtown	New York
Be The Dream		New York
Blue Ocean Institute*		New York
Brooklyn Society for Ethical Culture		New York
Capital District Local First*		New York
Capital Center for Conservation & Development*		New York
Capoeira-shop.com	New York	New York
Center for Agricultural Development & Entrepreneurship*		New York
Center for Biodiversity and Conservation, AMNH*		New York
Cherry Tree Association		New York

Citizens' Environmental Coalition*		New York
Clarkson Center for the Environment*		New York
Coalition on the Environment and Jewish Life*		New York
Coleman Raider International	Garrison	New York
Colgate University		New York
College of St. Benedict, St. John's Univ. Env. Studies Prog.	Queens	New York
Communications Coordination Committee for the UN	New York	New York
Community of the Holy Spirit		New York
Congregation of Christian Brothers	New Rochelle	New York
Conversations - TV Interview Series	New York	New York
Daughters of Wisdom USA Province	Islip	New York
Deepwater Experiential Education Project*		New York
Dyken Pond Environmental Education Center*		New York
Environmental Coalition*		New York
Earth	Basom	New York
Earth Pledge*		New York
Earth Society Foundation	New York	New York
EarthHeart	Buffalo	New York
Ecohumanist Organization, the	Long Island City	New York
Ecorevolution	New York	New York
Eddy Foundation*		New York
Education and Peace, Education Associates International	Rego Park	New York
Environmental Advocates of New York*		New York
Environmental Grantmakers Association*		New York
Environmental Defense Fund		New York
Environmental Studies Program. St. Lawrence University		New York
Federation of Sisters of Charity	New York	New York
Finger Lakes Land Trust		New York
Floating the Apple*		New York
Friends Academy*		New York
Friends of the Nature Preserve*		New York
Garden Conservatory*		New York
Global People's Assembly	New York	New York
Global Resource Action Center for the Environment (GRACE)		New York
Global Youth Action Network	New York	New York
Glenwood Center*		New York
Global Higher Ed for Sustainability Partnership - GHESP		New York
Good News Broadcast	New York	New York
GRACE*		New York
Great Lakes United		New York
Green May System		New York
Great South Bay Audubon Society*		New York
Green Guerillas*		New York
Green Map System*		New York
Group for the East End*		New York
Hawk Circle Wilderness*		New York
Hawthorne Valley Association*		New York
Heritage Foods USA*		New York
Hofstra University	Hempstead	New York
Horizons-on-the-Hudson	Salisbury Mills	New York
Hudson River Sloop Clearwater	Poughkeepsie	New York
Humankind	Tuxedo	New York
Indigenous Peoples Survival Foundation (IPSF)	New York	New York

Individual Associate, CIVICUS	New York	New York
Inspiration Point (bookstore)	Buffalo	New York
Institute of Ecosystem Studies*		New York
Institute for Global Spirituality	New York City	New York
Institute of Humanistic Science	Lansing	New York
Interfaith Center of New York	New York	New York
International Communities for Renewal of the Earth ICRE	New York	New York
International Community for Ecopsychology (ICE)		New York
International Consortium on Religion and Ecology (ICORE)	New York	New York
Int'l Institute for Sustainable Living-IISD Reporting Services	New York	New York
International Women's Writing Guild		New York
Interrupcion Fair Trade*		New York
John Denver Peace Cloth		New York
Keep It Real Discussion Forums		New York
Lake George Land Conservancy*		New York
Learned Evolution		New York
Learning Sustainablity Campaign		New York
The Lifebridge Foundation*		New York
Liz Claiborne Art Ortenberg Foundation		New York
Local Planet*		New York
The Lower Eastside Girls Club of New York*		New York
Maryknoll Mission Association of the Faithful	Maryknoll	New York
Media Savvy Connections		New York
Meristem*		New York
Millennium NGO Forum (a group of a 1000 NGO's)		New York
Mountain Top Arboretum*		New York
National Service Conference of The American Ethical Union	New York	New York
Natural History of the Adirondacks*		New York
The Nature Institute*		New York
Natural Resources Defense Council	New York	New York
Nature Institute	Ghent	New York
Network Alliance of Congregations Caring for Earth Center	Moriches	New York
New York Disaster Interfaith Services*		New York
New York Interfaith Power & Light*		New York
New York Sun Works*		New York
NEW-CUE*		New York
Niagara Heritage Partnership*		New York
North County School & Camp Treetops*		New York
NY Farms!*		New York
NYC Friends of Clearwater 20th Street	New York	New York
OneHeart Publishing Company		New York
Open Space Institute*		New York
Orange County Land Trust	Middletown	New York
Otsego County Conservation Association*		New York
Outstanding Renewal Enterprises Inc. [aka c]	New York	New York
Paul F. Brandwein Institute*		New York
Peaceable Kingdom	Ithaca	New York
Peconic Land Trust*		New York
Peekskill Coffee House	Peekskill	New York
The Pfeiffer Center*		New York
Phillies Bridge Farm Project	Gardiner	New York
Politics of Food Program	New York	New York
Porrow River Watershed Association		New York

Poughkeepsie Farm Project*		New York
Primary Environmental-International Peace Academy		New York
Project Unicorn South Salem		New York
Putnam Northern Westchester BOCES	Yorktown Heights	New York
Quail Hill Farm	Southampton	New York
Queens Peace Action	New York	New York
Queens, NY, Peace Action	Rego Park	New York
Raw	NYC	New York
RealClimate.org*		New York
Regional Farm & Food Project*		New York
Residents Committee to Protect the Adirondacks*		New York
Riverkeeper, Inc.*		New York
Riverside-Salem United Church of Christ	Grand Island	New York
Rocking the Boat*		New York
Rochester Food Not Bombs	Rochester	New York
Rochester Zen Center	Rochester	New York
Roger Tory Peterson Institute of Natural History*		New York
Roman Catholic Religious Cong. - Soc. of the Devine Word		New York
Roosevelt Institution – NY Office*		New York
Roxbury Farm*		New York
Rudolf Steiner Fellowship Foundation*		New York
SAFETALK Global		New York
Salamander Solutions		New York
Sane Aviation for Everyone, SAFE, Inc.	New York	New York
Sarah Lawrence College*		New York
Save the Mountain*		New York
Serpentine Art and Nature Commons	Staten Island	New York
SGI-USA	Brooklyn	New York
Sisters of Charity New York	New York	New York
Sisters Hill Farm*		New York
Sisters of St. Joseph	Watertown	New York
Sisters of the Presentation of the Blessed Virgin Mary	New Windsor	New York
Slow Food U.S.A.*		New York
Society of St. Ursula	Rhinebeck	New York
Sosa Entertainment		New York
Southold Program in Aquaculture Training (SPAT)*		New York
South North Development Initiative	New York	New York
St. Lawrence University Outdoor Program*		New York
St Pauls Center	New York	New York
Sterling Forest Partnership	Tuxedo	New York
Strategies for Development, Inc.	Hastings-on-Hudson	New York
St. Joseph's Neighborhood Center		New York
Synergos Institute, the	New York	New York
Stone Barns Center for Food and Agriculture*		New York
Sullivan Alliance for Sustainable Development*		New York
Sustainable South Bronx*		New York
Tamarind Foundation*		New York
The Sylvia Center at Katchkie Farm*		New York
The Albany Monthly Meeting - Religious Society of Friends		New York
The Association for the Protection of the Adirondacks	New York	New York
The Astrologers Fund, Inc	New York	New York
The Hastings Center	Garrison	New York
Touchstone Center for Children	New York	New York

Transportation Alternatives*		New York
Trillium Group		New York
Trinity Point Holistic Center	Plattsburgh	New York
Tropical Forestry Initiative*		New York
True Majority*		New York
Trust for Mutual Understanding		New York
Tug Hill Tomorrow Land Trust		New York
Universal Human Rights Coalition	Camden	New York
University - Colgate University		New York
Ursuline Sisters of Tildonk- US	Province	New York
Vassar College	Poughkeepsie	New York
Vervane Foundation	New York	New York
Vinmont Foundation		New York
VIVAT International	New York	New York
Waterkeepers Alliance*		New York
Watershed Agricultural Council*		New York
Wave Hill*		New York
Web Lab	New York	New York
Welless Institute of Greater Buffalo and Western New York	New York	New York
West Street School Geneva	Geneva	New York
We,The World	New York	New York
Wild America*		New York
Windham Chamber Music Festival*		New York
Women & Environment Dev. Organization - WEDO	New York	New York
World Goodwill New York		New York
World Ocean Observatory*		New York

North Carolina

Abolition Journal	Henersonville	North Carolina
Alliance for Preservation & Protection of Appalachian Lands		North Carolina
American Livestock Breeds Conservancy	Pittsboro	North Carolina
Appalachian Coalition for Just & Sustainable Communities*		North Carolina
Appalachian Voices*		North Carolina
Arthur Morgan School		North Carolina
Asheville Friends Meeting		North Carolina
Asheville Sustainable Earth and Global Ethics Foundation	Asheville	North Carolina
Being and Living Enterprrises, LTD.	Pine	North Carolina
CarolinaCape Fear Comm Coll/Univ of NC Wilmington	Wilmington	North Carolina
Carolina Kids' Conservancy		North Carolina
Carolina Mountain Land Conservancy		North Carolina
Center for Ecozoic Studies	Chapel Hill	North Carolina
Center for Education, Imagination & The Natural World		North Carolina
Center for the Environment at Catawba College*		North Carolina
Clean Water for North Carolina		North Carolina
Consensual Democracy	Winston-Salem	North Carolina
E. Carolina Univ-PhD Prog Coastal Resources Management	Greenville	North Carolina
EcoAccess, Inc.	Durham	North Carolina
Ecotone*		North Carolina
Elementality	Asheville	North Carolina
Elizabeth City Glass Company Inc	Elizabeth City	North Carolina
Environmental Leadership Center		North Carolina
Food Supply / Human Population Explosion Connection	Chapel Hill	North Carolina

Foothills Conservancy of North Carolina*		North Carolina
Friends of the Filipino People	Durham	North Carolina
Greenville Peace Committee	Greenville	North Carolina
Guilford College Environmental Studies Program*		North Carolina
Human Dimension	Raleigh	North Carolina
The Land Trust for the Little Tennessee*		North Carolina
Leaflight		North Carolina
Maryknoll Sisters, Hendersonville	Hendersonville	North Carolina
NAPCO	Sparta	North Carolina
Neuse River Foundation*		North Carolina
North Carolina Coastal Federation*		North Carolina
Odd Fellows	Winston-Salem	North Carolina
Piedmont Biofuels Cooperative*		North Carolina
Pogo Center for Appropriate Technology*		North Carolina
Rawleigh Woodworking	Greensboro	North Carolina
South Carolina Conservation Credit Exchange*		North Carolina
Southern Appalachian Forest Coalition*		North Carolina
Southern Appalachian Highlands Conservancy*		North Carolina
Southern Appalachian Yearly Meeting and Association		North Carolina
Southern Appalachian Biodiversity Project		North Carolina
Southern Dharma Retreat Center*		North Carolina
Southern Forests Network*		North Carolina
Southwings*		North Carolina
Stewards of the Earth	Asheville	North Carolina
stone circles*		North Carolina
Sustainables International, Inc.	Raleigh	North Carolina
The C.I.S. Consulting Group		North Carolina
The Servant Leadership School		North Carolina
Trading path Association*		North Carolina
Warren Wilson College Outdoor Leadership/Env.Studies Dept.		North Carolina
Wakling Cedar Online Literary Magazine	Asheville	North Carolina
Warren Wilson College		North Carolina
Wild South – NC Office*		North Carolina

North Dakota

Northern Plains Sustainable Agriculture Society*		North Dakota

Ohio

A Critical Decision Foundation	Miamisburg	Ohio
Blue Rock Station		Ohio
Brukner Nature Center		Ohio
Caribbean Island Conservancy	Columbus	Ohio
Cincinnati Nature Center*		Ohio
Cincinnati Waldorf School		Ohio
Citizens for Buckeye Basin Parks Inc.	Toledo	Ohio
Cleveland Museum of Natural History*		Ohio
The Community Solution*		Ohio
Community Land Cooperative of Cincinnati	Cincinnati	Ohio
Congregations of St. Joseph	Cleveland	Ohio
Crosscurrents International Institute	Sidney	Ohio
Crown Point Ecology Center		Ohio

Denison University Environmental Studies		Ohio
Dysart Defenders	Athens & Maumee	Ohio
Earth Speaks.org*		Ohio
Earth Day Coalition		Ohio
Enright Ridge Urban Eco-Village*		Ohio
Environmental Field Program, Antioch College		Ohio
Environmental Health Watch*		Ohio
Environmental Studies Program, Denison University	Granville	Ohio
Franciscan Justice and Peace Office	Cincinnati	Ohio
Friends of Lower Muskingum River*		Ohio
Good Food Co-op	Youngstown	Ohio
Gorman Heritage Farm*		Ohio
Great Lakes Region of Sisters of Charity	Cincinnati	Ohio
Healing the Earth and Each Other (HEEO)		Ohio
Highlands Nature Sanctuary	Bainbridge	Ohio
Hocking Voice		Ohio
Imago, Inc.	Cincinnati	Ohio
Justice Peace and Integrity of Creation (JPIC)	Cincinnati	Ohio
Little Beaver Creek Land Foundation*		Ohio
Miami University Institute of Environmental Science*		Ohio
Medical Mission Sisters	London	Ohio
Nature Center at Shaker Lakes*		Ohio
Nature's Nursery Ctr. for Wildlife Rehab & Conservation Education		Ohio
Ohio Leopold Education Project		Ohio
Ohio Valley Environmental Coalition		Ohio
Operation Botanic Rescue		Ohio
Park Conservation Committee		Ohio
Portsmouth-Piketon Residents for Env. Safety & Security*		Ohio
Robert Muller School of Fairview	Celina	Ohio
Rural Action		Ohio
Simply Living*		Ohio
Sisters of Charity of St. Augustine	Richfield	Ohio
Sisters of Charity of Cincinnati	Cincinnati	Ohio
Sisters of Charity of St. Augustine		Ohio
Sisters of St. Francis, Sylvania, OH	Sylvania	Ohio
Small Farm Research & Education Center*		Ohio
Stow Conservation Trust	Stow	Ohio
Toledo Coalition for Safe Energy		Ohio
Turning the Tide	Warren	Ohio
Wolf Creek Environmental Education Center*		Ohio

Oklahoma

Center for Appropriate Transport		Oklahoma
Kerr Center for Sustainable Agriculture		Oklahoma
Oklahoma City University	Oklahoma City	Oklahoma
Oklahoma Native Plant Society		Oklahoma
Phillips Theological Seminary	Bartlesville	Oklahoma
Scenic Rivers Association of Oklahoma	Bartlesville	Oklahoma

Oregon

Advancement Through Evolution Enterprises	Portland	Oregon
Alliance for Transportation Choice	Portland	Oregon
B Street Permaculture Project*		Oregon
Birch Creek Arts and Ecology Center*		Oregon
Bonneville Environmental Foundation*		Oregon
Cascadia Wildlands Project*		Oregon
Center for Diversity and the Environment*		Oregon
Center for Watershed and Community Health		Oregon
Central Oregon Environmental Center*		Oregon
Community Action Resource Enterprises (CARE)*		Oregon
Centro Cultural Cornelius		Oregon
Change Institute	Portland	Oregon
Citizens Democracy Watch	Florence	Oregon
City of Corvallis	Corvallis	Oregon
Columbia Riverkeeper		Oregon
Conservation Biology Institute		Oregon
Conservation for Central Oregon, The Recycling Team		Oregon
Co-Intelligence Institute, the	Eugene	Oregon
Douglas County Museum of Cultural and Natural History		Oregon
Eastern Oregon renewable Energies Nonprofit*		Oregon
ECLIPSE Portland		Oregon
Ecology Center of the Siskiyous		Oregon
Ecotrust*		Oregon
First Unitarian Church Portland OR	Portland	Oregon
Fishtrap, Inc.*		Oregon
Focus the Nation*		Oregon
Forest Service Employees for Environmental Ethics	Eugene	Oregon
47th Avenue Farm*		Oregon
Friends of the Buford Park & Mt. Pisgah		Oregon
Friends of Tyson Creek Park*		Oregon
Friends of Zenger Farm*		Oregon
Green Empowerment*		Oregon
Healthy Waters Institute*		Oregon
Honoring All Life Foundation	Ashland	Oregon
Interfaith Network for Earth Concerns*		Oregon
Jackson Bottom Wetlands Preserve		Oregon
John Inskeep Environmental Learning Center		Oregon
Klamath Riverkeeper*		Oregon
Klamath Watershed Partnership*		Oregon
Klamath Basin Ecosystem Foundation		Oregon
Klamath-Siskiyou Wildlands Center*		Oregon
Living Earth*		Oregon
Lomakatsi Restoration Project*		Oregon
Lost Valley Educational Center*		Oregon
Lower Nehalem Community Trust*		Oregon
Native Forest Council*		Oregon
Native Plant Society of Oregon	Eugene	Oregon
Natural Areas Association*		Oregon
Northwest Earth Institute*		Oregon
Northwest Youth Corps*		Oregon
Office of Justice & Peace, Archdiocese of Portland	Portland	Oregon

Oregon Folklife Program	Portland	Oregon
Oregon Tilth*		Oregon
Oxygen Collective*		Oregon
Pagan Awareness Network	Bend	Oregon
Peace From The Ashes	Beaverton	Oregon
Peace Team, the	Medford	Oregon
Resource Assistance for Rural Environments*		Oregon
River Network*		Oregon
Shambhalia Center & Nature Preserve*		Oregon
Siskiyou Environmental Education Center*		Oregon
Siskiyou Field Institute*		Oregon
The Siskiyou Project*		Oregon
Sitka Center for Art and Ecology	Otis	Oregon
Southern Oregon Land Conservancy		Oregon
Spring Creek Project*		Oregon
Step N2 Dlight Productions	Rico	Oregon
St. Mary's Academy	Portland	Oregon
Stop Abuse for Everyone*		Oregon
Sustainable Northwest*		Oregon
Trout Unlimited Chapter 678*		Oregon
Upper Deschutes Watershed Council*		Oregon
WaterWatch of Oregon*		Oregon
Western Environmental Law Center –	Eugene*	Oregon
Whole Systems Foundation		Oregon
Wild Salmon Center*		Oregon
Williams Creek Watershed Council		Oregon
Within Earthly Bounds*		Oregon
World Mind Society		Oregon
Write Around Portland - WRAP		Oregon
www.bookproject.org		Oregon

Pennsylvania

Action Center Inc/Energy Justice Network*		Pennsylvania
Action Wthout Borders / Idealist.org*		Pennsylvania
Allegheny Local River Advocates	Kennerdell	Pennsylvania
Allegheny Defense Project*		Pennsylvania
Alliance for a Sustainable Future	Ambler	Pennsylvania
AMD & ART*		Pennsylvania
Balance Health Center	Philadelphia	Pennsylvania
Bucks County Greens of Pennsylvania		Pennsylvania
Center for Coalfield Justice*		Pennsylvania
Changing Horizons Fund		Pennsylvania
Citizens Coal Council*		Pennsylvania
Church of Spiritual Humanism	Jenkintown	Pennsylvania
Claneil Foundation		Pennsylvania
Clinton Consulting Group		Pennsylvania
Concerned Citizens of The Delaware Valley		Pennsylvania
Creative Partnerships in Learning		Pennsylvania
Department of English, The Pennsylvania State University		Pennsylvania
Eastern PA Coalition for Abandoned Mine Reclamation*		Pennsylvania
Environmental Studies Program: Ursinus College*		Pennsylvania
Fairmont Water Works Interpretive Center*		Pennsylvania

FoodRoutes Network*		Pennsylvania
Forum on Religion & Ecology*		Pennsylvania
Friends of the Wissahickon*		Pennsylvania
Fruition Coalition, the	Philadelphia	Pennsylvania
Global Dialogue Institute	Haverford	Pennsylvania
Grey Nuns of the Sacred Heart	Philadelphia	Pennsylvania
High Mountain Medow Music	Philadelphia	Pennsylvania
Holland Architects Ltd	Philadelphia	Pennsylvania
i. Solve	Mechanicsburg	Pennsylvania
Julian Woods Community & School of Living		Pennsylvania
Kimberton Hills*		Pennsylvania
Life Spectrums Holistic Healing Conference & Retreat	Harrisburg	Pennsylvania
Mountain Meadow*		Pennsylvania
Mountain Watershed Association*		Pennsylvania
North Branch land Trust*		Pennsylvania
Order of the Rose, the	Catasauqua	Pennsylvania
Pax Christi USA	Erie	Pennsylvania
Peaceable Kingdom, Inc.	Whitehall	Pennsylvania
Peaceable Kingdom - Thinking Like A Mountain Institute		Pennsylvania
Pennsylvania Association for Sustainable Agriculture*		Pennsylvania
Pennsylvania Institute for Conservation Education*		Pennsylvania
Philadelphia University, Office of Spiritual Development		Pennsylvania
Roadtopeace*		Pennsylvania
SEA Way		Pennsylvania
Servants of the Immaculate Heart of Mary	Scranton	Pennsylvania
The Schuylkill Center for Environmental Education*		Pennsylvania
Sisters of Mercy of Dallas, Pennsylvania	Dallas	Pennsylvania
Sisters of SS. Cyril and Methosius	Danville	Pennsylvania
Sisters of St. Francis of Millvale	Pittsburgh	Pennsylvania
Sisters of Saint Joseph	Philadelphia	Pennsylvania
Sisters, Servants of the Immaculate Heart of Mary		Pennsylvania
SosteNica*		Pennsylvania
State College Friends Meeting		Pennsylvania
Strawberry Hill Foundation*		Pennsylvania
Strawberry Hill Nature Center & Preserve		Pennsylvania
Stroud water Research Center*		Pennsylvania
Student Environmental Action Coalition*		Pennsylvania
Sustainable Design Forum		Pennsylvania
Sustainable Lancaster*		Pennsylvania
The Thomas Merton Center*		Pennsylvania
The Threshold Foundation in Support of Youth*		Pennsylvania
Tuscarora Organic Growers Cooperative*		Pennsylvania
United States Citizens Aviation Watch	Philadelphia	Pennsylvania
University -Department of English-Pennsylvania State Univ.		Pennsylvania
University-Philadelphia Univ., Office of Spiritual Dev.	Philadelphia	Pennsylvania
Vicentian Sisters of Charity		Pennsylvania
The Village of Arts and Humanities*		Pennsylvania
Villanova University	Villanova	Pennsylvania
Vision Arrow	Thompson	Pennsylvania
Western Pennsylvania Watershed Program*		Pennsylvania
White Dog Community Enterprises*		Pennsylvania

Rhode Island

The Dancing Spirit Studio	Tiverton	Rhode Island
Friends of the Pawtuxet*		Rhode Island
National Network of Forest Practitioners*		Rhode Island
Norman Bird Sanctuary*		Rhode Island
The Ocean Project*		Rhode Island
Ocean View Foundation*		Rhode Island
Roger Williams Park Zoo/Rhode Island Zoological Soc	Boulder	Rhode Island

South Carolina

Culture & Heritage Museums*		South Carolina
Development Communications International	Columbia	South Carolina
Drayton Hall Museum		South Carolina
Forest Watch		South Carolina
Hub City Writers Project*		South Carolina
John Bachman Group - Sierra Club*		South Carolina
South Carolina Coastal Conservation League		South Carolina
S.C. Sustainable Universities Initiative, Univ. of South Carolina		South Carolina
The L.U.C.K.Y. Program*		South Carolina
Lowcountry Local First*		South Carolina
University of South Carolina Sustainable Universities Initiative		South Carolina
Upstate Forever*		South Carolina
Write for Change	Clemson	South Carolina

South Dakota

Adams Homestead and Nature Preserve*		South Dakota
Dakota Technics		South Dakota
Slip Up Creek Prairie Science Center*		South Dakota

Tennessee

Cohn Adult Learning Center*		Tennessee
Environmental Ministry Network	Nashville	Tennessee
Great Smoky Mountains Institute at Tremont*		Tennessee
Mountain Justice Summer*		Tennessee
New Horizon Montessori School*		Tennessee
Save Our Cumberland Mountains*		Tennessee
Sequatchie Valley Institute	Whitwell	Tennessee
Swan Conservation Trust		Tennessee
Tennessee Clean Water Action		Tennessee
Lookout Mountain Land Trust		Tennessee
Memphis Friends Meeting	Memphis	Tennessee
Nature's Way Montessori School		Tennessee
New Horizon Montessori School		Tennessee
The Trustees of Reservations - Islands*		Tennessee
United Mountain Defense*		Tennessee

Texas

Austin Nature 7 Science Center*		Texas
Austin Youth River Watch*		Texas
Bexar Audubon	San Antonio	Texas
Center for Environmental Research at Hornsby Bend*		Texas
Center for Maximum Potential Building Systems		Texas
Center for Study of Environment and Society*		Texas
Childers Commercial Group	Austin	Texas
Citizens Environmental Coalition*		Texas
Citizens for Healthy Growth	Denton	Texas
DFW Green Alliance	Dallas	Texas
Discovery Program at Camp Allen*		Texas
EduQuest International	Houston	Texas
Environmental Institute of Houston		Texas
Gateway to the Heart 501(c) 3 Religious Ed. Organization	Dripping Springs	Texas
GEMUN, Global Elementary Model United Nations	Arlington	Texas
The Good Tern Foundation*		Texas
Houston Arboretum & Nature Center*		Texas
International Association for Human Values	San Antonio	Texas
Katy Prairie Conservancy*		Texas
Knights of Gaia	Austin	Texas
The Lady Bird Johnson Wildflower Center*		Texas
Metropolitan Partnership for Energy	San Antonio	Texas
Moore Works	San Antonio	Texas
Namaste Cafe	Indianola	Texas
One World Rhythms	Dallas	Texas
Partnership For the Environment	Dallas	Texas
Partnership Group of Midland, Texas	Midland	Texas
PEACEMAKERS Inc	Dallas	Texas
River Legacy Foundation*		Texas
Robert Muller School	Arlington	Texas
Saint David's Episcopal Church	Austin	Texas
School of Ageless Wisdom	Arlington	Texas
Service Transmaritime Inc.	Laredo	Texas
Sibley Nature Center*		Texas
Sisters of Charity of the Incarnate Word	San Antonio	Texas
Skaglund Hill Environmental Education Center	Arlington	Texas
Sustainable Dallas*		Texas
University of Texas - Houston, School of Public Health	Houston	Texas
Texas Association for Environmental Education*		Texas
U.S. Province of Sisters of Charity of the Incarante Word	San Antonio	Texas
Urban Harvest*		Texas
Vox Sophia Publishing	Arlington	Texas
West Texas Associates of the Sisters of the Living Word		Texas

Utah

Air Terminal Gifts, Inc.	Salt Lake City	Utah
Allen and Alice Stokes Nature Center	Logan Canyon	Utah
Business Many One Networks, Inc	Salt Lake City	Utah
Canyonlands Field Institute*		Utah
County of San Juan		Utah

Ellen Meloy Fund for Desert Writers*		Utah
Headwaters		Utah
Intermountain Lodging		Utah
Living Rivers*		Utah
Manzana Springs Vegetable Farm*		Utah
Ogden Nature Center*		Utah
One Love Lifestyles Magazine		Utah
Plateau Restoration & Conservation Adventures*		Utah
Soldier Hollow Charter School*		Utah
Southern Utah Wilderness Alliance*		Utah
Stokes Nature Center*		Utah
Swaner EcoCenter*		Utah
Tracy Aviary*		Utah
TreeUtah		Utah
Utah Conservation Corps*		Utah
Utah Society for Environmental Education		Utah
Wasatch Community Gardens*		Utah
Weber Pathways*		Utah

Vermont

ACoRN: Addison Eounty Relococalization Network*		Vermont
AgRefresh	Burlington	Vermont
Apeiron Foundation, the	Coventry	Vermont
Arcana Gardens & Greenhouses*		Vermont
Audubon Vermont*		Vermont
Awakening Sanctuary, Inc.	Monkton	Vermont
Ben & Jerry's Foundation		Vermont
Town of Bethel, Vermont		Vermont
Burlington Friends Meeting -Religious Society of Friends	Burlington	Vermont
Businesses for the Northern Forest		Vermont
Catamount Ranch*		Vermont
Center for Whole Communities*		Vermont
Children of the Earth	South Burlington	Vermont
City Council of Burlington		Vermont
City of Burlington	Burlington	Vermont
City of Montpelier, Vermont (State Capital)	Montpelier	Vermont
Connecticut River Watershed Council*		Vermont
Connecticut Riverfest*		Vermont
COVER Home Repair*		Vermont
The DREAM Program*		Vermont
Equinox Preservation Trust*		Vermont
Farm and Wilderness Foundation*		Vermont
First Unitarian Univeralist Society of Burlington	Burlington	Vermont
Forest Watch*		Vermont
Four Winds Nature Institute*		Vermont
Friends Committee on Unity with Nature		Vermont
Friends of the Mad River		Vermont
Full Moon Community Association*		Vermont
Global Community Initiatives*		Vermont
Global Living Project	East Corinth	Vermont
Goddard College Environmental & Sustainability Studies*		Vermont
Green Mountain College*		Vermont

Institute for Spiritual Development	Burlington	Vermont
Institute for Sustainable Communities	Montpelier	Vermont
Islands and Highlands Environmental Consultancy		Vermont
Keeping Track*		Vermont
Keewaydin Environmental Education Center*		Vermont
Living Future*		Vermont
Londonderry Inn, the	South Londonderry	Vermont
Longoneil Enterprises, Ltd.	Newfane	Vermont
Maple Wind Farm*		Vermont
Merck Forest and Farmland Center*		Vermont
Middlebury College Environmental Affairs*		Vermont
Middlebury Friends Meeting (Quakers)	East Middlebury	Vermont
Middlebury Vermont Area Clergy		Vermont
Mountain School	Vershire	Vermont
New England Grassroots Environment Fund	Montpelier	Vermont
Noise Pollution Clearinghouse	Montpelier	Vermont
North American Coalition on Religion and Ecology (NACRE)		Vermont
North Universalist Chapel Society	Woodstock	Vermont
Ocean Arks International*		Vermont
Otter Creek Audubon	Middlebury	Vermont
Orton Family Foundation*		Vermont
Peace & Justice Center	Burlington	Vermont
People of Addison County Together, Inc. (PACT)	Middlebury	Vermont
Principality of My Vermont, the	Rutland	Vermont
Quaker Earthcare Witness	Burlington	Vermont
Save Our World		Vermont
Shelburne Farms	Shelburne	Vermont
Sisters of Mercy of Vermont	Burlington	Vermont
Sisters of Mercy, Northeast Justice Team	Burlington	Vermont
Smallholders Association of Vermont, Inc	East Middlebury	Vermont
Smokey House Center*		Vermont
SolarFest: Energy Education Through the Arts	Middletown Springs	Vermont
Spirit in Nature Vermont		Vermont
Step It Up*		Vermont
Sterling College*		Vermont
Sustainability Institute*		Vermont
Sustainable Living Network of Randolph, VT	Randolph	Vermont
The University of Vermont	Burlington	Vermont
Upper Valley Trails Alliance*		Vermont
Three D Dairy	Middletown Springs	Vermont
Three Mountain Papers	Warren	Vermont
Town of Bristol, Vermont	Bristol	Vermont
Town of Charlotte, Vermont		Vermont
Town of Granby, Vermont 367 Lund Lane	Granby Valley	Vermont
Town of Hinesburg, Vermont	Hinesburg	Vermont
Town of Huntington, Vermont	Huntington	Vermont
Town of Isle La Motte, Vermont	Isle La Motte	Vermont
Town of Lincoln, Vermont	Lincoln	Vermont
Town of Marlboro, Vermont	Marlboro	Vermont
Town of Marshfield, Vermont	Marshfield	Vermont
Town of Middlebury, Vermont	Middlebury	Vermont
Town of Monkton, Vermont	Monkton	Vermont
Town of Norwich, Vermont	Norwich	Vermont

Town of Plainfield, Vermont	Plainfield	Vermont
Town of Randolph, Vermont	Randolph	Vermont
Town of Ripton, Vermont	Ripton	Vermont
Town of Starksboro, Vermont	Starksboro	Vermont
Town of Warren, Vermont	Warren	Vermont
Town of Weston, Vermont	Weston	Vermont
Town of Weybridge, Vermont	Weybridge	Vermont
Unitarian Universalists for Ethical Treatment of Animals	Burlington	Vermont
United Plant Savers & Sage Mountain Herbal Retreat Center		Vermont
University of Vermont, Environmental Program	Burlington	Vermont
University - Vermont Law School	South Royalton	Vermont
Vermont Bicycle & Pedestrian Coalition*		Vermont
Vermont Businesses for Social Responsibility	South Burlington	Vermont
Vermont Children's Forum		Vermont
Vermont Commons*		Vermont
Vermont Commons School	South Burlington	Vermont
Vermont Community Works		Vermont
Vermont Conference, United Church of Christ	Burlington	Vermont
Vermont Housing and Conservation Board		Vermont
Vermont Humane Federation		Vermont
Vermont Institute of Natural Science (VINS)*		Vermont
Vermont Law School		Vermont
Vermont Natural Resources Council		Vermont
Vermont Public Interest research Group (VPIRG)*		Vermont
Vermont SWEEP **(**State-wide Environmental Education Programs)		Vermont
Vermont Wilderness School*		Vermont
Vermont Zen Center	Shelburne	Vermont
Vermont Youth Conservation Corps*		Vermont
Vermont Zen Center*		Vermont
Vital Communities*		Vermont
Voices of the Land	Manchester	Vermont
Volunteers For Peace	Belmont	Vermont
Watershed Center*		Vermont
Westing Associates, Environment, Security, & Education	Putney	Vermont
Whole Systems Design*		Vermont
Wilderness Friends Meeting (Quaker)	Wallingford	Vermont
Wildlands Project, the	Richmond	Vermont
Willowell Foundation		Vermont
World Species List*		Vermont
www.Ark-Of-Hope.org	Bethel	Vermont
Yestermorrow Design / Build School*		Vermont
Youth Horticulture Program - UVM Extension*		Vermont

Virginia

AEH Institute	Reston	Virginia
Allbright Enterprises	Reston	Virginia
American Association of Yoga in Daily Life	Alexandria	Virginia
blue moon fund*		Virginia
Blue Ridge Center for Environmental Stewardeship*		Virginia
Earth Force*		Virginia
Eastern Mennonite University*		Virginia
Center for Health, Environment and Justice*		Virginia

Earth Mama Music/ Rouse House Music	Independence	Virginia
EarthPagan Books	Fredericksburg	Virginia
Environment News Service (ENS)	Alexandria	Virginia
Environmental News Service		Virginia
First Peoples Worldwide		Virginia
Friends of the Rappahannock*		Virginia
Goose Creek Monthly Meeting of Religious Soc. of Friends (Quakers)		Virginia
The Hill School*		Virginia
Hollins University Environmental Studies*		Virginia
Homeplanet Defense Institute - HDI	McLean	Virginia
Institute for Nature and Leadership*		Virginia
Jane Goodall Institute	Arlington	Virginia
Jim Caffrey Images	Arlington	Virginia
Lilith's Tribe	Richmond	Virginia
Living Education Center for Ecology & the Arts		Virginia
Millennium Institute	Arlington	Virginia
National Wildlife Federation, the		Virginia
Radford University		Virginia
RappFLOW*		Virginia
Rare – Inspiring Conservation*		Virginia
Rural School and Community Trust*		Virginia
Shenandoah resource Conservation and Development*		Virginia
Southern Environmental Law Center*		Virginia
3D Life Adventures*		Virginia
Tom's Creek Basin Vision Group		Virginia
Valley Conservation Council*		Virginia
Virginia Clean Cities*		Virginia
Virginia Office of Environmental Education*		Virginia
Virginia Save Our Streams Program*		Virginia
Washington Regional Network for Livable Communities	Reston	Virginia
Western Virginia Land Trust*		Virginia
William McDonough + Partners-Architecture	Charlottesville	Virginia

Washington

21 Acres*		Washington
Alternative Health Talk	Seattle	Washington
Altitude. A Leadership Consulting LLC.	Seattle	Washington
Antioch University Seattle, B.A. Program		Washington
Antioch University Seattle, Center for Programs		Washington
Antioch University Seattle, The Center for Creative Change		Washington
Attraction Retreat	Bellingham	Washington
Au Sable Institute of Env. Studies –	Pacific Rim*	Washington
Beam Reach Marine Science School*		Washington
Bellevue Community College	Bellevue	Washington
Big Mind Media	Langley	Washington
Biodiversity Northwest*		Washington
Bloedel Reserve		Washington
Cascade Bicycle Club Education Foundation*		Washington
Cascadia Media Alliance	Seattle	Washington
Celtic Prayers.Org		Washington
Center for Creative Change*		Washington
Central Basin Audubon Society*		Washington

Chelan-Douglas Land Trust		Washington
Church Council of Greater Seattle		Washington
City of Bellingham		Washington
Climate Solutions		Washington
Communitas	Bremerton	Washington
Community Land Trust of Waldron Island		Washington
Conservation Northwest*		Washington
Context Consulting Inc	Seattle	Washington
Daughters Sisters Project, the	Bainbridge Island	Washington
Digital Environmental Political Activists (DEPA)		Washington
Dudley Foundation	Bellingham	Washington
EarthCorps*		Washington
Earth Day Network	Seattle	Washington
Earth Ministry	Seattle	Washington
East Lake Washington Audubon*		Washington
East Shore Earth Corps		Washington
Eastside Friends Meeting (Quaker) of Bellevue	Bellevue	Washington
Educating For Humanity	Coupeville	Washington
Educating for Humanity Institute, the	Clinton	Washington
Environmental & Adventure School	Bothell	Washington
Foundation for life Change*		Washington
Friends of the San Juans		Washington
Global Higher Education for Sustainability Partnership GHESP		Washington
The Grass Roots Garbage Gang*		Washington
Green Party of San Juan County		Washington
Green Party of Skagit County	Anacortes	Washington
Hate-Free Zone Campaign of Washington*		Washington
Hazel Wolfe Environmental Film Network*		Washington
Heritge Institute, the	Clinton	Washington
Homewaters Project*		Washington
Humanists of North Puget Sound		Washington
Innisfree Association		Washington
Institute for Children's Environmental Health	Freeland	Washington
Institute for Educational Inquiry	Seattle	Washington
Institute of Noetic Sciences NW Regional Community	Bellevue	Washington
International Bicycle Fund		Washington
IronStraw Institute*		Washington
IslandWood*		Washington
Justice, Peace & Integrity of Creation-Wheaton Franciscans		Washington
Kestrel Tool Ltd		Washington
Kooskooskie Commons		Washington
LIOS~The Leadership Institute of Seattle	Seattle	Washington
Locavores*		Washington
Lopez Community Land Trust - LCLT		Washington
Lopez Island Hospice & Home Support	Lopez Island	Washington
Lopez Island Quaker Worship Group		Washington
L&O Enterprises	Seattle	Washington
Mangrove Action Project*		Washington
Mercer Slough Environmental Education Center*		Washington
Methow Conservancy		Washington
NaturaLeadership	Vashon	Washington
Neighborkids*		Washington
New Road Map Foundation	Seattle	Washington

NLP Northwest, Inc.	Anacortes	Washington
Northwest Environmental Education Council	Seattle	Washington
Northwest Intentional Communities Association	Bothell	Washington
Northwest Service Academy*		Washington
Olympic Park Associates		Washington
Olympic Park Institute*		Washington
Orcas Island Odd Fellows Lodge #88	Orcas Island	Washington
Organic Seed Alliance*		Washington
Organic Volunteers*		Washington
Organizing Committee - Earth Day(s)	Bainbridge Island	Washington
Pacific Lutheran University	Tacoma	Washington
People for Environmental Action & Community Health*		Washington
People Web, the	Seattle	Washington
Rite of Passage Journeys*		Washington
Ross Chapin Architects	Langley	Washington
Ruth H Brown Foundation	Seattle	Washington
Salish Sea Expeditions*		Washington
San Juan Community Home Trust	Friday Harbor	Washington
San Juan County		Washington
Save Our Wild Salmon*		Washington
Sea Resources*		Washington
Seattle Local Peoples Assembly	Seattle	Washington
Seattle University	Seattle	Washington
Seattle Wisdom School	Seattle	Washington
Shining Star Productions	Everson	Washington
Sisters of Providence Mother Joseph Province	Spokane	Washington
Sisters of the Holy Names of Jesus and Mary	Spokane	Washington
Snow Leopard Trust*		Washington
Songbird Foundation	Burton	Washington
Songhouse Productions		Washington
SoundCircle Center for Arts and Anthroposophy		Washington
Starfeather	Edmonds	Washington
Starflower Foundation*		Washington
Student Activist Coalition at Pacific Lutheran University	Tacoma	Washington
Studio Strong	Langley	Washington
St. Leo Parish Eco-Spirit Group	Tacoma	Washington
The United Churches of Olympia	Olympia	Washington
Tirawa Consulting, Inc.	Medina	Washington
Unity of Woodinville	Woodinville	Washington
University - Student Activist Coalition at Pacific Lutheran		Washington
VOXRX.ORG	Seattle	Washington
Voyager Montessori Elementary School	Bainbridge Island	Washington
Washington Physicians for Social Responsibility		Washington
Washington Wilderness Coalition*		Washington
Westland Gardens	Seattle	Washington
Whatcom Land Trust*		Washington
Whidbey Institute	Seattle	Washington
Wild Fish Conservancy*		Washington
Wilderness Awareness School*		Washington
The Windward Center*		Washington
WorldWire: News on Global Issues	Seattle	Washington

West Virginia

The Alliance for Appalachia*		West Virginia
American Conservation Film Festival*		West Virginia
Appalachian Coal Country Watershed Team*		West Virginia
Appalachian Trial Conservancy*		West Virginia
Augusta Heritage Center*		West Virginia
Big Laurel Learning Center, Inc.	Kermit	West Virginia
Canaan Valley Institute*		West Virginia
Coal River Mountain Watch*		West Virginia
Claymont Society for Continuous Education	Charles Town	West Virginia
Eastern Coal Regional Roundtable*		West Virginia
Friends of the Second Creek		West Virginia
Mountain Sustainability Project*		West Virginia
Ohio valley Environmental Coalition*		West Virginia
Sisters of St. Joseph of Wheeling	Wheeling	West Virginia
Web of Life Ecology Center of Big Laurel Learning Center Inc.		West Virginia
West Virginia Rivers Coalition*		West Virginia

Wisconsin

Aldo Leopold Foundation*		Wisconsin
Anishinaabe Niijii/Protect the Earth		Wisconsin
Bay Towel, Inc	Green Bay	Wisconsin
Beloit Monthly Meeting of Friends (Quakers)	Beloit	Wisconsin
Bicycle Federation of Wisconsin		Wisconsin
Biodiversity Project*		Wisconsin
Citizens for Safe Water Around Badger		Wisconsin
City of Wauwatosa	Wauwatosa	Wisconsin
Community Conservation	Gays Mills	Wisconsin
Community Garden Partnership*		Wisconsin
Congregation of St. Agnes Leadership Team	Fond du Lac	Wisconsin
CSA	Milwaukee	Wisconsin
Dominican Sisters from Racine	Racine	Wisconsin
EarthWINS	Shawano	Wisconsin
Ecolution	Fond du Lac	Wisconsin
Ecospirituality Group at Sinsinawa Mound, the	Sinsinawa	Wisconsin
Fitchburg Fields*		Wisconsin
Fox / Wolf Rivers Environmental History Project*		Wisconsin
Franciscan Spirituality Center*		Wisconsin
Friends of Lake Wingra		Wisconsin
Friends of Muraviovka Park*		Wisconsin
Gathering Waters Conservancy*		Wisconsin
Green Slow Moving Vehicle*		Wisconsin
Inland Sea Society*		Wisconsin
Lakeland College	Sheboygan	Wisconsin
Leopold Education Project - WI*		Wisconsin
Michael Fields Agricultural Institute*		Wisconsin
MinGei Center for Creation Spirituality		Wisconsin
Nature Net*		Wisconsin
New Moon Productions	Milwaukee	Wisconsin
North American Lake Management Society*		Wisconsin
Nuke Watch	Luck	Wisconsin

Peaceways - Young General Assembly		Wisconsin
Philadelphia Community Farm*		Wisconsin
Pleasant Ridge Waldorf School	Viroqua	Wisconsin
Potter's Farm*		Wisconsin
Racine Dominicans Administrative Offices	Racine	Wisconsin
River Alliance of Wisconsin*		Wisconsin
River Bend Nature Center*		Wisconsin
Riveredge Nature Center*		Wisconsin
Ruffolo Design Ltd.	Webster	Wisconsin
The Sauk Prairie Conservation Alliance*		Wisconsin
Sigrid Olson Environmental Institute*		Wisconsin
Sinsinawa Dominican Central Council	Sinsinawa	Wisconsin
Sinsinawa Dominican Sisters of the Southern Province	Sinsinawa	Wisconsin
School Sisters of Notre Dame	Elm Grove	Wisconsin
Student Environmental Action Coalition - Oshkosh	Oshkosh	Wisconsin
SUNSEED Eco-Education Center*		Wisconsin
Tall Grass Farm		Wisconsin
TAUWP - University of Wisconsin - Oshkosh	Oshkosh	Wisconsin
University of Wisconsin – Madison Arboretum*		Wisconsin
University of Wisconsin Oshkosh	Oshkosh	Wisconsin
University of Wisconsin Oshkosh Faculty Senate Wisconsin	Oshkosh	Wisconsin
University of Wisconsin Oshkosh Senate Academic Staff	Oshkosh	Wisconsin
University of Wisconsin Oshkosh Student Association	Oshkosh	Wisconsin
Univ of Wisconsin Oshkosh Classified Staff Advis.Council	Oshkosh	Wisconsin
Urban Center for Sustainability	Milwaukee	Wisconsin
Urban Ecology Center		Wisconsin
Watershed Wisdom, Shorewood High School*		Wisconsin
Wild Ones: Native Plants, Natural Landscapes*		Wisconsin
Winnebago County Wisconsin Labor Council AFL-CIO	Oshkosh	Wisconsin
Wisconsin Center for Environmental Education*		Wisconsin
Wisconsin League of Conservation Voters*		Wisconsin
Wisconsin Partners for SustainAbility*		Wisconsin
Wisconsin Stewardship Network*		Wisconsin
Wisconsin Sec. of State	Madison	Wisconsin
Zephyr Community Farm		Wisconsin

Wyoming

The Bauen Camp*		Wyoming
Buffalo Bill Historical Center*		Wyoming
Jackson Hole Chamber of Commerce	Jackson	Wyoming
Jackson Hole Conservation Alliance		Wyoming
Murie Center		Wyoming
Natural Outdoor Leadership School (NOLS)*		Wyoming
Teton Science Schools*		Wyoming

Orion Grassroots Network list by state:
Source:http://webarchive.org/web/20061001170238/http///.online.org/pages/ogn/vieworg.cfm?ob=st (or) Source:http://www.orionsociety.org/pages/ogn/earthcharter/endorsees.html
Source:http://web.archive.org/web/200809164059/http://www.orionsociety.org/page/ogn/vieworg.cfm?ob=st
Earth Charter public database of endorsers as of 2008:
Source: http://eccommons.dabbledb.com/publish/earthcharterorganizationalendorsers/

Index